AFRICA

Progress Through Cooperation

Previous publications:
THE PROMISE OF WORLD TENSIONS, edited by Harlan Cleveland, 1961
RESTLESS NATIONS: A *Study of World Tensions and Development*, 1962
LATIN AMERICA: EVOLUTION OR EXPLOSION?, edited by Mildred Adams, 1963

SOUTH ASIA PACIFIC CRISIS: *National Development and the World Community*, edited by Margaret Grant, 1964

Conferences sponsored by the Council on World Tensions:
REMOVING ROADBLOCKS TO WORLD PEACE, New York City, 1957
STEPS TOWARD PEACE, Bern, Switzerland, 1958
INDIAN DEMOCRACY IN THE ASIAN BACKGROUND, Bombay, India, 1960
CONFERENCE ON WORLD TENSIONS, University of Chicago, 1960
SEMINAR ON WORLD TENSIONS, Geneva, Switzerland, 1960
TENSIONS OF ECONOMIC DEVELOPMENT IN SOUTHEAST ASIA, University of Bombay, 1961
OXFORD CONFERENCE ON TENSIONS IN DEVELOPMENT, New College, Oxford, 1961
CONFERENCE ON TENSIONS IN DEVELOPMENT IN THE WESTERN HEMISPHERE, University of Bahía, Brazil, 1962
CONFERENCE ON DEVELOPMENT AND COOPERATION IN THE SOUTH ASIA PACIFIC REGION, University of Malaya, Kuala Lumpur, Malaysia, 1964
AFRICAN CONFERENCE ON PROGRESS THROUGH COOPERATION, Makerere University College, Kampala, Uganda, 1965

AFRICA

Chief S. O. Adebo
Adam Pierre Adossama
Leona Baumgartner
Bernard Chidzero
Everett R. Clinchy
Sir Andrew Cohen
Gershon Collier
Chief H. O. Davies
A. S. Dhawan
René Foch
Jiri Hajek
Paul G. Hoffman
Louis Ignacio-Pinto
W. Senteza Kajubi
Albert Kervyn
Pumla E. Kisosonkole
Sir Arthur Lewis
Tom J. Mboya
Leo Model
François A. N'Liba-N'Guimbous
A. Milton Obote
Samuel N. Odaka
Taieb Slim
Maitama Sule
Barbara Ward
Walter H. Wheeler, Jr.
Whitney Young, Jr.

Progress Through Cooperation

Edited by JOHN KAREFA-SMART

Introduction by CHIEF S. O. ADEBO

Council on World Tensions

DODD, MEAD & COMPANY

New York 1966

The Council on World Tensions, a private, nonprofit, and nonpolitical organization, has conducted studies and high-level international conferences on practical steps toward peace based on better economic and social conditions for peoples of all nations. The conferences have been organized in cooperation with universities in different parts of the world.

The Council has helped to inform public opinion by distributing its publications in cooperation with educational, civic, economic, religious, and communications agencies. It has also cooperated on programs with national organizations such as the National Education Association and the Junior Chamber International.

The Council has made the wide variety of information and opinions published in its books available to the public. However, the authors are responsible for their statements of fact and opinion.

Library of Congress Catalog Card Number: 66-12809

Printed in the United States of America
by Vail-Ballou Press, Inc., Binghamton, New York

916
AC258a

COUNCIL ON WORLD TENSIONS

325 East 41st Street, New York, New York 10017

18818

CONTENTS

FOREWORD—*Everett R. Clinchy*   xi

INTRODUCTION—*Chief S. O. Adebo*   xiii

A CONTINENT OF NEIGHBORS—*Paul G. Hoffman*   1

PROBLEMS OF PROGRESS THROUGH COOPERATION
—*A. Milton Obote*   11

PROFILE OF AFRICAN INDEPENDENCE—*Barbara Ward*   18

THE NEED FOR COOPERATION IN AFRICA—*Tom J. Mboya*   31

I. PROBLEMS OF COOPERATION WITHIN
    NATIONS

    COOPERATION WITHIN NATIONS—*Chief H. O. Davies*   39

    THE CIVIL SERVICE IN NEWLY INDEPENDENT COUNTRIES
    —*Chief S. O. Adebo*   45

    PROBLEMS OF DEVELOPMENT: THE EXPERIENCE OF
    TUNISIA—*Taieb Slim*   54

II. AFRICAN SOLIDARITY AND
    INTERNATIONAL COOPERATION

    INDEPENDENT AFRICA IN SEARCH OF INTERDEPENDENCE
    —*Louis Ignacio-Pinto*   67

    AFRICA IN TRANSITION—*Sir Andrew Cohen*   74

    POLITICAL AND ECONOMIC PROBLEMS OF AFRICA
    —*Maitama Sule*   83

THE ROLE OF THE UNITED NATIONS IN AFRICAN CO-
OPERATION AND DEVELOPMENT—*Gershon Collier*   93
THE HUMAN COMMUNITY—*Barbara Ward*   100

III. THE AFRICAN ECONOMY

ASPECTS OF ECONOMIC DEVELOPMENT—*Sir Arthur Lewis*   115
PLANNING IN AN AFRICAN ECONOMY, WITH PARTICULAR
REFERENCE TO KENYA—*Tom J. Mboya*   131
PROGRESS THROUGH COOPERATION
—*François A. N'Liba-N'Guimbous*   138
PRIVATE CAPITAL AND ECONOMIC DEVELOPMENT
—*Leo Model*   148

IV. PROBLEMS OF SOCIAL DEVELOPMENT,
EDUCATION, AND CULTURE

SOCIAL PROBLEMS OF DEVELOPING COUNTRIES
—*Pumla E. Kisosonkole*   153
HEALTH AND WELFARE SERVICES IN DEVELOPMENT
PLANNING—*John Karefa-Smart*   163
PRIORITIES IN INVESTMENT IN EDUCATION
—*W. Senteza Kajubi*   171
EDUCATIONAL PROBLEMS IN THE DEVELOPING
COUNTRIES—*Adam Pierre Adossama*   183

V. INTERCONTINENTAL VIEWS ON
COOPERATION AND DEVELOPMENT

COOPERATION IN AFRICA AND IN THE UNITED NATIONS
—*Samuel N. Odaka*   197
STEPS TOWARD UNITY IN EUROPE AND IN AFRICA
—*René Foch*   203
UNIVERSAL PROBLEMS OF DEVELOPMENT
—*A. S. Dhawan*   207

SOME NOTES ON SCIENCE AND TECHNOLOGY
—*Leona Baumgartner*   210

THE RATIONALE OF COOPERATION
—*Walter H. Wheeler, Jr.*   215

AFRICAN PROBLEMS: CZECHOSLOVAKIA'S APPROACH
—*Jiri Hajek*   219

SUMMARY OF DISCUSSIONS

AFRICAN PROGRESS THROUGH COOPERATION
—*John Karefa-Smart*   225

COMMITTEE I   PROBLEMS OF COOPERATION WITHIN
                NATIONS—*Whitney Young, Jr.*   228

COMMITTEE II   AFRICAN SOLIDARITY AND INTERNA-
                TIONAL COOPERATION
                —*Albert Kervyn*   239

COMMITTEE III   THE AFRICAN ECONOMY
                —*Bernard Chidzero*   248

COMMITTEE IV   DEVELOPMENT OF HUMAN RESOURCES:
                EDUCATION, CULTURE, AND SOCIAL
                PROBLEMS—*W. Senteza Kajubi*   266

APPENDIX

A. Biographical Notes   279
B. Organization of the African Conference   286

FOREWORD

The great transformations in human life which science and engineering are bringing about in the twentieth century are clearly manifest in Africa. There is the biological revolution's conquest of disease, with the concomitant danger of too great population numbers stealing the gains of machine production; the knowledge industry's contribution to mass education, with the accompanying threat from the science of contemporary destructive weapons; and the twentieth century's creation of a beginning of what Teilhard de Chardin calls the noösphere, wherein common knowledge communicated by general literacy, travel, and telstar television is creating new intellectual and spiritual powers for man. But accompanying this human evolution to a higher level of world community consciousness are the escalated instincts to exploit, to hate, do violence and exercise genocidal murder.

This book looks at the human predicament through the African window. African biology, economics, politics, education, religion, nationalism, and trans-national dreams are integral parts of the plural problems all of mankind is experiencing. These pages illuminate the human condition from Cairo to Capetown. For the thoughtful reader this book sheds light on all other continents as well as on Africa.

The Council on World Tensions thanks the writers of these chapters, an expression of gratitude every reader will share. The Council wishes to thank particularly H. E. Chief S. O. Adebo's committee of African leaders who fixed the targets and drew up the agenda of this African Conference on *Progress Through Cooperation*. To Dr. Margaret Grant, Executive Director of the

Council and formerly a United Nations expert on social and economic affairs, goes our grateful appreciation for an extraordinary administrative job in carrying out the Conference plans, and serving as co-ordinator of the position papers. To Paul Hoffman we give our thanks for work from the outset of the whole program through his presidency during the sessions. We thank our Chairman of the Board, Walter H. Wheeler, Jr., for the burdens he carried so well in obtaining funds to match the Ford Foundation's grant. Prime Minister A. Milton Obote, Principal Lule, and the many Makerere University College hosts earned the plaudits of all Conference participants. As this Conference was planned by Africans, arranged in Uganda by Africans, this volume is edited by a writer and physician from South of the Sahara: we thank Dr. John Karefa-Smart of Sierra Leone for his work as editor and rapporteur.

Beyond all that is said about Africa's need for capital and tools, increased gross national product and markets, this book is a universal call to restore our souls and to stir our capacity for spiritual disquiet.

EVERETT R. CLINCHY

INTRODUCTION

CHIEF S. O. ADEBO

Ambassador of Nigeria
to the United Nations

This volume contains the speeches and papers prepared for the African Conference on Progress Through Cooperation, organized by the Council on World Tensions in association with Makerere University College and held on the University campus in Kampala, Uganda, May 9–15, 1965.

The purpose of the Conference was to study ways in which the African nations can speed up their economic and social development, meet the pressing needs of their peoples, raise their standards of living, and establish fruitful relationships among the groups within their own borders as well as with other nations of the world community. Practical ways were sought for countries to make more effective use of their own resources and of aid from others in order to establish the economic and social foundations for peace.

With a Foreword from the pen of Everett R. Clinchy, internationalist and President of the Council on World Tensions, and an opening chapter, "A Continent of Neighbors," by Paul Hoffman, one of the greatest friends of the "new" nations, there is no real need for another Introduction to this book.

However, I should like to use this opportunity to pay tribute to all those whose services made the Kampala Conference the success it was. Pride of place on the list must be given to The Ford Foundation, whose financial generosity made it possible to hold the Conference at all. This is, of course, only one of the many valuable services that this remarkable Foundation renders to Africa—and to the world. We are not forgetting the other contributors to whom gratitude is due for providing the necessary matching funds to supplement the Foundation grant.

Money alone, however, accomplishes nothing. Someone has to put it to work. This function in our case was performed by the Council on World Tensions, under the splendid leadership of Dr. Clinchy, Mr. Hoffman and Mr. Walter H. Wheeler, Jr., Chairman of the Council. Great credit is due to them for their excellent performance of it. If they do not mind my saying so, these gentlemen displayed an acute sense of judgment in appointing such an admirable Executive Director, Dr. Margaret Grant, to help with the management of the Council's affairs. I cannot imagine any project entrusted to Dr. Grant failing to succeed, provided all others concerned cooperate.

In this case all others cooperated beautifully. Who were these others? The Council was anxious that the Kampala Conference should deal primarily with African problems, be attended mainly by Africans, and organized in accordance with African advice. They therefore set up an Advisory Committee composed almost wholly of African ambassadors in New York who, fortunately, responded wholeheartedly to the call. It was this Committee which, among other things, settled the topics for discussion and advised on the list of participants.

That list was not easy to prepare because, in order to maintain the private and informal nature of the discussions, the total number naturally had to be limited. There were thirty-six independent African countries from all of which participants were desired; it was also intended to invite African participants from the yet unfree areas of Africa; and, in order to assure the cross-fertilization of ideas between Africa and the rest of the world—one of the principal aims of the Conference—a strong contingent of participants from Europe, the Americas, and elsewhere outside Africa was needed. Not all the persons invited from African or non-African countries were able to accept, but the attendance list was, nevertheless, impressive.

Discussion at conferences is greatly facilitated when participants are able to have in advance papers on the items on the agenda, prepared by knowledgeable persons, which pinpoint the issues and can serve as a basis for at least the opening shots in the debate. It is not always easy to secure advance studies, but the Kampala Conference was more fortunate than most in this respect. There was, indeed, a wealth of papers from distinguished statesmen, educators, and others with knowledge and experience of the subjects on which they wrote. All their papers are being published in this volume, together with the addresses of distinguished speakers and summary records of the proceedings in each of the committees into which the Conference was divided for effective working, as well as in plenary sessions.

For any person interested in the theme of the Conference and desirous of becoming more informed on the problems of our continent, there is, of course, no substitute for actual participation in the exciting dialogues that took place at Kampala. Unfortunately, not all such friends of Africa could be there. For those who were not, this publication provides an opportunity to gain a well-rounded idea of what was done there. It is my hope that it will be read by thousands, since only in this way can the frank exchange of knowledge and experience and the practical suggestions which emerged have the wide influence they deserve among the many persons actively involved in the problems of the developing nations. Only thus is it possible to secure adequate value for the expenditure of money by the financial sponsors, and the expenditure of time, thought, and energy by all concerned in organizing this great Conference.

Like its predecessors in the World Tensions series, Kampala was not intended necessarily to produce decisions, or resolutions, much less a blueprint for the development of all Africa, or a sure cure for all our political, economic, and social headaches. Its objective was

the modest one of bringing intelligent minds into confrontation
on those problems so that the issues become clearer, along with
the implications of alternative solutions. All those I have met who
had the privilege of joining in this Conference seem to have no
doubt that this objective was amply achieved. I am one of the un-
lucky ones who did not have that privilege. But I have no difficulty, from a perusal of the manuscripts for this book, in conclud-
ing that the great debate in Kampala on African problems was
more than worth while, and that we should make every possible
effort to find some means of continuing it in other countries of the
continent.

A CONTINENT OF NEIGHBORS

PAUL G. HOFFMAN

Managing Director, United Nations Special Fund

It would take a great deal of daring for anyone to say that he truly knows Africa. Indeed, the mere use of *Africa* as a collective term can easily be misleading. For this great continent that spans more than seventy degrees of latitude and six thousand years of history dazzles the mind with its diversity of climates and cultures, economies and social systems, racial backgrounds, religious beliefs, and shades of political persuasion. Moreover, so alive is Africa with growth and change that expertise in any of these areas is subject to overnight obsolescence.

Yet there is one Africa with which I can claim a certain familiarity. It is not the Africa of the headlines, the Africa of crisis and conflict, the Africa divided against itself. It is the Africa of compelling and consistent purpose that last year brought its gross national product to the highest point in history. It is the Africa which is working on a continental scale to improve the life of its people, and cooperating for that purpose on scores of development projects. It is the Africa whose responsible and forward-looking leadership honors this Conference by its presence.

This Africa is by no means exclusively preoccupied with its own problems. On the contrary, as their activity in every organ of the United Nations has shown, the countries of Africa are deeply concerned with the outside world and fully committed to playing a constructive role in its affairs. This concern and commitment spring from a recognition that when a nation casts itself loose from foreign rule, it is swept immediately into the mainstream of the great global trends of the times.

In our era, one of the most pervasive and important of these trends is technological change. Scientific progress, rapid and revolutionary beyond anything in history, has altered the basic state of man more drastically in a single lifetime than in the sum total of all previous centuries. I am fully aware that this is a truism. But I am fully convinced that it cannot be too often or too forcefully repeated. For ours *is* the first generation with the power to wipe out hunger, disease, destitution, and despair. Equally, it *is* the first generation with the power to wipe out perhaps half of humanity and nine-tenths of human progress in one brief nuclear spasm. Thus it *is* the first generation in history to be presented with a choice both absolutely clear and utterly inescapable—unite and prosper or divide and perish.

The decision is easy to define. Yet it seems terribly difficult for mankind to take. Astronauts have circled the globe in eighty minutes. Jet aircraft make person-to-person contact between the most distant centers a matter of a handful of hours. Within microseconds, satellite television can link the continents, eye-to-eye and voice-to-voice. But we have thus far failed to accept what these facts so clearly imply—the reality of our world as a very small neighborhood, and the necessity of learning to live with our neighbors on reasonably good terms though we may not always love them or their way of life.

Of recent years, there has been growing acceptance of the idea that the world must be made safe for diversity. The Middle Ages were blighted by utterly futile religious wars—wars that persisted until there was belated agreement to "live and let live." We must not permit the remainder of this century to be darkened by wars over ideology. Rather let us promote further progress toward building a world where nations may violently disagree without resorting to violence.

Does all this mean that in our new and compact world nationalism has become, like the human appendix, a useless and even dangerous vestige of the past? I do not think so. Diseased and distorted nationalism can, of course, poison the whole world's body politic. But for countries, as for individuals, a healthy sense of identity, a strong sense of security, a reasonable sense of self-respect, and a realistic sense of purpose are absolute prerequisites to forming good relationships with others. Developing this kind of nationalism is, moreover, an indispensable first step toward the acceptance of international responsibilities, and thus toward meaningful cooperation in regional and global affairs.

This is why the great experiment in nation-building which Africa is carrying out in this decade may well prove decisive not only for her own peoples but for the future of humanity. Africa with its fresh-minted independence—its fluidity, drive, and diversity—its chance to profit from the successes and failures of other regions—this Africa of the 1960's has a unique opportunity to create a continent of true neighbors. And as Africa increasingly speaks with one voice, she may increasingly impress the world with the truth of her own ancient proverb: "When was honey ever made by one bee in the hive?"

Thus this African Conference on Progress Through Cooperation offers uncommon opportunities. The distinguished participants come from a host of national backgrounds, command extensive and varied experience, hold strong and challenging viewpoints. Under ground rules guaranteeing the strictest privacy, they will have full freedom to open to each other their hearts as well as their minds. The agenda is wide—covering Africa's problems of national development, internal cohesiveness, and external cooperation.

Within this general framework, ample opportunity has been provided to examine, among other matters, the specifics of what Africa can do to speed its own social and economic progress, and what Africa can contribute to speeding such progress in the rest of the world. These are matters that command our most thoughtful and imaginative consideration. For I feel very strongly that the key to healthy nation-building, and to the development of true neigh-borliness among nations, must today be sought as much in the social and economic as in the political spheres.

I base this belief on a number of grounds. To begin with, there can be little doubt that a reasonably sound economy, a broad-based educational system, and a cohesive society are the rock-bottom prerequisites for true nationhood. Unschooled people can contribute little to nation-building. Sick people and hungry people care little about nation-building. People inadequately clothed and inadequately housed have little concern to spare for nation-building. And people who can find no meaningful place for themselves in a nation's social structure have no interest in national stability. Thus, one of the first tasks of nation-building is the creation of an economic and social framework within which people can enjoy full human dignity, and employ their full human talents in forwarding their own and their country's welfare.

If a country is to achieve real economic and social health, and fully independent nationhood, its progress must largely be sustained from within. The people and leaders of a country must assume primary responsibility for their own development, and their own land must supply the bulk of the resources needed. Developing countries do, of course, require outside capital investment, together with technical assistance that will enable them to attract such investment and to use it with greatest effectiveness. But the role such external assistance can play, while vital, is at the same time strictly limited.

For in social and economic development, it is not the end goals alone that are meaningful. The difficult and demanding steps which most countries must take in order to raise substantially the living standards of their people are, of themselves, contributory to solidifying nationhood at home and cementing good relationships abroad. To this I can testify from my experience as Administrator of the Marshall Plan for European recovery.

In 1948, Europe was a continent physically shattered by the most terrible war in all of human history, and deeply scarred in spirit by the twenty years of disillusion and divisiveness which had preceded that war. Nothing, in those days, seemed more visionary than a revival of European unity in even the most rudimentary form. Yet I had a strong feeling that, given the common goal of economic and social reconstruction and a method for working in cooperation toward this goal, there could be a healing of ancient wounds and the birth of a new understanding. So, in large measure, it proved to be. Europe today, with all its disagreements, is more closely united economically and politically than at any time since its nations achieved their modern form.

There is, of course, no question that the specific problems involved in European recovery were very different from those which the countries of Africa now face in their drive for self-development. Yet the unifying forces—domestic and international—which Africa's efforts for progress can generate should be no less strong and enduring. For in Africa, as in Europe, a basic characteristic of human behavior is involved.

It is a sad commentary on human nature, but none the less universally true, that unity is often thwarted by antagonisms of political, cultural, racial, national, or historic origin. Nations which before the world rightfully demand an immediate end to all forms of discrimination sometimes themselves fail to accord a full measure of respect to other nations or, in fact, to particular groups of their own citizens. Sometimes more than good will is needed. It would seem that the development of effective unity—national or international—often requires the presence of a common enemy too strong to be defeated without a common effort.

The peoples of Africa have, as did the peoples of Europe, not one but many such common enemies. Hunger, disease, poverty, ignorance, too much unemployment and too little opportunity—it seems almost superfluous to name these killers of the body and cripplers of the spirit, for they are old and familiar foes. Yet Africa can overcome them and it can do so largely in this generation. Its land has the wealth, its peoples have the will, and modern technology now makes available the way.

Already the peoples and nations of Africa are exploring the many paths of practical cooperation, among themselves and with the rest of the world, that are necessary for the eventual attainment of this great goal. And Africa's rapid accumulation of development experience over recent years means that her leaders can more and more find on their own continent, rather than overseas, guidelines to successful action.

I personally believe that the African peoples and nations will pioneer entirely new approaches to collaboration in social and economic development, for Africa's problems and Africa's potentials have their own unique identity. In so pioneering they cannot fail to progress toward national, regional, and finally continental unity of purpose. The dynamics of working together for essential common ends, and of doing so under urgent pressure for worth-while results, dictate such an evolution.

There are, of course, many different national approaches to achieving economic and social progress, as well as many forms of international cooperation that can help to speed this process. However, in the opinion of African leaders for whose insight and experience I have the deepest respect, there are certain key issues that, to one degree or another, affect the continent virtually as a whole.

One question that immediately arises concerns the relative merits of national and regional development. This is a complex and difficult problem that cannot usefully be defined in "either-or" terms, nor successfully resolved on the basis of generalized theories. Almost invariably it is the nature of the needs to be met, and of the resources available to meet them, that will dictate the decision. For example, one of the first projects to be approved by the Governing Council of the United Nations Special Fund was neither national nor regional but intercontinental in scope—an integrated attack on the desert locust ranging from the Atlantic Coast of Africa to East Pakistan. Other needs dictate other approaches. Thus one of the most recently approved Fund-assisted projects brings together Guinea, Mali, Mauritania, and Senegal to study possibilities for regulating the Senegal River, whose waters they share. Similar practical considerations have led African Governments and the Fund to join forces in nine other regional approaches, and on 144 national projects.

The determination of development priorities is another pressing problem throughout Africa. This is due not only to the obvious necessity for making the most productive possible use of scarce resources, and for avoiding errors in planning that can have greatly adverse long-range effects. The lack of clear priorities can also generate severe national tensions as each group's special needs are argued while basic needs go unfulfilled. Regional tensions, too, are likely to be sparked, since no nation can plan its own development with confidence or economic efficiency while the development plans of its neighbors are unknown. Finally, undue delay in establishing development priorities makes it difficult for a country to formulate sound and rational requests for technical assistance or to attract growth capital from abroad.

There is general agreement that in order to make such decisions on a truly sound basis, African countries urgently need much more detailed and precise information on practically every aspect of their natural and human resources than is presently available to them. Fuller and more accurate resource inventories would also greatly speed the flow of capital investment. Unfortunately, over the last five years, technical and economic research in many critical areas has actually diminished.

Another unresolved issue in Africa's development efforts is that of public versus private enterprise. If there ever was an issue which should be approached pragmatically, it is this. Africa needs a rapid increase in the production of agricultural and industrial goods. Whether this can best be achieved under public or private enterprise or a mixture of both is for the government concerned to decide. Whatever that decision, it is absolutely essential that African nationals be given immediate opportunities to play a far larger role in the economic life of their countries. This gives governments the difficult task of deciding how to foster domestic participation without losing the benefits which external participation may provide.

African economists and statesmen with whom I have talked are taking a realistic view of other long-term problems as well. High on the list is the necessity of bringing down tariff barriers against each other's products as quickly and as completely as possible. Africa's leaders are also well aware that the industrialized nations are becoming more self-sufficient in terms of their need for many primary commodities, making prospects for certain basic exports from Africa increasingly unfavorable. This has not only led many African countries to expand and diversify exports to their present major customers in the industrialized world; it has also encouraged them to undertake a serious search for methods of stimulating greater and more profitable trade with new customers in the developing nations of the globe.

There is no doubt that Africa has rich, rich reserves of natural and human resources. But, as the world's experience shows, all countries tend to make better and fuller use of their physical resources than of their human. By way of example, it is rather hard to conceive of a nation's neglecting its diamond mines or overlooking its petroleum deposits. Yet human potentials of immeasurably greater worth are often wasted, and frequently for most unreasonable reasons. This is not only a great injustice; it is terribly costly as well. For human resources are by far the most valuable of a nation's assets. Indeed, while today's technology can almost always devise quite adequate substitutes for any natural resource that may be in short supply, the human contribution remains irreplaceable.

Thus Africa, like every other region on earth, is challenged to make the very most of her human resources. And, as in other regions, that challenge is fourfold. First, to offer every human being the greatest possible chance to develop himself, or herself, and to contribute to the development of the country, without discrimination of any kind on any basis. Second, to help create the new outlooks and attitudes that Africa's new aspirations require—while preserving and building upon the important values inherent in many of Africa's old customs and tested ways of life. Third, to make training available in all the vocational, technical, managerial, and administrative skills of which Africa finds itself in such desperately short supply, and to provide this training on a quantity basis at quality levels. Fourth, to expand opportunities for basic education, of adults as well as of children. For, in the final analysis, nations are not built by skilled workers or technicians or scientists or even civil servants alone, but by men and women with the generalized knowledge and interests that are essential to the exercise of responsible citizenship.

The problems touched on here are not only serious in their effects but complex in their causes and stubbornly resistant to solution. Indeed, the economic, social, political, and humanistic goals toward which the nations of Africa are striving with passionate and purposeful conviction must sometimes seem to have a mirage-like quality. Yet, as Africa's people feel and as Africa's leaders know, this is clearly not the case. Progress is painful. Progress is slow. But progress is being made. And conferences such as this one can do much to accelerate progress, not only on this continent but throughout the world. For both Africa and its neighbors have hard-won experience of much value which can be shared with mutual profit.

The nations of the industrialized world, for example, have had their own long struggle for economic and social progress. That struggle, even today, is by no means over and won. Its history is replete with costly errors and time-consuming experiments which the nations of Africa, forewarned, may well be able to avoid. One clear lesson emerging from this experience is the great importance of approaching social and economic problems with a high degree of pragmatism, and of testing all likely-seeming theories on a small scale before applying them on a large one. Another discovery which Africa may find relevant to its own needs is the fact that disagreement on ideological and political questions need not, and should not, prevent effective cooperation on practical problems, both international and domestic.

Finally, as the industrialized nations are constantly rediscovering in attempting to solve their own economic problems, there is simply no substitute for persistence. To quote a recent report by a respected organization of professionals in the field: "We must persevere, *often for years*, to achieve . . . a constructive change in national policy on even a single one of our problems."

But the coin of shared experience has its other side. Daily and dramatically, the impressive achievements being hammered out on this continent show the world how much can be accomplished when nations have the dedication and discipline to work toward a great vision, step by practical step. Furthermore, and at a critically important time, Africa is showing the determination to rely on and work through the United Nations, as the chief instrument for assuring peace and progress on its own continent and in the world. This cannot fail to have a profound and beneficial impact.

What we are seeking here, and what we have the ability to achieve, is not a bland and soothing consensus, but the free and constructive exchange of ideas which is essential to understanding. From this there can emerge new and more fruitful forms of cooperation. And while cooperation alone cannot solve all of Africa's problems or the world's, it is in cooperation alone that we shall find the strength and the wisdom to make real progress in the days and years ahead.

PROBLEMS OF PROGRESS THROUGH COOPERATION

A. MILTON OBOTE

Prime Minister of Uganda

On behalf of the Government and people of Uganda, I am privileged to welcome you. We are pleased with your decision to hold this Conference here in Uganda and with the honor which the Council on World Tensions has shown us in holding the Conference in association with Makerere University College.

We hope that your discussions will lead to significant and dynamic cooperation in social and economic development. Within and among the African nations, as well as in the developed nations, the need and the concern for the development of the social and economic resources of the African nations is a common point of agreement. This I consider a most important basic factor, because it has enabled African nations to carry out projects which they would otherwise not have attempted. It is in the hope of its remaining constant that they have drawn up plans, or are doing so. The interest and desire of developed countries to assist African nations—whether motivated by humanitarianism or selfishness—have been significant and welcome, establishing a common ground of agreement between African nations and developed nations. There is, however, some evidence that this factor is becoming increasingly a serious source of instability within African nations, and between one another.

The struggle for independence was characterized by politics. This was not surprising. A nation seeking independence is preoccupied with politics. When it becomes independent, political affairs continue, but the development of social services and economic resources becomes urgent and demanding. It is not surprising that on independence day some of the biggest newspaper headlines report offers by developed countries to assist in social and economic development. African leaders welcome such offers and describe them in laudatory terms.

A disturbing trend, however, soon develops. The providers of aid begin to compete for the ears either of the government as a whole, or of individuals in and outside the government—and aid itself soon appears to be an instrument of instability. This situation may develop to a point where the providers of aid assume and expect immunity from criticism of some of their policies by the recipients of aid. Because of this mistaken approach to human relations by both the East and the West, most African states are walking on a tight-rope.

With all respect to the great countries in the East and West, I would say that the world is not in a condition today—and I doubt it ever was—when one should refrain from expressing honest criticism simply because of favors received or hoped for. Those nations which are loosely banded together as "nonaligned" often feel very strongly that the actions of the big powers do not always take account of the fact of their independence and right to self-determination. In spite of this, future historians reviewing the present era may well judge that it was the existence of a powerful body of opinion not automatically aligned to a power bloc which saved the world from a nuclear holocaust. It would be a poor reward if the historical results proved to be that development assistance to the nonaligned were reduced or stopped.

The prime responsibility for the extension of the area of conflict in Africa between the East and the West rests with the power blocs. Surely what they must now do is to seek a new field for cooperation among themselves in helping the poorer nations.

Most countries tie their aid wholly or partly to purchases of their goods or services. One cannot always blame them for this. If they are in balance-of-payment difficulties, they cannot give away what they have not got. But there is an additional complication. They like to parcel up their aid tightly in specified projects, which is administratively convenient and presumably attractive for public relations purposes. But this means that the African nations may have to take most of their equipment for a project from one source, whether or not this is the best arrangement. Suppose, for instance, we in Uganda wanted to experiment with growing swamp rice on the shores of one of our lakes. It might turn out that the best combination for this purpose would be American equipment and some Chinese advisers. It is questionable whether we would get assistance for a project put together on this basis. Yet, if we could, it might be of value not only to us but to other nations concerned. At the very least, the United States and Chinese citizens would have to learn to cooperate at the personal level and would probably discover that their opposite number was, as the saying goes, "not a bad chap after all."

There are many facets of this problem, and what appears to be the right answer is a major problem in itself. This is the promotion of cooperation among African nations in order to keep a solid and united front, not only in the way they analyze the social and economic problems facing them, but also in the solutions they put forward in spite of their varied social and economic circumstances. This unity of action seems to be the one thing that some developed countries do not want, but it is likely to make those developed countries realize the seriousness of the issues involved.

Furthermore, the international trading nations working through the United Nations constitute a colossal economic lever which decides and moves slowly. In some cases, it appears that they do not decide at all, because some members of the developed countries would not take certain actions unless other members agreed. This is apparent, for instance, when one considers the issue of Preferences. At the 1964 UN Conference in Geneva, Britain offered to extend the Commonwealth Preference system to all developing countries if the other developed countries would reciprocate. The other developed countries would not reciprocate and therefore no action is likely to be taken on this matter. The result is clear. The failure of the developed countries to agree leads the African nations to look to their various ex-colonial powers. So long as some of their urgent needs can be met by the ex-colonial powers, the African nations feel less impelled to cooperate with each other in an effort to press the developed nations to take joint positive action to assist African development.

The range of problems needing cooperation among African nations is very wide. Some are historical. Attempts have been made to tackle these problems and the incidence of contact is increasing —frequently at the political level. But this will have to be greatly broadened so that more effective contact will lead to exchange of goods and services and a much wider personal, social, and cultural involvement.

The fundamental difficulty is, of course, that Africa is a big continent with great natural barriers by way of rivers, deserts, mountains, and dense forests. There are also formidable language barriers. Huge investments in communications will be necessary to link the continent internally, to change the mine-to-coast orientation of roads and railways, and to make it as easy—for example—for us in Kampala to telephone the four hundred miles to Kigali as the four thousand miles to London.

In the development of Africa, we shall have to look to the developed countries for continued assistance. The whole subject of development assistance has generated such a spate of reports and conferences that it is unnecessary for me to dwell on the details now. I wish to emphasize only one point. The development of economically backward areas with capital, skill, and enterprise provided by those more developed is in what may be called the main line of history. This is irrespective of the institutional arrangements, such as whether the enterprises are public or private, whether financed by grants, loans, or investments, or whether the outside agencies are national or international. Underutilized resources of fertile land, minerals, and human beings in some regions inevitably tend to attract more capital, enterprise, and skill than other regions where these are relatively less plentiful.

The great barriers and the difficulties of finance make the case for regional cooperation in schemes highly important. In East Africa we already have a great deal of cooperation between Uganda, Kenya, and Tanzania. The full extent of this cooperation may not always be appreciated—perhaps because of exaggerated reports about differences of opinion among us. I would like to point out that our joint agencies and common policies include such major subjects as transport, communications, trade, and taxation. It is true that the intercountry agreements on the allocations of manufacturing industries are the most difficult to achieve. Our experiences bear this out. But we have nevertheless made some progress. Perhaps our basic difficulty has been that the East African countries inherited from colonial times methods and types of cooperation which had been imposed by the metropolitan power and which had had somewhat different effects in the individual countries. It was hardly to be expected that these institutions could be taken over in their entirety and function smoothly when these countries became independent. But the will to cooperate has so far overcome many obstacles, and I have no doubt we shall continue to work together.

Perhaps the greatest single obstacle to cooperation within East Africa is the political structure of Uganda, which has a federal constitution. Those who know the complex operation of federal constitutions will understand our difficulties. There are, of course, other factors related to the different programs of development for the three countries and what each country inherited at the time of independence. There are also drawbacks in internal budgets. I think it would be true to say that African leaders—not only in Uganda and East Africa—have shown tremendous drive, immense vision and enthusiasm for the development of their various economies and cooperation within their own states, on regional levels and on a continental level. They realize that without vision there will be no fulfillment of the economic and social development plans which have been drawn up.

The people also have shown tremendous capacity to make the best use of the available natural resources. Governments have made studies of the necessary economic and social projects, taking into account before the projects are started the best means of effecting development. International agencies, foreign countries, and foreign enterprises have participated in the development of our social and economic projects.

Personnel remains a big problem, and the hand of the well-meaning, conservative past among our people is still being held over their eyes and impeding their vision. The old ways of doing things, the vested interests, the assumption that everything will be all right without change, remain obstacles. The very advantages of the continent, its warmth and fertility, also stand in the way. On the other hand, there are strong demands on governments to provide immediately social services—demands which must be watched carefully lest they distort the shape of a country's development.

Not much imagination is needed in calling for more money to spend on education, except to decide what shall be taught, to whom, and why. Everyone wants education, and everyone is out to produce as much of it as possible. Schools and colleges are being built and teachers are produced as fast as funds become available. The outside world encourages and assists in this expenditure.

The same applies to health. It is both fashionable and civilized. So clinics and hospitals are built. Doctors and nurses are produced as fast as the money can be found.

Nor is there any disagreement about the need for defense, law, and order. Money can always be found for this protection in an uneasy world. But the bill to pay for the public debt and other international obligations begins to rise, and its rise must inevitably accelerate. This brings in problems of budget deficits and balance-of-payments deficits. When these arise, a country's small external assets and foreign loans will stop. There is plenty of international money for projects which are viable both domestically—because they pay their way—and externally, because a country has the means of servicing loans. The danger is that a country may move into a position in which she has viable projects for development domestically but no longer has the means of making overseas payments.

This brings a dilemma—whether to retrench and allow a development program to fall behind by curtailment of social services, or to increase revenue dramatically out of the proceeds of effective and high-yielding development and production. The apparent third course, of taxation by inflation, is only a palliative. It can solve temporarily the internal budgetary problem, but it cannot resolve in the long term the balance-of-payments problem, or encourage foreign investment.

Faced with this choice, we in Uganda have taken the course of effective revenue-earning development. This means that the same enthusiasm in favor of social services must be applied to animal industry, improving the quality of coffee and cotton, substituting home manufactures for imports of cotton piece goods, and all other economic activities that bring in money. These activities are too vast and involved to be left solely to commercial enterprises to develop on conventional lines.

Uganda, along with other African states, has a problem of implementing development projects that does not face the developed countries, in that large-scale development must be promoted by the government, even if not finally executed or financed by it. The government's function, therefore, is not simply that of inspiration or control, but also one of physically getting projects underway. African nations need and want cooperation in getting off the ground projects which they have already worked out. This is a major point for study by the African Conference on Progress through Cooperation.

PROFILE OF AFRICAN INDEPENDENCE

BARBARA WARD

Economist, Author, and Lecturer
United Kingdom

When historians look back on the first phase of African independence, they may be inclined to stress one overriding factor—the degree to which outside pressures impinge on the new states at a time when those states are trying to establish at home their own national identity. Africa is not alone in this. The ending of empires, even peacefully, is often the signal for new forces to press in, seeking influence and even control. Europe fought two world wars to determine who should fill the "vacuum" of waning Turkish imperialism, and some would say the issue is still unsettled. Yet if one compares Africa's present position with, for example, that of Latin America in the last century, it seems clear that Africa's evolution is proving much more "open" and hence vulnerable.

There are a number of reasons for this. Technology has pulled the world together. Under no conditions would Africa of the jet-plane age resemble Latin America of the pack-horse age. An embryonic world society, centered in the United Nations, has drawn Africa's new leaders instantly onto the world stage—and as they go to the world, the world inevitably comes to them. In the United Nations, they have discovered a majority of states with a similar background and heritage, coming out of a century of Western colonial control. Such a field of common experience beyond Africa's boundaries inevitably draws African interest outwards and outside interest back in again.

Something of the same magnetic field appears in the issue of race relations. A secular experience of racial discrimination at the hands of the white man common to many nations of the world keeps the current of interest and action flowing in and out of the African continent. In addition, the southern part of Africa—the last large area of the world under Western colonial or settler control—helps to concentrate world-wide attention on the ending of the colonial century rather than on the problems of the post-colonial epoch.

Above all, the colonial issue in Africa has been drawn to the heart of the world's ideological dispute. The Leninist interpretation of imperialism and neo-colonialism fits Africa into a world-wide theory of the Cold War waged between "reactionary" and "emergent" states. It projects into Africa ideas and interpretations of a global nature. None of this universalizing of issues was apparent in earlier centuries. In fact, not since the wars of religion in Europe or the Moslem conquests of the seventh and eighth centuries have faith and force been so closely allied.

The difficulty about this central—and inevitable—preoccupation with the colonial issue in the context of the Cold War is that, while it decreases the likelihood of an African consensus on the needs and future policies of the continent, it tends to increase the risks and complexities of outside interest and even intervention. The whole issue is ambiguous, since at least two radically different interpretations of exactly where the colonial issue stands today confront each other in Africa. Broadly speaking, the Western powers (with the exception of Portugal) believe that the phase has closed. In conformity with the principles of self-determination and national independence first asserted in the American and French Revolutions and given world-wide application in President Wilson's Fourteen Points of 1918, they have, they believe, accepted their colonies' claim to self-government and peacefully agreed to remove outside control. The British are proud of the fact that

African states, on achieving independence, have decided to stay in the voluntary partnership of the Commonwealth. A majority of French-speaking states have entered a voluntary but even closer association with the European Common Market. This, the Westerners feel, would hardly have come about if long and bloody struggles had preceded the break. Even where the fight was prolonged and fierce—as in the single case of Algeria—not all good will was lost, not all links were broken.

The Western powers also tend to feel that the connection with Europe helped to give Africa some of the preconditions of nationhood. They point to the missionary efforts in education, to the founding of postwar universities. They argue that Western investment and Western purchases of Africa's products have launched the states on economic modernization, and that a continuance of close economic relationships in the future will serve the interests of both sides. They underline the postwar reversal of earlier colonial policy—that colonies should pay their own way—and the rapid growth in direct economic assistance which, from all Western sources, has been running at an average of more than one billion dollars a year,* the bulk of it from French and other Euro-

*   OFFICIAL AID TO AFRICA
          (Excluding Egypt and South Africa)
              (*Millions of Dollars*)

	1964		1962–64		1959–64	
USA	380		1367		2227	
AID		189		743		1327
Food for Peace		153		487		693
Export-Import Bank		13		90		148
Peace Corps, etc.		25		47		59
W. Europe and EEC	811		2885		5638	
Other Free World	43		203		329	
World Bank Group	109		221		495	
UN Special Fund and EFTA	63		141		181	
Free World Total:	1406		4817		8870	
Soviet Bloc	413		658		1099	
Total:	1819		5475		9969	

NOTE: The above figures are taken from official sources.

pean sources. Western governments probably feel less confident now about their direct political legacy to the new states. They question whether either the "Westminster model" or a multiplicity of parties, European-style, best suits the new nations in their early attempts to build unity on the basis of varied ethnic and tribal groups. But Westerners believe that they did transfer power to genuine national leaders and left behind a valuable tradition of a plural society and the rule of law. They tend therefore to support and sympathize with existing leaders and to regard attempts to unseat them and radically redistribute political power as subversion and treason.

It would be difficult to conceive of a more opposite interpretation of the African scene than that put forward from the other end of the political spectrum. One cannot perhaps talk of a single Communist view of the colonial situation, for there appear to be significant differences between the Soviet and the Chinese approaches. The Chinese are in a better position to identify themselves with the "world-wide struggle against colonialism and racial discrimination," since they are themselves emerging from an uncomfortable century of being jostled and attacked by outside powers, first Western, then Japanese. They have also endured racial discrimination at the hands of white peoples.

The Russians, on the contrary, are European and white, and they can, in some interpretations of history, be accused of maintaining dominion over colored peoples in Asia. This is a significant factor in China's desire to keep the Soviet Union *out* of the Afro-Asian association. And although, since Mr. Khrushchev's fall from power, the theoretical points at issue between Moscow and Peiping have become more obscure, it does seem that the two Communist power centers differ on the degree of force that will be needed to produce a single world order of Communist states, the Chinese arguing that Western imperialism must be driven out by violence if necessary, the Russians suggesting that there may be nonviolent roads to socialism and that violence could produce an atomic war after which, in Khrushchev's chilling phrase, "the living will envy the dead."

These differences—which are likely to produce varying emphases and interpretations in African policy—do not, however, extend
to the whole field of Communist-African relations. The Communists argue that only the aroused will of the peoples of Africa has
enabled them to throw off imperial control and even now the
process is not complete. The Westerners are determined to maintain their economic dominance in Africa, which has been highly
profitable to them but is sheer exploitation from the point of view
of Africa, its peoples, and its resources. The aim of economic aid is
to tie the new, still weak economies to dominant markets and corporations abroad, thus ensuring that Africa's minerals are shipped
off to the West without adequate returns to Africa, and that its
raw materials will be made available to the capitalist countries at
low and fluctuating prices.

Also, since the "strings" on aid may not tie up the deal adequately, Communists say, the Western powers go further and set
up local puppet governments whose members, in return for heavy
bribes, are prepared to cooperate with the Western monopolists to
sell the nations' economic birthright for what one might be
tempted to call a mess of profits, if the profits remained in local
hands, which, by definition, they do not. From this Communist
analysis follows the presumption that national leaders who maintain friendly relations with the West are in all probability lackeys
of capitalism, and that "the aroused will of the people," having got
rid of their colonial masters, must now get rid of them. Liberation
is thus not complete until every link westward is broken.

At this point a Western countercriticism becomes relevant.
Throughout human history, the withdrawal of one form of imperial control has often been the signal for other power systems to
come in and fill the vacuum. True, in the twentieth century, the
effort is being made—for the first time—to affirm the basic right of
small nations not to be ruled and controlled by powerful neighbors
and to build up, in the United Nations, an instrument which can
safeguard their independence. But the Western powers question
whether the Communist recognition of this right may not be heav-

ily overlaid by the presuppositions of Marxist ideology. If, by definition, no state is "free" until it is Communist, then non-
Communist states cannot claim the rights of freedom. "Liberation" can mean not simply the end of old forms of control but the
imposition of new ones. The Soviet army freed Poland from Nazi
imperialism and imposed control from Moscow instead. If such an
evolution is possible in Europe, so argue the Western powers, may
not the risk be the same in Africa? Russia and China are very large
states in comparison with, say, the Congo (Brazzaville) or
Burundi. Is it certain that complete reliance on the Communist
grants may not substitute a new form of outside control for the
diminishing influence of the French or Belgians?

An outside observer can define the terms of the dispute, since it
is world-wide and an essential part in the dialectical dialogue of
mankind. It is much more difficult to describe African reactions to
the debate since they are drawn from the unconscious roots of
Africa's own history and from a more and more conscious attempt
to find a specifically African response. Moreover, there is not one
single African response but a spectrum of reaction from radical to
conservative, different leaders and different countries emphasizing
differing aspects of the debate, and the debate itself shifting under
the impact of changing events.

But perhaps from outside one can assess the weight of some of
the arguments and thus gauge the often contrary pressures under
which African governments have to work. Links with the West
have the advantage of familiarity and custom. Language, education, professional experience make an African more at home in
London or Paris than in Moscow or Shanghai or, for that matter,
Bonn. And since thousands of Africans are now educated in the
United States, the same familiarity, on the basis of the English
language, is growing up. This direct contact with the old metropolitan powers presumably allows educated Africans to realize how
widespread the local Western commitment to anti-colonialism
really is. And this, in turn, underpins belief that the ex-colonial

powers, once gone, are not likely to return. Even when, as in East
Africa in early 1964, British troops were invited to reinforce local
authority, they were gone again before the end of the year. On the
other hand, residence in some areas in the West—for instance, the
Southern USA—gives the African visitor a less comfortable picture
of Western liberalism.

Turning to economic interests, one can argue that Western
links do give Africa access to the wealthiest countries in the world,
with the largest markets and the greatest supplies of surplus capital. The flow of aid continues. In fact, British aid to East Africa
has sharply increased. For over a decade, France has been paying
its African associates more than world prices for such products as
coffee and groundnuts. And even though these discriminations are
to cease in the latest agreements between the Common Market
and its African associates, the European governments have undertaken to increase their grants to the Africans to help them to diversify their economies. Meanwhile, in the wake of the UN Conference on Trade and Development (UNCTAD) at Geneva,
most European governments are giving more serious thought to
means of stabilizing the prices of raw materials and providing the
developing nations with balance-of-payments support.

In the field of capital, the share of local states in the return to
be gained from investment seems certain to grow. Not only can
sovereign governments experiment more widely in tax policies
which retain more of the enterprise's earnings in the host country;
companies themselves are working out formulas which offer more
of the realities of partnership. The 50–50 division of profits between the Liberian American Minerals Company (LAMCO) and
the Liberian Government is a case in point. The Nigerian Government has been able to negotiate equally favorable arrangements
with Shell Oil. In a different field, the British Government has
started buying out European farmers in Kenya and giving long-
term loans for the resettlement of Africans on the released land.

So far, no government in Africa has been ready to neglect these
advantages. The government of Sekou Touré in Guinea is at

the radical end of the spectrum. But it has achieved a workable relationship with the Compagnie Internationale pour la Production d'Alumine, commonly known as FRIA, the aluminum consortium developing Guinea's bauxite. Similarly, Dr. Nkrumah enjoys excellent relations with Kaiser Aluminum Company, whose cooperation is essential to the success of the Volta River Scheme. Most African governments underline their desire for foreign investment and betray little fear that they will not be able to control the local activities of foreign investors.

Yet the issue creates a malaise, and when we turn to the credibility of the Communist accounts of colonialism, high in the list are memories of past exploitation, of decades during which Africa gained little from foreign enterprise beyond the customs duties used to cover the costs of colonial administration and unskilled wages for Africans—often migrant at that. The vast mineral wealth of Africa's South has advantaged the local Africans only by the "trickle-down" process, and only in the Union of South Africa has this had widespread economic effects. And there the economic effects are nullified by political discrimination.

The extreme fluctuations in the prices of tropical products, the degree to which all middleman profits in such activities as shipping, marketing, insurance, remain in Western hands, Western tariff discrimination against local processing—all can add up to a pretty ruthless picture of the rich getting what they can out of the poor. The very disproportion in economic power between such giants as the United States—or indeed, the vast American corporations—and the micro-states of Africa reinforces the feeling that even if the elephant is amiable, there is hardly room for him in the bath. And past history—from the Kimberley diamonds onwards—is used to argue that he is not always amiable.

Nor is it only the past. Foreign investment is linked with the recent carving out of mineral enclaves from pre-existent colonial territories: Mauretania out of French West Africa, Gabon out of French Equatorial Africa, and the setting up there of very large Western mining interests. Here, it is argued, are the archetypes of neo-colonialism—complacent local governments kept in power by foreign interests and, when necessary, by foreign arms. The attempt at secession in Katanga has been interpreted in the same sense and its leaders marked as "neo-colonialist puppets."

All this malaise and uncertainty are, of course, reinforced a thousandfold by the continuance of colonial and racial domination in Africa's South. There is no need to labor the point, but it is important to underline its link with the picture of Western capitalist powers unwilling to give up their allegedly monopolistic exploitation of African wealth. Angola and Mozambique are not only under colonial domination; they control the internationally owned Benguela and Beria Railways and hence the major outlets for Rhodesian copper. South Africa is not only ruled by a racial minority; it contains approximately one billion dollars of British investment, as well as about 25 per cent of America's total investments in Africa and 90 per cent of America's investment in manufacturing in Africa. Imperialism and capitalism, racial discrimination and Western investment, African exploitation and white wealth are believed to meet in southern Africa and to yoke the Leninist identification of "late forms of capitalism" with the continuance of the colonial system.

What does Africa make of these rival interpretations of its destiny? In general, perhaps, it is learning to live with them. Most African governments approach the matter pragmatically, picking out now this thesis, now that, according to their local needs and interests. All are united on the urgent necessity of ending colonial and racial dominance in the South. All are anxious to encourage foreign investment under proper safeguards. All want to trade with West *and* East. All joined the 77 nations of UNCTAD to demand more equitable distribution of the world's commerce and capital. All, inheriting the paternalistic tradition of colonial economic control, and largely lacking local entrepreneurs, intend that government shall play a large part in economic activity. Most would describe this policy as some version of "African Socialism," in which old communal traditions are combined with modern concepts of planning. Virtually all agree that, for some time to come, governments of national union or single-party governments will be needed to make possible the forging of the nation and the unification of the state. In fact, it would almost seem that consensus politics might have a reasonable chance in Africa, since, on so many great issues, governments do not appear to be very far apart.

In practice, however, the issue is much more troublesome. Wherever governments are strong, frontiers stable, social pressures manageable, ethnic and tribal strains under control, the ideological debate about Africa's future does not impinge on local security. But many states are not in this condition. Colonial frontiers are often an arbitrary inheritance and irredentism is the result—as on the frontiers of Somalia. Internal cohesion between tribes is often far from complete. The social structures of some states include unresolved conflicts between privileged groups and the mass of the poor. Feudal leaders on the Saharan fringe, for instance, or dominant professional and business classes in the more developed communities enjoy living standards and opportunities closed to the majority, and the gap becomes steadily more apparent as cities grow and unemployment tends to increase. Many African states are, therefore, exposed to strong pressures for change. And the more these pressures undermine the stability of government, the more the ideological debate becomes a further factor of division.

It is an old story. Divisions within states in Southeast Asia were entry points for the outsiders. Japan was able to preserve independence in the sixteenth century only by heroic self-isolation. India after the collapse of the Moguls presents the same picture. Internal weakness invites external intervention, and when the world is polarized between rival doctrines, the intervention will be all the more likely and all the more lethal. What is a war of liberation to the Communists is an act of subversion to the West. If either radicals or moderates turn to outside sources of help, the country is quickly sucked into the whirlpool of the Cold War.

For these reasons, the Congo has proved, so far, a turning point in the development of African independence. Up to 1960, the newly founded states were sufficiently stable and united to determine their own destiny, to explore new relations with East and West, to decide their own part in the world's fierce debate. But the Congolese, lacking all proper preparation for independence, fell apart and have hardly recovered their unity since. In the struggle, internal forces have looked for outside support, the various efforts of secession—in Katanga, in the Eastern provinces—calling on outside assistance. Today, after the withdrawal of the UN experiment to secure international control above the pressure of rival factions, a civil war still rages, embittering the internal divisions of all Africa, sharpening ideological differences, and creating the climate and the opportunity for further external intervention.

Nor is it difficult, in the light of these last five anguished years, to project into the future the appallingly divisive effects of the existing crisis. The deep rift over the Congo is dangerous enough. But if the struggle for African liberation in the Portuguese territories, in Southern Rhodesia and the Union of South Africa becomes entangled with the world-wide hostility between East and West, the southern lands could become not only the scene of a prolonged and bloody racial struggle but conceivably the flash point of escalation to nuclear war.

Can Africa in its own interest abate its own divisions and lessen the risks of outside pressure and intervention? That there is a strong internal drive toward African unity seems beyond question. The Organization of African Unity (OAU) exists. Various subsidiary organs of unity—the Economic Commission for Africa (ECA), the African Development Bank—exist. They do so in spite of the divisions of Africa into French-speaking states attached, in the majority, to a close association with Europe and to the Union Africaine et Malagache, in spite of the British Commonwealth partnership, in spite of such local associations as the East African Common Services Organization.

Again, a certain amount of economic assistance to Africa is al-

ready being channeled through international agencies—the World
Bank, the International Development Association (IDA), the UN
Special Fund, the affiliated UN agencies. New organs of unity
such as the ECA at Addis Ababa could accelerate the trend.
At various times, the African states have attempted to mediate
their own disputes—over Somalia, over the Sahara. Their *ad hoc*
body to settle the Congolese dispute is still in being, but it has not
yet achieved a basis for mediation. And this fact is perhaps the key
to the relative ineffectiveness so far of the OAU's attempt to secure the autonomy of its efforts. The organization is already deeply
divided between conservative and radical elements and has not
found a stance above the battle of its constituent members. A
completely *African* interpretation of today's crisis has not yet
emerged. Africa is, like other continents, caught in the toils of the
Cold War, and its freedom of action is correspondingly reduced.

Yet the last five years offer some clues to wider unity and more
effective African initiatives. Wherever the OAU can act on the
basis of majority opinion, the risks of outside interference are correspondingly reduced. If wider authority and greater resources are
needed, the United Nations is a safer instrument of pacification
than rival appeals to rival great powers. At present, the UN is
hamstrung by the Great-Power dispute over peace-keeping and over
the authority to control peace-keeping. But it would seem to be
profoundly in the interests of African states—moderate or radical,
right or left—to ensure that the United Nations can still act as po-
liceman, conciliator, and assistance-giver, provided the states most
concerned with a dispute or a region wish UN jurisdiction to be
introduced.

This is not simply an issue of peace-keeping. In view of the fatal
lack of preparation for self-government given to Africans in such
territories as Angola and Mozambique, international assistance on
a massive scale would be needed after independence to prevent
even worse versions of the Congo's tragedy. But such assistance
can safely come only from the United Nations. Thus, the present
would seem the very last time at which Africa should acquiesce in

a weakening of the powers and responsibility either of the organization in general or of the General Assembly in particular.

In a world driven by ideology, the small powers will founder if they are drawn into the maelstrom. As Dr. Nkrumah has often remarked: "When the bull elephants fight, the grass is trampled down." But the African states will avoid the bull elephants and keep their freedom of action only if they know how to keep clear of the Great-Power struggle themselves and how to establish their own independent bases for action. Ultimately, no outside power can intervene effectively unless the invitation comes from within. And the invitations will cease only when Africans themselves realize effectively and fully the implications of their own unity.

THE NEED FOR COOPERATION IN AFRICA

TOM J. MBOYA

Minister for Economic Planning
Kenya

There is little argument about the need for cooperation to promote peace and progress. In fact, wherever African leaders meet, they readily agree that Africa must unite in order to achieve full and total independence and to eliminate poverty, disease, and lack of education. It is when we come to the political and economic factors involved in this cooperation that difficulties start.

I am one of those who remain firmly optimistic about the future of cooperation in Africa. Some would like us to believe that in Africa there are too many problems, contradictions, and ambitions to allow for unity and cooperation. I do not accept their view. In fact, I would say that such people have looked at Africa only very superficially.

This continent is not yet completely free, and the majority of the independent states are not even a decade old. Thus, in some parts, we are still faced with the struggle for independence itself. Some key African territories are denied the right and opportunity to participate in or contribute to continental cooperation by virtue of the fact that they remain under colonial rule or, as in South Africa, under a minority racist regime.

Another factor which must be taken into account is the economic structure inherited by African states on becoming independent. The departing colonial masters did not leave our countries with the institutions or structure suited for cooperation. For us to cooperate fully within Africa, we will need some degree of disengagement from the strings and commitments inherited at the time of independence. We will also need to adjust some of our local institutions in order to allow for cooperation.

Last but not least, a newly independent country is faced with grave problems of unemployment; of scarce resources, including manpower; of foreign exchange and balance of payments; and the need to ensure political stability. It is natural that the new nation is immediately concerned with its own very urgent domestic programs. Practically every new state has produced her economic plan in the first year of independence, usually designed to meet immediate and long-term economic and political problems at home. If there is to be real cooperation in Africa, all such plans would have to be harmonized and coordinated through some agreed formula.

The conditions which we inherited at the time of independence are of two categories. The first relates to the nature of the economy at home. Very often this economy is based entirely on private investment from outside, controlled by parent companies or by groups residing in the capital of the former colonial powers. Our currency remains tied to that of the former colonial power. Within the country we have achieved independence, but almost the entire economy may be in the hands of noncitizens. Aware of their power, these people often state publicly that our policies must be geared to encourage their stay or they will leave our country and stop any further investment and expansion! Our people walk about our towns and see all the major shops, business premises, and industrial and commercial undertakings still in the hands of noncitizens and non-Africans. They are bound to ask: "Where is this independence that we are supposed to have gained?"

The second category relates to the economic and social systems which were developed during the years of colonialism to emulate and even complement those of the metropolitan country. Because the colonial powers needed certain raw materials, our countries were developed so as to specialize in those particular products, as well as to suit the market requirements of the metropolitan country. Other sectors of the economy were neglected, and no real trade or even contact was encouraged with other areas of Africa. This resulted in "vertical trade," on a north-south line from Africa to Europe. Perhaps the extent to which these conditions impede rapid steps toward greater cooperation in Africa is not realized.

Further, each government is under political pressures at home to "deliver the goods" at once, to provide expanding social services, and to Africanize the economy at the same time. With our limited resources in domestic capital for investment, lack of trained manpower, and foreign exchange problems, we find ourselves in a dilemma. We are faced with critical issues and choices at home, and in order to move at all toward our declared goals, we must rely on the cooperation and assistance of friendly countries abroad.

Each state in Africa is confronted with a period of multiple transition problems set in motion by the attainment of independence. We must move from a subsistence economy to a money economy; from an economy dependent on agriculture to a more balanced growth; and from a development of natural resources for the benefit of others to a development of human and natural resources for our own people. These problems, together with the critical shortages we have inherited, tend to force each country to mobilize its resources, as well as those that may be offered by a former colonial power and any new friends, exclusively to meet its individual urgent needs.

We are encouraged to think that cooperation can wait, and that political union should be postponed until we have put our different houses in order! It is clear that international agencies, outside forces, and Cold-War power politics have a tremendous opportunity to put off, to undermine and even subvert, Africa's efforts toward cooperation—that is, if they choose to exploit and manipulate our immediate national fears, anxieties, and needs.

Our desire for cooperation within Africa and the machinery set up toward that goal will need the sympathy and understanding of our friends outside Africa, including international institutions such as the World Bank, the UN Special Fund, and various foundations. In the final analysis, however, cooperation in Africa must come from African initiative. The machinery for cooperation must be designed by the African states themselves to meet our specific and peculiar needs.

It is common among African leaders to talk of economic independence as a corollary of political independence. We see this in national terms and seek to give it priority without bringing in our neighbors or other regions. Perhaps this is one point that we need to clarify for ourselves in order to pave the way for greater cooperation. It should be clear that what we seek as a long-term goal is effective partnership and *interdependence*. We want to Africanize our national economies to provide for fuller participation by our own people. We want to ensure equitable distribution of incomes and wealth, and to set up a society based on our concept of mutual social responsibility. At both the national and the continental levels, we want to have a full say in matters concerned with world trade and other economic policies in which we are now involved as members of the family of nations of the world. We reject any idea of trusteeship or patronage exercised on our behalf by former colonial powers, or by any power groups involved in the Cold War.

I doubt whether there is any place in the world today for the concept of national economic independence. Full economic independence is possible only in subsistence economies and today we should be emphasizing the economic interdependence of the nations of the world. Our real task is to achieve greater prosperity and economic growth by taking advantage of the opportunities for national and regional economic specialization which modern science and technological innovation have made available.

There is little dispute about the need for cooperation between African states and the more developed countries of the world. Without this cooperation, our development plans would come to a standstill. However, the weakness at present is that aid is entirely determined by the particular needs of our individual states. Each state negotiates separately, and often in competition with others. The donor countries or investors are free to pick and choose and even to dictate the terms by playing one country off against another, or by inducing one country to undermine the terms offered by a neighboring state. While I would like to hope for the sympathy and understanding of the more developed countries, and ask them to desist from taking advantage of us, I am inclined to feel that, human nature being what it is, the answer will come only through unity and cooperation among the African states at regional and subregional levels, that is, through moving toward a regional economy.

Within Africa we need to cooperate in order to conserve our scarce resources and to use them more effectively. We can do this by harmonizing and coordinating plans in the various subregions and by agreeing on joint projects that require heavy investments, e.g., development of power, communications, and higher education. We also need to cooperate in order to speak and negotiate more effectively with regard to markets and prices for our products. We need to cooperate in the fields of research and training by sharing experiences and achievements, and thus avoid waste through duplication of efforts and facilities. And we need to cooperate so that we can more quickly achieve diversification in our economies through intra-African trade.

Today some African states have a surplus in agricultural commodities such as meat, fruits, and vegetables, while others are importing these same products from outside the continent, because this is easier than establishing trade with countries in Africa. Some African countries have even mortgaged their entire production of certain agricultural products to countries abroad for a long time to come, regardless of market and price changes, to the detriment of their agricultural expansion and of Africa generally. Clearly, with the growing trend in Europe and elsewhere for many nations that had traditionally imported African raw materials to look for alternative synthetics or for production within their own borders, we must urgently consider the possibilities of developing within Africa our own markets for agricultural and other African products.

To develop trade and economic cooperation in Africa, international communications and monetary cooperation are essential. To gain the full benefits of scientific and technological innovation, industry and research must cooperate and, when necessary, be organized on a supranational basis. Tourism is another area where cooperation is needed. Here there is a great urgency for improved communications. The modern tourist wants to see as many African countries as possible in a short time.

Another area for cooperation relates to the scarcity of trained manpower, especially of technicians, specialists, and advisers. Most African states have come to accept without question the presence of experts and advisers from the developed countries. There is a tendency to overlook the growing accumulation in some African countries of knowledge and experience in problems of agriculture, soil culture, animal husbandry, veterinary services, research, cooperatives, and the like, and the increasing number of Africans qualified as experts and advisers. We need to make greater use of any experience, knowledge, and trained personnel available within our continent. This will stimulate our young people to strive harder for recognition, and our institutions to aim higher in their training programs. It will provide competent people who can see our problems from a realistic African viewpoint. There is no substitute for the expert who feels he is part of the problem and who has a commitment with the destiny of the continent or nation in which he is working.

The self-seeking uses to which foreign aid can be put and the dangers of neo-colonialism make yet a further case for cooperation in Africa. Our policy of nonalignment is easily undermined so long as we operate in isolation. Most of our states are too small in a modern economic context to avoid continued exploitation or political manipulation. Individually, we are unable to put an end to the threat of neo-colonialism or to create an atmosphere of genuine independence in which we will not have to look over our shoulders to see what the different world powers think of our decisions or actions. If we are to cooperate meaningfully, it is necessary for the international agencies and foreign countries working with us to recognize that Africa is determined to develop policies and programs that are genuinely African and to avoid a merely satellite relationship with nations.

Although it may appear that nothing dramatic or spectacular has been achieved toward cooperation, some very decisive steps have already been taken. Here in East Africa we have the common market and the Common Service Organization. We are exploring ways to modernize and strengthen the common market and to establish a larger market and area of cooperation with some of our neighbors. The recent Conference of the Economic Commission for Africa agreed on the establishment of subregional organizations and resolved to take practical steps to promote intra-African trade in the subregions and thence in the whole region. The problem of communications was given absolute priority; I hope it will not be long before practical measures are taken in this field. The need to train planners and other personnel was also given priority, and the Institute at Dakar is to be used fully for this purpose. We should also take account of the joint studies and cooperation among the nations of the Senegal River Basin, among the Central African states, and the talks among the states of the Magreb. Perhaps even more important is the establishment of the African Development Bank.

There is much hope among us regarding the future of the Organization of African Unity. Here is the opportunity for working out political policies and for harmonizing political with economic goals on a subregional and regional basis. It is not possible to discuss economic cooperation without noting certain political implications, for economic policies are the responsibility of political governments. The OAU holds a unique position insofar as cooperation among African governments is concerned. Most of us would like to feel that the OAU will succeed, if not in bringing about union government, at least in helping us to achieve a greater degree of cooperation through the consultative machinery created within itself, and through the meetings of heads of states and of ministers in the different commissions. In fields like the development of power, of institutions for higher education and technical training, there is great scope for us to come together, even before agreeing on political union and associations, to plan jointly and use our limited resources in these very expensive investment projects.

Africa is determined to maintain relations with the more developed countries. But these relations will need to be on a completely new basis. Apart from the objective of closing the gap between the "have" and "have-not" nations, there is a general need to recognize the changed circumstances of Africa in relation to the rest of the world, as the result of independence and self-determination. No one can put the clock back.

Much has been said about international cooperation and foreign aid and its benefits. But a more ideal form of cooperation is that of "aid through trade," which can help reduce the dependence of African nations on aid through gifts and loans. Yet aid through increased trade is possible only through greater cooperation, both among African nations and between them and the outside world, in order to create a more balanced pattern of trade. We must, therefore, make sure that this is fully understood by the multilateral agencies, especially when implementing the decisions of the UN Conference on Trade and Development.

This Conference provides for all of us a unique opportunity to study and understand the problems of cooperation and to share some of our anxieties. I would like to hope that similar conferences will be held in other parts of Africa in the near future.

I. Problems of Cooperation Within Nations

COOPERATION WITHIN NATIONS

CHIEF H. O. DAVIES

Federal Minister of State, Nigeria

A newly emergent and developing state is a nation in its infancy. We are here concerned with the problems of tension and conflict experienced in the effort to evolve a nation out of a state.

A state is a legal concept of a geographical unit or group of geographical units which is vested with sovereignty. A nation, on the other hand, is a group of people who are conscious of their relation to each other. No one is born with the consciousness of being a member of a nation. Unless members of a state become aware of their relations with other members of that state, they are not a nation. Thus a state may embrace more than one nation; indeed, common experience in Africa is that a state comprises several *petits nations*.

The ideal goal, of course, is to weld the *petits nations* into one nation, so that the state and the nation may coincide. The Nigerian national anthem contains the lines:

> O God of all creation,
> Grant this our one request.

Help us to build a nation
Where no man is oppressed.

This ideal of a larger nation has been carried forward among neighboring states in their efforts to merge and form a larger nation.

Originally, a nation was a group of individuals having a common ethnic origin, speaking a common tongue, and conscious of their common relations. Usually a nation so conceived is a very small group—sometimes referred to as a clan or a tribe.

Several nations, however, have fused into one in the face of common suffering, like earthquakes, flood, pestilence, famine, or war. Recently, colonization tended to weld several *petits nations* into one, and people of different ethnic stocks and diverse languages have recognized themselves as belonging to one nation. Colonial territories like Cyprus, the Malay States, Nigeria, Kenya, and British Guiana are examples.

Common danger may also bring different nations together. At the height of Nazi aggression against Europe, Sir Winston Churchill proposed a union between France and the United Kingdom. Any further effort to integrate European countries now stems from a fear of Communist aggression and possibly of American economic domination.

The Organization of African Unity is a humble beginning by a group of small African states in the face of mighty powers and the Cold War. Yet it confronts many problems of both a general and a specific nature.

1. A nation's equilibrium can be upset when there is an intensive immigration of people alien to the nation, people who might have conflicting interests. Immigration may be caused by refugee pressures resulting from wars or revolution; by the vagaries of trade or adventure, such as a gold rush or a search for arable land. The Indians employed in the construction of the East African Railways settled down after the operation and became the nucleus of the Indian *petit nation* in each of the East African states. Adventure

brought the white settler in quest of fertile, arable land in East Africa.

2. Another factor of disequilibrium may be the withdrawal of the binding force of common danger, common suffering, or common authority. The evil emergence of tribalism in the developing states in some cases coincides with the end of colonization. "Misery acquaints a man with strange bedfellows." When misery disappears, a new atmosphere is created.

The end of colonization ushered in for the ruling local elite the opportunity to exercise power, for the first time, and to control and allocate wealth. The immensity of the task of nation-building, the novelty of the situation, human weakness when faced with the temptation to use power and wealth for private benefit, and, generally, lack of understanding of new systems of government—all these combine to engender rivalry between the elites of the different *petits nations*. The conflicting interests which had been dormant under the colonial masters now come to the surface.

3. Other causes of disequilibrium can be diverse religious beliefs, when embraced either by different sections of the existing *petits nations* or by the indigenous groups as against the immigrants. Nigeria and the Sudan are divided into Christian and Muslim halves. In Nigeria this has not affected the political atmosphere, but it is one of the upsetting factors in the Sudan. In both, of course, different religious beliefs are held by different ethnic groups.

4. In their struggle for power, the elites within the state, or even within the nation, divide on the issue of ideology. Each set of leaders presents its programs for benefiting the entire populace. Most of the European states, before the last World War, were split on the issues of Capitalism, Socialism, and Communism. In the developing African states, the tendency is to split between Labor and Capital. Thus the efforts of the leaders of a state to evolve a nation are bedeviled by conflicting ethnic, religious, and ideological interests.

On the basis of this analysis, we can discuss the subject of co-operation within nations, assuming that the nation is an infant and that its problems are those of growth. The obvious solution for religious or ideological conflict lies in education, which engenders not only tolerance, but also a consciousness that all religious beliefs are meant to serve one common end—the Fatherhood of God and the brotherhood of man.

The conflict of interests between different ethnic groups is more serious. This is generally referred to as tribalism. The solution seems to lie in the discovery of new and more permanent integrating forces to take the place of transient common dangers and common suffering. The need is for positive common interest, instead of the negative forces of colonization, fear, aggression, war, or revolution.

Most newly independent African states have embarked on schemes of rapid economic development, with the avowed object of raising the standard of living of their citizens. These schemes, dealing with common needs and requiring common effort, can be made a strong unifying force.

Rapid economic growth may imply foregoing immediate consumption in order to have more goods and services in the future; it may mean inconvenience to the individual, or to one section of the nation in the interest of the whole nation; it may imply the subordination of legitimate political activities in order to enable the nation to attract much-desired foreign aid. Citizens may be called upon to effect savings and to invest such savings in loan capital for national development. They may be called upon to pay heavy taxes as part of the resources required for the same purpose. Private properties may be appropriated for the purpose of public development, and the owners may ill afford to give them up or may consider the compensation price inadequate. Labor may be allocated to a field different from that which it likes or in which it can be most efficient.

Several new states declare that they would give all facilities to foreign investors, that they would not indulge in nationalization or expropriation without adequate compensation. But the barometer on which potential foreign creditors or investors keep their constant gaze is the general atmosphere, particularly in the political field, of the intending borrower state. Hence it becomes a matter of national importance for the politicians to observe discipline in their acts and utterances if they are not unduly to embarrass their governments in their quests for foreign aid.

Indeed, a borrower state may insist that loans should have no strings attached. So long as this means that the borrower is not expected to participate actively in ideological warfare, it is likely to be understood and appreciated by the lender country. But it is a sad illusion to expect any lender country to assist a borrower country which indulges in subversion or acts inimical to the interest of the lender. This appears to me to be plain common sense; yet some citizens of a borrowing nation carry the game of nonalignment to the point of playing one lender against another, and of assuming a hostile attitude to the lender country as a subtle blackmail calculated to extract further loans.

Another important area in which cooperation can be improved is that of citizens' attitudes toward private foreign investment. It is foolish in the extreme for any country to create infrastructure capacities, if such capacities are not to be utilized for the production of goods and services. Where indigenous private capital is not available, it is in the best interest of the country to encourage private foreign capital to fill the gap. Studied hostility to such private foreign investment, based on insensate political feelings, actually amounts to noncooperation with the government in the field of economic development.

If development schemes are pursued with singleness of purpose, and every discipline is observed to ensure the necessary foreign aid, then a step in the right direction has been taken. What is required further is assurance to all citizens of equal political and economic opportunities, irrespective of ethnic, racial, religious, or class differences.

Several states have endeavored to meet the challenge of ideological conflict by adopting a one-party system of democratic government. This has the merit of making it possible for the entire people to face economic development with very little friction. In the long run, a one-party system of government would appear to involve suppression or negation of the fundamental human right of freedom of conscience and of association. In the short run, however, the matter may be viewed as one of priority of objectives. The issue of economic development is so vital that few sacrifices are too much to make it succeed.

In state and nation, the great need is for selfless, dedicated leadership that is acceptable to all groups and levels of society. Misguided opposition and petty party rivalry can have no place here. Only thus will be achieved the disciplined fellowship from which a new sense of common interest and common loyalty is forged. This is the way of cooperation within the states. Without such cooperation the state is insecure, and international relations or attempts at integration among states are merely illusory.

It should be mentioned that colonization has not been an unmitigated evil. It has introduced the metropolitan language as a *lingua franca*, and it has fused a good deal of the metropolitan culture into most of the conflicting *petits nations*. These are factors which aid communication and cooperation. The development of international communication and trade has also created an atmosphere in which cooperation among the states can increase. It is left to the leaders of the new states to place cooperation at the very top of their priority schedule.

THE CIVIL SERVICE IN NEWLY INDEPENDENT COUNTRIES

CHIEF S. O. ADEBO

Ambassador of Nigeria
to the United Nations

The role of the civil service is an important one in any country, whatever its political system. Even in the USA, where many politicians, businessmen, and industrialists do their best to keep the activities of government to the barest minimum, those activities have been increasing. This cannot be avoided in a world in which national defense is the greatest preoccupation of the country, and in which no government, however ideologically oriented, can with impunity avoid an increasing level of expenditure on social welfare.

In most countries the term *civil service* is used, as it is in this paper, only for that part of the public service which is manned by "career" people. Others, who are "politically" appointed to take charge of the direction of a government department or agency on behalf of the government in power—whether or not politicians—are public servants but not civil servants within this definition. Their appointment is not governed by a code of recruitment regulations prescribing requisite qualifications and/or experience; they hold their offices in a more real sense than civil servants "during pleasure," and they are removable "without cause shown." In some countries, only one or two top positions in each department

45

or agency are reserved for these appointed—as opposed to "re-cruited"—personnel; in others, the reserved positions include offices lower down in the departmental or agency hierarchy. Again, in some countries, notably the United Kingdom, each government department has two heads: a Minister—a politician appointed to take the political decisions, and a Permanent Secretary—a civil servant whose duties are to advise the Minister in the considera-tion of issues requiring a decision, and to supervise the carrying out of the decision by the Civil Service.

Obviously, the candidate seeking a career will be more attracted by a civil service in which he can rise to the very top echelon than by one in which the top is denied him because it is reserved for political appointees. Also, the greater the attractions, the better the quality of the candidates who will present themselves. It is therefore not surprising that civil services which offer the greatest opportunities in terms of final status are the most efficient in the world.

By the same token, since the greater the scope of activities di-rectly undertaken by a government, the greater the opportunities that its civil service would have to offer, the civil service of a coun-try with a more "socialist" leaning tends to be correspondingly larger than that of a country whose citizens are wedded to the clas-sical idea of a government's role in society. The efficiency or ineffi-ciency of the civil service of the socialist type of country will ac-cordingly affect the country's fortunes in a correspondingly greater degree.

But whatever the political system, the crucial importance of the civil service is undeniable. Without minimizing the vital role of po-litical leaders, it is no exaggeration to say that a country with an inefficient or corrupt civil service cannot be a great, stable, and happy country. Indeed, one of the most important tasks of the po-litical leaders is to try to secure a civil service of top quality. It is not sufficient for the party in power to initiate sound policies; the soundest policy can be frustrated by an inefficient civil service. Even where policy is not completely frustrated, it can be shorn of part of its effectiveness and the government thereby denied some or all of the political advantages that should be secured from it.

On the other hand, while an efficient civil service is not a substitute for sound policies, it has been known to help a country to tick along without damage to the common man during a period of political doldrums. The most striking case of this is probably the performance of the French Civil Service during the period of the Third Republic when the Government was changing hands at an average interval of six months, so that no Government had enough tenure to formulate and implement its policies before it was superseded by another. In spite of the lack of political direction, life for the average Frenchman was not visibly affected, thanks to the magnificent quality of the Civil Service.

There are, of course, other examples. In 1964, the general election in one country of Europe produced an inconclusive result, the negotiation for a new administration went on and on, and the country was without a government for months. The civil service of that country does not have quite the reputation of the French, but it did manage to pull the country through its leaderless period. In the United Kingdom, by the nature of its Constitution, written and unwritten, there is never a time when, as a matter of law, there is not a Government. When a Government resigns, the Prime Minister and his Ministerial colleagues continue on a provisional, albeit lame-duck, basis until a new Government is formed and takes over. There are few countries in which the civil service performs a more important or appreciated role than in Britain, for many reasons. For instance, the British make no pretense of giving a politician a portfolio because of his profound knowledge of the contents of it; rather, he is appointed to provide the department with political direction and leadership, and to ensure that it implements the new Government's policy in its special area of activity. For example, a medical doctor is not as a rule appointed as Minister of Health—although it has been known to happen, with results which many Britons consider not entirely satisfactory. There is one important exception to this rule, dictated by the nature of the responsibilities: Ministers in charge of legal departments must be not only qualified but eminent lawyers.

If the civil service is of great importance to a developed country, it is of vital importance to a newly independent country. It could make all the difference between survival as a reasonably well-ordered country and degeneration into chaos, because of the special handicaps to good government that usually exist there. The new political leaders may be first-rate in their unselfish love of country. They may be full of determination to govern their country justly and well. They may include individuals who have proved successful in their respective professions or other callings. Even with these advantages—which are invariably all present in the leadership of a newly independent country—the political leaders will require a specially dedicated and highly efficient civil service to help their administration achieve the success they desire. Why?

1. In many cases, the leaders will have had, before independence, relatively little experience in government. In no case will they have had experience of complete control of their country's affairs. Unfortunately, in government, more than in some other fields of activity, the only real way to learn is by performing. The British have a habit of granting to their colonies a halfway status in self-determination before complete independence, called "internal self-government." During such a period the local people run practically the whole of the internal show themselves, the metropolitan power retaining jurisdiction over the colony's foreign relations, but also a residual power in respect to internal affairs judged essential for the exercise of the foreign-affairs jurisdiction. This period constitutes an opportunity for local leaders to gain valuable political experience—although the sharing of responsibility creates its own delicate problems, and the indigenous leadership, understandably, never wishes to see it continue for longer than can be helped. But even such experience falls short of that which only full control of affairs can bring. During the period following independence, the civil service has a special responsibility to keep the ship on an even keel while the captain and his mates learn their jobs.

2. A newly independent country is inevitably a nation in a hurry. It is a "developing" country, in the sense of being an underdeveloped country with a lot of ground to make up. In a world in which the natural tendency is for the gap between the developed and the underdeveloped to widen, the political leaders of a new nation, with full control of affairs in their own hands for the first time, can hardly be blamed for aspiring to do a great deal in as short a time as possible. This imposes a great strain upon the country's civil service.

3. A third kind of problem applies particularly to those countries in sub-Saharan Africa. Even by the date of independence, a great many of the key posts in the civil service may be in the hands of foreigners, mostly nationals of the old metropolitan power. The proportion of posts so held has varied from country to country. In some, as a result of spirited agitation by their native leaders prior to independence, and a cooperative response on the part of the Colonial Government, the position in this respect was not so bad. For instance, by October 1960, when Nigeria attained independence, all the top policy-making administrative posts, and all but a handful of the top professional and technical posts in one of the Regional Governments, were in indigenous hands. A similar position was attained in a second Regional Government some two years later; in the third Regional Government and in the Federal Government, the storming of the "overseas officer" citadels took rather longer but has now been accomplished. Other newly independent countries have not been so fortunate, the administrative take-over requiring a longer time. Long or short, the special problems of the transition add an extra dimension to the problems of the civil service.

4. Finally, upon independence, some adjustment is usually necessary in the relations that previously existed between the politician and the civil servant. This point can best be explained by the story of the Indian politician who, shortly before his country became independent, was asked what he thought of the Indian Civil Service. He replied that it was an institution for which he

cared very little, because in his opinion the Indian civil servant was not Indian or civil or a servant of the people. Needless to say, this was not the general view held by the majority of Indian politicians before independence, for the Indian Civil Service has always been a truly great service. But it does point up a certain dichotomy that usually exists between the civil servants in a country struggling for freedom and the politicians involved in that struggle. Such a civil service is usually "colonial" in structure and in composition. It is not intended as an instrument of democratic government; a colonial government does not pretend to be democratic. The senior civil servants do not work directly under Ministers; they are not subject to Ministerial supervision or control. The top control post is held by one of themselves, the Governor. They are not, therefore, servants of the people or of their elected Ministers, in the sense in which they will and must become after independence. In some places, in fact, during the struggle for independence, some senior civil servants regarded and treated as "agitators" the indigenous leaders who assumed ministerial positions upon independence. The politicians could hardly be expected to nurse cordial sentiments for these future servants of theirs.

How can a newly independent country overcome these problems? How can it develop and maintain a civil service of the quality requisite for its needs?

In the first place, the government must make up its mind as to the kind of civil service it wants. Is it one in which appointments and promotions will be made strictly on merit, one insulated from political influence although loyally implementing the policies of the government in power? Or is it one in which the members, apart from any question of qualification or experience for their jobs, will be required to show that they are favorably disposed toward, or even members of, the governing party? My opinion is that the former attitude is to be preferred in any case, and that it is the only kind that can work satisfactorily in a country with a multiparty system of government. It also happens to be the only one with which I am personally acquainted.

In the second place, efficiency is achieved by good educational preparation, sound selection procedures, and a properly organized post-appointment development program. The preselection requirements will, of course, depend upon the office to be filled. In my experience, the specifications taken over from the colonial era are not invariably appropriate for the purposes of the more dynamic administration that a nationalist government naturally contemplates. The selection procedures will partly depend on whether one is recruiting for a "politically oriented" service or for the other kind. But a sound procedure results in the avoidance of complete misfits and of the waste of time and money that efforts to develop the undevelopable involve.

Post-appointment training includes arrangements for assisting or encouraging the official to develop his capabilities with time and increasing experience. There will be cases in which formal instruction at an institution (for example, a Staff College) would help. In others, and especially for persons in senior positions, the best means of development would be participation in seminars and conferences. At all levels there is no complete substitute for the self-development that the official acquires by reading, and by learning from the good example of his seniors. Here, again, it is advisable for the newly independent country to review the post-appointment training arrangements previously in force, since in most cases they are likely to be found inadequate for the purposes of the new service.

The problem of replacing the erstwhile "foreign" holders of key policy-making positions in the service by local officials is a delicate operation. It should not be recklessly rushed, nor should it be unduly delayed. It should be planned with care, executed with firmness and, as far as possible, with the cooperation of those to be displaced, many of whom will give their support if the plan is frankly discussed with them beforehand. The following extract from a talk I gave two years ago in Washington in the William A. Jump—I. Thomas McKillop Memorial Lecture Series, shows how such an exercise was carried out under one of the Regional Governments of Nigeria:

So we decided that training was of the essence of the solution to our problem, and therefore in both those regions to which I referred, the Eastern and the Western, a big program of training was put into action. We sent officials all over the world; some of them to this country, some to Britain, and a few to Germany. We have not regretted the expenditure of time and money involved.

We had to train very fast and very hard. (That was one way in which we tried to meet the emergency.) But however good the training may be, it is still very essential for the public administrator to learn a lot at his desk. To meet this problem we instituted an emergency program of appointing supernumerary officers to understudy the European heads of departments. It was a very bold scheme indeed. There were a great many skeptics who said it would not work. I did not blame them at all. The British Governor of Western Nigeria told me quite frankly, but I think erroneously, that it would fail. I told him that whether or not it would fail, it was the only thing that had any chance at all of success and we had to try it.

We were not looking simply for college graduates. We were looking for people who combined good intelligence with a flair for administration, people who were educable, people who had the energy and the enthusiasm to face the problems which we had to overcome. We appointed six such persons, comparatively young—four of them were graduates, two were not—and we at once attached them to six heads of departments. Now if that had been all we did I am quite sure that we would have failed, but that was not all. The scheme as originally formulated was for these people merely to sit by the head of department and learn how the latter dealt with papers. But from personal experience and that of my few colleagues who were working with me, we knew that you could only learn to govern by governing. There was no other way. You could see a man govern for twenty years, but you could not begin to do it until you yourself had tried your hand at governing. So whenever the head of a department went on vacation we did not allow his number two to take over. We sent his number two on vacation at the same time to save him embarrassment, and we put the supernumerary Nigerian official in the place of the department head. So the Nigerian official tried his hand at administering the department. It was a very bold scheme, bold in conception, bold in execution. It was called a gamble by quite a few people, but I am glad to say it was a gamble that paid off. The senior official did not go away for too long. British officials in Nigeria at that time used to go for three months' vacation at a stretch, which was plenty of time in which a man could learn to govern or misgovern, but it was not long enough for him to sink the boat. The boat was still there when the substantive director of the department returned, and we were able to say whether the supernumerary official had fulfilled our expectations.

I am glad to be able to tell you that all six of the people whom we took on at that time are now securely in charge of their different departments of the Western Nigeria Civil Service. A lot more who were taken on later are also in charge of departments. Today there is not a single department of that service that is not being controlled by a Nigerian official. What these officials lacked in the way of long experience was made up by their enthusiasm and their eagerness to learn. It is wonderful how much energy people can put in when they are faced with an emergency. It is like being at war. It is wonderful how much production people will put in, how much suffering they will undergo, if they feel that there is an emergency in which their own interests are engaged.

PROBLEMS OF DEVELOPMENT:
The Experience of Tunisia

TAIEB SLIM

*Ambassador of Tunisia to
the United Nations*

International cooperation is the great invention of our time. In the first place it meets the need for economic and social development in all nations, and more particularly in the developing countries. Furthermore, it constitutes one of the most important contributions to the achievement of world peace and the strengthening of the bonds of friendship between peoples. Since the Second World War the *rapprochement* between peoples and the acceptance of the principles of the United Nations have prepared the way politically and psychologically for the work of international cooperation. The tireless efforts of the UN and its specialized agencies, and the encouraging results they have obtained, have modified the outmoded views of the colonial powers on aid to the countries previously under their domination. To gain a better understanding of this irreversible progress toward cooperation, we must go back a little and consider the situation historically.

THE COLONIAL PERIOD

At the end of the First World War we find, on the one hand, the Union of Soviet Socialist Republics mobilizing all the living forces of the nation in order to set up a Marxist regime which alone—in the view of the Soviet leaders—was capable of developing in a rational and effective manner all the country's resources. The immense revolutionary task in which the USSR was engaged almost completely isolated it from the rest of the world.

On the other hand, we find that the great European powers, which had just emerged victorious from the war, needed to strengthen their colonial domination, or even to extend it to other parts of the world, if they were to recover. With some exceptions (such as Japan, Ethiopia, Liberia, and Yemen) all the countries of Africa and Asia underwent colonial domination and were administered by foreign powers. Their territories provided the markets needed as an outlet for manufactured goods from the various metropolitan countries and supplied inexhaustible resources of raw materials which assisted the industrialization and economic development of Europe.

Thus the world economic system was based on colonial exploitation to the detriment of the indigenous peoples. This system could neither facilitate the economic development of hundreds of millions of Africans and Asians nor hasten their social development or the promotion of democratic institutions in their countries. We therefore witnessed some degree of equilibrium and even agreement among the various colonial powers with a view to maintaining their domination. But this equilibrium and agreement were themselves precarious because of the competition and rivalry among the colonial powers.

Gradually, however, Wilsonian ideas on self-determination and the various rebellions of oppressed peoples created a sense of awareness among those peoples and a determination to liberate themselves. Nationalist movements were born in Asia, Africa, and the Middle East; the struggle for independence of the colonial territories began to take shape. One has only to mention the main nationalist movements in Asia, inspired by the leaders of the Indian Congress and of French Indochina, the Destour Parti du Peuple Algérien, the Istiqlal parties in North Africa, and others, to realize the scope of this national awareness and the fierce resolve of the people to regain their freedom.

World War II, however, and the Nazi and Fascist threats to the democratic regimes, temporarily silenced the claims of the oppressed peoples. It was only at the end of this war that a fresh process of decolonization was set in motion. Moreover, the intervention in world affairs of the great American democracy gave birth to new hope among the colonized peoples.

Great Britain, one of the largest colonial powers, had begun to realize that its relations in the Indian subcontinent would have to be reshaped if its major interests in that part of the world were to be safeguarded. It therefore granted the claims of the Indian nationalists, and at their leaders' request agreed to recognize the independence of India, Pakistan, and Burma in 1947. This change in the relations between a major colonial power and the territories which formed its empire marked an extremely important date for the world. It opened the way to an era of emancipation for all colonial peoples. Indian independence triggered an irreversible process of decolonization, offering an example and a stimulus to other national liberation movements.

Between 1947 and 1957 almost all the countries of Asia (with the exception of the Malay States and the British protectorate of Borneo) joined the concert of free nations, as well as five new states in Africa (the French protectorates of Tunisia and Morocco, the Sudan, Libya, and Ghana). The process of decolonization continued with renewed energy and vigor through struggles of armed resistance, such as the Algerian war. In the few years from 1957 to 1963, the number of African and Asian states that gained their independence more than doubled, rising from 27 to 57.

With political independence, all the African, Asian, and Caribbean states were faced in a really acute and urgent way with the complex problems of international politics, national reorganization, economic development, social emancipation, and other responsibilities as sovereign states. However, the membership of these newly independent states in the United Nations opened up new horizons for them in the search for an economic and social equilibrium to meet the aspirations of their peoples. In Article 1 of the UN Charter they found a statement of the principles for which they had long fought:

To develop friendly relations among nations based on respect for the principle of equal rights and self-determination of peoples, and to take other appropriate measures to strengthen universal peace; To achieve international cooperation in solving international problems of an economic, social, cultural, or humanitarian character, and in promoting and encouraging respect for human rights and for fundamental freedoms for all without distinction as to race, sex, language, or religion.

Chapter IX of the Charter deals with international economic and social cooperation, and here Article 55 acknowledges that it is "with a view to the creation of conditions of stability and well-being which are necessary for peaceful and friendly relations among nations based on respect for the principle of equal rights and self-determination of peoples" that economic and social cooperation must be introduced in order to ensure progress and development.

Thus the new nations found in the Charter the ultimate objectives they had sworn to reach as free and sovereign nations:

the strengthening of peace,

the establishment and recognition of freedom and justice for all,

the liquidation of colonialism, and

the creation of a new economic order.

Problems After Independence

The most urgent problems that arise for newly independent countries are multiple, varied, and complex, and include political, economic, and social factors. First and most important is the establishment of a sound regime enjoying lasting political stability and supported by the country's political parties. Once the colonial power has departed, the entire regime has to be recast and equipped with new institutions which take into account the need for human progress, the traditions of the country, and the aspirations of the people. It is not always easy—experience in Africa and

Asia has more than once proved this point—to set up an acceptable regime which precisely meets these needs.

Nevertheless, before any attempt can be made at national reconstruction or economic and social development, it is essential to build up a solid and stable regime. Its stability will prove lasting only if it is based on the full confidence of the people in the political leaders who are responsible for managing their affairs. To achieve this, these leaders must constantly seek to persuade and educate the masses, explaining and defining the objectives to be attained.

The second problem is that of setting up a balanced and sound administration which will carry out its tasks with maximum integrity and efficiency. In internal affairs, this involves the existence or the training of qualified personnel who can grasp the problems, propose and prepare economic and social development projects and programs, and supervise their execution.

The newly independent states must also face up to the problems of external politics. Each must begin to reshape its relationship with the former colonial power, establishing new ties based on mutual respect, understanding, and the protection of their mutual interests. In my view, this readjustment is crucial. It can be achieved without conflict, leaving the door wide open to fruitful cooperation in all fields and avoiding any violent break. Through mutual assistance, the complexes created by a narrow and chauvinistic sense of nationalism can be overcome.

Other problems which the newly independent countries must meet are those arising from the aftermath of colonialism and attempts at economic domination. Neo-colonialism greatly impedes the progress of these new states and may even jeopardize the stability of their regimes.

There is the further question of political options. Since the creation of the Organization of African Unity, these options take their place for us in Africa within the framework of intra-African interests, involving the question of commitment to one or other of the great powers which divide the world, or of nonalignment.

Other no less important problems concerning Africa's international situation call for collective responsibility in certain questions and for intra-African solidarity in the solution of others.

THE STRUGGLE AGAINST UNDERDEVELOPMENT

The most onerous and urgent task which the newly independent states must undertake is the struggle against underdevelopment. To ensure the well-being of their peoples and to raise their standard of living, these states must: (1) provide equal education for all and fight against illiteracy; (2) provide work for all and combat unemployment; (3) draw up general plans to combat unemployment and underdevelopment in all fields.

Economic development is undoubtedly the first objective. Various approaches have been adopted by different states, in the light of their special economic and social conditions. Natural resources and human potential, the geographical situation and relations with the former metropolitan country, which vary from one country to another, are determining factors in the preparation of a valid development plan. The approach adopted must meet the requirements of each country's political system in accordance with its traditional values and its own particular structures.

THE EXPERIENCE OF TUNISIA

The Tunisian approach to economic development illustrates the need to mobilize all the living forces of the nation in the struggle against underdevelopment.

What was the state of the Tunisian economy following independence? Like all African countries, Tunisia had undergone colonial rule. Its economic life had been subject to the evil consequences resulting from the application of the notorious "colonial pact" concluded between the great powers, which had divided the world into zones of influence and exploitation. For this reason, the former directors of the Protectorate had never envisaged for Tunisia a coherent, balanced, and sound economic development policy which would allow its population to raise their standard of living.

On the contrary, by encouraging colonial settlement, the Protectorate had created a number of artificial enclaves which existed in closed circuit, sharing their profits with the rest of the population only to a derisible extent.

These enclaves could be found in every sector of the country's economic life. In agriculture, for instance, we were faced in 1956 with an alarming situation. There were:

4700 foreign-held farms comprising 600,000 hectares of the finest Tunisian land;

5000 modern Tunisian farmers working 400,000 hectares, including 150,000 hectares under cereals cultivated by rotation; and 450,000 small properties divided among the remaining 3.5 million hectares of more or less arable land, i.e., an average of 7 hectares per property.

In view of the low average technical level of the Tunisian farmer and the financial means at his disposal, we were very doubtful about his ability to contribute effectively to the economic development of the country.

In industry the same phenomenon could be observed. For many years Tunisian industry had consisted exclusively of extraction (lead, iron, and phosphates) and was dominated, of course, by foreign companies, which alone had investment capital at their disposal. Processing industries were almost nonexistent in 1956, as were consumer goods, which were imported in a fully finished state. The excuses put forward to explain this industrial backwardness were the usual ones: the cost of power, the scarcity of water, the absence of capital, the lack of skilled manpower, the limited market, and so on.

To complete the picture, a bare living was earned by craftsmen using archaic methods, living in neglect, without any financial resources or technical aids. There could be no question of relying on this sector, such as it was, to make any sort of contribution to the economic development of the country.

As for the sector which includes banking, finance, insurance, and the like, in 1956 it accounted for 23 per cent of the active population and provided 46 per cent of the gross national product, as compared with 9 per cent and 2 per cent, respectively, for the industrial sector. This in no way reflects an advanced economic state, but simply shows the excessive development of commerce and the existence of a multiplicity of small traders of no interest to the national economy. It barely conceals the low level or absence of genuinely productive tertiary branches in banking, engineering, or basic research.

Thus in 1956 the Tunisian Government inherited an economic situation dominated in all sectors by outside forces whose only aim was to maximize the profit from their enterprises, regardless of the higher interests of Tunisia and the need for a balanced, over-all development. The basic features of this situation were the disarticulation of the national economy, which was made directly dependent on the French economy, and the accentuation of various natural imbalances, both economic and social, which were already a serious handicap to any form of development.

Tunisia's achievement of political independence put an end to this dangerous strategy and obliged the government to undertake an organic and functional decolonization of the national economy by eliminating vestiges of foreign economic power. Once this basic stage had been passed, it was up to the entire nation to decide on the most effective means and the basic objectives for a harmonious, integrated development. To do this, Tunisia chose the method of planning, which had already achieved concrete results in countries that had followed the path of discipline and sacrifice to overcome underdevelopment.

For three years, the Tunisian authorities undertook a systematic study and analysis of the country's entire human and natural resources in order to reveal their strength and their weaknesses and to determine the prospects for rapid development on a sound basis in accordance with Tunisia's situation and possibilities. The people as a whole were then invited to discuss these prospects, which governed the ultimate objectives of the development plan and the means to carry it out. This task was undertaken by the

Destour Socialist Party and government officials. They organized democratic public meetings in party cells, isolated areas, towns, and country districts in order to explain to the population the aims of the plan—sometimes altering the methods for its implementation, not only to obtain the country's agreement but to ensure the enthusiastic participation of the entire nation in the thrilling work it was called upon to perform.

For maximum success in any economic and social development plan, it is absolutely essential to be able to count on certain basic political and psychological factors and on a competent and trustworthy technical and administrative staff. Tunisia had the good fortune to possess a mass political party organized and built on a democratic basis, government officials enjoying wide support among the population, and an efficient and competent administrative machine.

The Tunisian people, of whom an overwhelming majority are from the middle and working class, naturally supported all the efforts made to raise their living standards and to help them join the caravan of nations advancing toward greater progress and civilization. Although political independence has restored to Tunisians their national dignity, it still remains to free them from unemployment, poverty, and ignorance.

Thus the object of planning was the promotion of man, the defense of his freedoms—in a word, the humanization of society, in which all the efforts of individuals, groups, and the state would be combined. Once the basic aims of the plan had been established and approved by the nation, it was necessary to determine the means of carrying it out, the stages to be gone through, and the priorities to be observed.

An initial three-year plan was drawn up and put into operation as of 1960. Its main goals were to introduce measures designed to release the Tunisian economy from its organic and operational ties with the former colonial power in agriculture, industry, and finance; to integrate the colonial sector in the national economy; and to *Tunisify* the enclaves which had remained in foreign hands.

The plan also introduced reforms in institutional structures in order to place economic power on a democratic basis and to adapt the administrative machine to the requirements of rapid over-all development. Similar reforms were undertaken in social structures, with a view to bringing about a more equitable distribution of incomes and remedying regional disequilibrium so that natural and human resources could be used to the full.

This vigorous plan could not achieve the desired results by using the technical and financial resources of Tunisia alone. The construction of new roads, harbors, and modern airports, of more hospitals, schools, and decent houses, could not be undertaken without foreign aid. In addition, the training of personnel at all levels, the struggle against illiteracy, and the implementation of a social, economic, and cultural policy required international technical assistance. Thus Tunisia, like all developing countries, must rely on others for both technical help and capital investment in the earlier stages of the plan.

INTERNATIONAL COOPERATION

Naturally, one of the main aims of the Tunisian plan is self-help. Aid in any form must not lead to a permanent and intolerable state of dependence for the receiving country, which should rightly beware of economic neo-colonialism. Nor should it be a cause of laziness and wastefulness in the developing countries. These dangers explain the failure of the efforts of certain countries in their fight against underdevelopment, and the caution and sometimes unacceptable demands of the countries that provide capital. The gradual and harmonious application of a development plan should lead over the years to a reduction in foreign technical and financial assistance, thus freeing the economies of the developing countries from any kind of dependence that would weaken their sovereignty.

Like other developing countries which were brought face to face with two concepts of aid—bilateral and multilateral—Tunisia had to meet this problem. Bilateral agreements have certain positive features which can lead to fruitful cooperation between the great powers and the developing countries, provided there are no unacceptable political conditions. To the extent that donor countries have eliminated any attempt at domination, thus demonstrating their understanding of the problems of the developing countries and their respect for the latter's sovereignty, agreements have been signed in which both parties were fully satisfied. Unfortunately, this type of agreement could not exceed a certain framework and scope and was incapable in itself of solving many different development problems with any large measure of success. A much wider framework was needed, based on greater understanding on the part of the financial powers and a stronger sense of international solidarity.

The United Nations and its specialized agencies have constantly sought to apply this concept. While the Expanded Program of Technical Assistance and, more recently, the Special Fund have substantially assisted the developing countries in economic studies, research, and vocational training at all levels, an immense amount of work remains to be done. Enormous effort and sacrifice will be required from the entire world if a sincere attempt is to be made to eliminate disease, ignorance, and poverty. It is because the difficulties which the underdeveloped countries are now experiencing involve international peace and security that an appeal has been made for the support and solidarity of all nations in the task of creating a harmonious world order.

The first tangible manifestation of this sense of international solidarity could be a reform of international financing institutions, making their regulations more flexible and the conditions on which loans are granted to developing countries more accessible. Regional development banks could then be set up in greater numbers so that they would be nearer their field of operations. This would give them a better understanding of the problems which face the developing countries, and help them to find the proper solutions with a full knowledge of the facts.

This program could be combined with the strengthening and

diversification of the work of the UN regional economic commissions, in particular, the Economic Commission for Africa (ECA), which for several years has carried out extremely important work in all spheres of African economic life. Here, again, special emphasis should be placed on the regional approach to development; climatic conditions, natural resources, and products in a particular group of countries are a convincing argument in favor of combining their potential with a view to the rapid and balanced development of the region.

The international trade system should also be revised to provide tariff advantages and preferences which would help the developing countries to find an outlet for their products in the markets of the rich countries, thus obtaining the capital needed for development. The UN Conference on Trade and Development has as its task the examination of all these questions in the light of the evolution of the developing countries and the problems with which they are faced. At the first session of the Conference, in Geneva in 1964, a large number of recommendations and resolutions were adopted, intended either to correct former methods or to shape a new framework accommodating the principles and objectives on which to build a new trade system. While these resolutions and recommendations did not receive the support of all countries, particularly the highly developed ones, most of the serious problems facing the developing countries were examined and set before the conscience of the world, and outline solutions were proposed.

Henceforth it is up to the world community to decide whether it wishes to give concrete form to this move toward international solidarity, without which the world will degenerate into decadence and ruin, by means of sincere joint efforts to construct a new order free from such scourges as poverty, disease, and ignorance. If this new order is achieved, world peace will be strengthened, sources of conflict will be eliminated, and man will eventually emerge the greater from the ordeal he has gone through.

II. African Solidarity and International Cooperation

INDEPENDENT AFRICA IN SEARCH OF INTERDEPENDENCE

LOUIS IGNACIO-PINTO

Ambassador of Dahomey to Washington and Ottawa
Permanent Representative to the United Nations

During a period of upheaval and change in the world, it is right to examine the question of independent Africa in search of interdependence. Africa today, plunged into a kind of immense melting pot, is seething with different tendencies, the results of which are difficult to foresee. What does interdependence mean for an independent Africa?

To begin with, we must agree on a definition of the term *Africa*. Although I am one of the most enthusiastic supporters of African unity, I feel we should face facts and acknowledge that at present Africa is far from a single political entity. In the continent today are various states, each of whose governments jealously watches over its sovereignty, although all proclaim their desire for unity. Here, however, I shall use the term *Africa* as denoting a single entity, not only because it is convenient but because, as unity is the avowed aim of every good African, we had better get used to it right now.

Africa, after lying under the colonial yoke for centuries in some parts and for decades in others, has been involved since World War II in the irrevocable cycle of its liberation. This is not the place for diatribes against the colonialists and other imperialists, who have been vituperated so often that the effect produced by such language today is like flogging a dead horse. Instead, I shall attempt to analyze independence as it has developed in Africa, and then, in the light of the results—whether good or bad—see how Africa should pursue the goal of interdependence, which is known in the international world as *cooperation*.

Long Live Independence! Down with Colonialists and Imperialists! Africa for the Africans! These have been the slogans repeated by all Africans in good standing since the end of World War II. I would not deny them, since I had the privilege of playing an active part in the struggle for the freedom of my own country.

However, it should be acknowledged that, in most countries, the passage from colonial domination to independence happily took place without too much violence—with the exception of the Algerian war and the Mau Mau revolt in Kenya. It is a sign of the times that in both the former French colonies (except for Guinea, which opted for a violent break by voting "No" in the 1958 referendum) and the former British colonies, independence was achieved by negotiation.

Once independence and sovereignty were won, and after the enthusiastic celebrations died down, it became necessary to face up to the heavy responsibilities thus entailed. At that moment, like a child who comes of age and must assume responsibility for himself, the African countries had to confront the glaring reality that it is not all that easy to live in independence.

The ex-French colonies in West Africa and Equatorial Africa immediately realized the disadvantages of going their separate ways toward independence, in other words of allowing themselves to be "Balkanized" instead of remaining together in the two large groups formed by the old Occidental French Africa (AOF) and

Equatorial French Africa (AEF). Furthermore, contrary to the great hopes expressed for a brighter future, providing all the desired prosperity and progress, independence turned out to be a cripplingly heavy burden for all new nations.

Of course, certain African leaders bravely attempted to face up to these difficult problems by adopting the principles of particular ideologies in an effort to find a political solution. But in the light of the tragic events in Congo-Leopoldville and other glaring instances of frontier violations, as well as certain financial ventures, it was soon realized that politics alone could not solve the problems posed by the accession to independence. On the contrary, the democratic freedoms so recently and dearly won were sometimes quickly forgotten, if not eliminated. Some regard the political upheavals now taking place as sufficient evidence for agreeing with René Dumont that "African has got off to a bad start."

In my view, Africa has not got off to such a bad start. In fact, the disturbing or even alarming events we have witnessed are only growing pains. When we compare them with the many changes of regime in the Western countries and elsewhere, we have no cause to complain too bitterly about current events in Africa. We should rather congratulate ourselves that the tragic happenings we deplore in one or two areas of Africa have not spread and plunged the entire continent into uncontrollable and bloody revolution or catastrophic chaos.

I believe that present troubles and anomalies are an ordeal we must go through, but one which will prove to be the crucible in which the gold is separated from the dross. Africa will certainly survive them and will eventually advance along the path toward true progress which will assure improvement in the living standards of its peoples. In any case, it seems that the lesson has been learned and that the "politics first" attitude, dear to certain African heads of state, is rightly being abandoned. Obviously, the African people cannot forever be satisfied with shouting "Long Live Independence," or other purely political slogans, when they are hungry, in rags, sick, or badly cared for.

As they grow increasingly aware of the disadvantages of a purely political organization of Africa and of its Balkanization, some heads of state are beginning to pay more attention to economic development and are endeavoring to remedy the disastrous effects of Balkanization. Thus we have witnessed various attempts at greater unity, such as the formation of the Monrovia group, the Casablanca group, the Union Africaine et Malagache (UAM), composed of the former French colonies of the AOF, the AEF, and Madagascar, which became the Union Africaine et Malagache de Coopération Economique (UAMCE) after the creation of the OAU in May 1963 and is now known as the Organisation Commune Africaine et Malagache (OCAM). We can only applaud the perspicacity of those heads of state who were instrumental in the formation of these groups, which help to bring the former colonized territories together on a sounder basis.

There can be no doubt that, in order to promote the rational and balanced development of their countries, Africans must go beyond the concept of a multiplicity of small states and tiny ministries and must set up larger units, thereby eliminating the need for useless administrative, representational, and prestige expenditure. The funds so released could be profitably invested to the greater benefit of the African people.

I hope you do not misunderstand me. I am in favor of African unity as proposed by the OAU, but as a realist I am less keen on the idea that it should be converted at once into a unified political body with a "continental government," as urged by my eminent friend President Nkrumah.

Of course we must take a broad view of Africa. Those who cherish this ambition are right, and I personally could not agree more with the view that the division of Africa, and the whole world, into larger or smaller states with absolute sovereignty leads to rivalry and even war. In any case, it would not lead to the much desired progress.

Surely it would be preferable, with a view to increasing the effectiveness of development work, for the African states to begin by practicing among themselves the African solidarity they preach. At the moment it seems to exist only as a weapon to be used against colonialists and imperialists, while we stand by helpless in the face of the unbelievable fact that African nationals from a neighboring country are being brutally expelled by other Africans, in flagrant violation of the most elementary of human rights. Thus appears that hateful feeling—xenophobia—which was held in check during the colonial era.

To achieve their destiny, at a time when scientists are opening the way toward the conquest of space, it is necessary and salutary that Africans should look inward and remain faithful to their traditions of wisdom and moderation. They should reappraise the fact of independence, which is far more than decolonization. Are there not many African rulers who treat their own nationals little better than the colonial administrators of yesteryear treated their former subject peoples? I do not wish to appear here as a merciless judge; my aim is to attempt to determine objectively where the trouble lies and try to find ways of putting things right.

To promote the development and progress that all of us wish to see in Africa, we must also look upward and, drawing upon the principles of the United Nations Charter, transcend the notion of independence for a lot of little states, paying heed to this maxim of La Rochefoucauld: "People who concentrate on little things usually become incapable of greater things." I am convinced that Africa is heading toward a great future, but only provided that Africans make the effort to transcend all that remains of the aftermath of colonialism and tribalism.

A proof that this transcendence is taking place can be seen in the fact that almost all the African states that have gained their independence—even those that won it by some degree of violence —have turned to their former colonizers for help. Such was the case of two states in East Africa which in 1964 appealed to Her Britannic Majesty's Government for English troops to support the local authorities against the rebels. In Central Africa the French Army intervened to restore order after a palace revolution. I disapprove of this kind of assistance! The fact remains, however, that it was at the request of the heads of state, themselves, that the ex-colonizers provided assistance.

I shall not dwell on this kind of aid, since I would prefer to examine the cultural and economic aspects of the problem of maintaining contact with the former colonial power. We must have the courage to acknowledge the fact that colonization was an abject state of affairs, being for many centuries an instrument of oppression and exploitation. But in all sincerity we must also acknowledge that all was not for the worst, nor were all colonials necessarily despicable colonialists. Every cloud has its silver lining; in return for the sufferings the colonized peoples had to put up with, whether they liked it or not, they were given an opportunity of pitting their wits against those of the colonialists. The result, in some countries at least, was that the colonized people proved to be a match for their master, assimilating his culture in his schools and universities, and creating bonds of friendship and esteem between them that were maintained after independence.

In addition to these cultural factors, we must also consider the material factors. It is undeniable that the infrastructure of the colonized countries left behind by the colonizer, from which the newly independent states now benefit, constitutes useful equipment for progress. This is why we may claim that, by maintaining their ties with the former metropolitan countries, the independent African states are gaining the means to develop their economies on a sound basis and to raise their populations' standards of living. It explains why certain ex-French colonies have remained within the French community, just as certain former British colonies have remained within the Commonwealth. Through these continuing contacts they have access to the main channels of world trade and are able to take advantage of the resulting financial and commercial benefits.

Thus the need for economic development obliges the African states to seek cultural, technical, and financial help from their former colonizers, or, in default of this, from other governments in the Eastern or Western blocs. Thus, in addition to bilateral ties, subject in a greater or lesser degree to caution, new multilateral ties are created which extend interdependence. This is good, for no ideological considerations should be involved when it comes to benefiting from economic aid to advance progress.

As I see it, there is no harm in this, for today, more than ever before, we must deliberately turn our backs on sordid methods of mercantilism, commerce, speculation, and the unilateral exploitation of the wealth of our land. Africa's great advantage today lies in its broad representation within the United Nations, where it has free contact with the entire world, allowing it to cooperate with all nations. The UN is the lifeline of the newly independent African states. Some knotty points have still to be settled before cooperation can be complete; the problems of South Africa and of the territories occupied by Portugal—Angola, Mozambique, and Portuguese Guinea—must be solved sooner or later.

Since this is the International Cooperation Year launched by the UN, I should like to express the hope that the independent African states will eventually realize that the future of their continent depends on them alone. This future will be for better or worse to the extent that they accept or do not accept the fact that in our time independence must be approached from the standpoint of interdependence. In other words, at some point the old idea of sovereignty must be dropped, and Africans must begin to practice among themselves the virtues of sincere and constructive cooperation.

There is a long way to go before the spirit of interdependence permeates the African states, but the path which leads toward this high ideal lies open. We have only to abandon rivalries, envy, racial or religious prejudices; then, free at last from hatred, anxiety, and fear, we can make a fruitful contribution to the birth of a new world in which men will be linked by bonds of love. I feel sure that every good, self-respecting African who is aware of the intermediary role which Africa can play in the world should be able to subscribe to this ideal and help to make it a living reality.

AFRICA IN TRANSITION

SIR ANDREW COHEN

Ministry of Overseas Development
United Kingdom

In discussing the problems of aid and cooperation between developed and developing countries, I suppose I speak as a representative of a developed country. But if there is a barrier between us—and in this world of the 1960's I do not think there is—then certainly I have been fortunate enough to have chances to see across it. Many friends here know my crime sheet as an old African war horse—first as a back-room boy in Whitehall during the great period of political transformation in Africa started by the last Labour Government; then here as an administrator trying to pack a generation's change into a Governor's five-year term; then with the United Nations during the period of the great accession of African states; and finally again back in Whitehall, but in a wholly new organization geared to the individual needs of the new world. It was fortunate that first the Department of Technical Cooperation was organized, then the Overseas Development Ministry (ODM) in 1964 and 1965.

On the basis of this experience, may I venture a few general thoughts?

First, we in Britain, in the West generally, and I have no doubt in Russia as well, believe that the development relationship between industrialized and developing countries is a long-term relationship—not years, not decades, but perhaps generations. You will, we believe, look to us for cooperation in this for a long time to come, although in changing and developing patterns.

As Sir Arthur Lewis has said in his splendidly comprehensive paper, which I shall draw upon as on a rich mine of wisdom and experience, Africa needs massive foreign aid to sustain a growth rate of between 4 and 5 per cent per annum. This means a prolonged, wide-ranging, and complex job to be done, requiring continuing application, the acquisition and replenishment of knowledge, and close and sympathetic contacts between the developed world and the African countries.

Now a word on some of the key areas of help. I will not talk about money. Capital aid is, of course, crucial and it raises many problems of absorbing interest to all of us who are aid practitioners —terms of aid, tying or untying, local costs, to mention some which concern East Africa particularly. I want rather to mention some of the specialized subjects of particular importance in the field of technical assistance. We British in this region of the world —like the French in West Africa—have close historical ties with the newly independent countries. Through their great national movements they won their independence from us; or, as we would say, through our foresight and wisdom we granted them independence. The truth, of course, lies between the two views; independence came about through interrelated pressures. But independence did not of itself solve all their economic and social problems, nor could it have been delayed until these problems were solved.

Independence gave a great impetus forward to greater efforts and progress in education, agriculture, economic development, and other areas. We see the results of that today. But it came to these countries at a time when they were still exceedingly short of trained and experienced men and women to help run their services. We are glad to continue helping them through the large numbers of British officials, teachers, and others now working here. The number of British officials in Uganda, Kenya, and Tanzania at the end of 1964 was 5500. We are still, at the request of your governments, recruiting large numbers—610 in 1962; 633 in 1963; and 872 in 1964.

This is the massive kind of help that stems from our past historical ties. I believe that your governments will wish it to continue for quite a time ahead. It may even be extended to new fields. I refer to the Overseas Development and Service bill now before Parliament. But, looking further ahead, this may not be the most needed kind of technical help. The most important help in the future will be specialized help—just as it is now in India, Pakistan, Latin America, and countries like Jamaica. Let me give you a few examples.

In the field of *education*, which underlies all development, we shall continue to give bulk help as long as you want us to, for example, through secondary-school teachers from Britain. But we expect increasingly also to help by sending out experts in many specialized problems, such as the organization of teacher training, curriculum development, technological aids for education, including instructional television, manpower studies, school design and building, educational research, and perhaps in fields where education policy impinges on general development policy in the economic and social spheres.

Agriculture is the livelihood of the vast majority in the developing countries. It is vitally important to all development and much needs to be done. Some special fields where we should increase our capacity to help are the building up of extension services, agricultural research and education, credit arrangements, marketing, and cooperative development.

Economic planning and development administration (including transport economics and the economics of education). In this crucial field your countries have shown that they are anxious to secure help from outside experts and advisers, many of whom have come from the International Bank and the United Nations, as well as from individual countries. These experts have made important contributions, but to give full effect to the help they bring, there must be local machinery and trained personnel able to convert their reports into action.

Here we are inhibited by the world shortage of economists and statisticians, not only in the developing countries but in all the developed countries as well, including my own. Help must therefore take the form of supplying experts and providing training arrangements—nothing can be more important.

Industrial development. There will be need for much highly specialized help in both the public and the private sectors—help in industrial and commercial management training, in accountancy and banking, project identification, feasibility studies, establishing industrial estates, building up development banks, and organizing industrial training.

Research. I fully agree with Sir Arthur Lewis that scientific and technological research must have the highest priority. Research, which tends to produce results slowly, is in danger of not getting its proper due, in countries where experts and resources are scarce, in the struggle for priority against activities which can show more immediate results. But knowledge of the physical environment, of the technological possibilities, and of economic and social factors bearing on development is vitally necessary. The scientific and technological revolution of the last generation will prove as important in the long run as the political transformation which has brought all your countries to independence. If research services, surveys, and technological progress are not pushed forward vigorously, the gap between the richer and poorer countries must continue to widen.

Research is particularly suitable to cooperation between countries because it knows no frontiers. That is why we in Britain have made a special effort to help maintain your research services in this area of East Africa. As some of you know, we are bearing half the cost of your East African Regional Research Stations in agriculture, forestry, animal health, medicine, pest control, etc. But these stations represent only a small part of what ideally is needed. How can these research services be more effectively carried on by cooperation between us? Have international organizations done enough in this vital field?

Finally, a word on *population control*. This is perhaps the greatest development problem of Asia. It may not yet have assumed as much importance in East Africa, but, as malaria eradication goes forward, it is likely to become a big social and economic problem, just as I believe it will in Britain itself. So far we have only a limited capacity to help in this field, but we are working to develop our resources, as the United States has already done. This is a crucial area for technical cooperation.

I have mentioned these fields of activity as key examples of specialized cooperation which we may look to in the future. If you accept the premise that these things are of vital importance, what needs to be done?

1. We in Britain must develop our capacity to help in various ways, such as the organization of resources of manpower; the creation of additional capacity in our specialized institutions to be made available for service overseas; links between our institutions in Britain and overseas outside government, but with government help.

2. Where shortages of skilled manpower exist (e.g., economists), we must:

Increase the capacity of our universities to produce these experts;

Provide special training and research facilities to encourage people to study the problems of developing countries;

Create opportunities for medium- or long-term employment to attract people into the field;

Encourage those British people already having overseas experience in these fields to continue to work in technical cooperation. The French have done much in this, and we a good deal. But we must do more, and the ODM is working hard on this. The United States is also, I believe, planning in this field.

3. We must also throw aside the shibboleths of the past, and abandon any trace of neo-colonialist thinking or attitudes which

may inhibit our usefulness. We must make sure that it remains dead and buried. In greater detail, this means that:

We must no longer believe we have some sort of moral responsibility —even in our own minds or hearts—for the actions of independent countries for which we used once to be responsible. We must avoid applying to them judgments and attitudes we would never apply to other independent countries.

The granting of aid should not be linked with our judgments on political matters which are not our concern. Similarly, economic and social policy decisions are not for us, but for the governments and parliaments of these countries.

We must constantly strive to help developing countries who want our help to develop their know how and their resources of skilled manpower, so that they do not have to rely so heavily on outside skills as at present.

Neo-colonialism is not a one-way but a two-way street, just as the colonial relationship itself was. As there used to be the colonial rulers and the people and their leaders, so now there are the independent countries and the former metropolitan powers. Just as we on our side regard it as essential to avoid all neo-colonialist attitudes, so we hope that you will avoid your side of neo-colonialism.

Your side of it, I think, would be allowing attitudes and emotions which grew up during the colonial period in relation to the colonial rulers to persist now that you are independent. It would be seeing neo-colonial bogies even where they do not exist; believing that people from our countries who come to work with you or to advise you are neo-colonialist in their outlook when they are not; refusing to treat us as equals because you suspect we are still adopting superior or we-know-better attitudes. I cannot say that I see much sign of this reverse neo-colonialism in Uganda; but then, I do not find it easy to see faults in this country which is so close to my heart. Yet I believe that up and down Africa this neo-colonialist feeling in reverse does continue to exist here and there. It would help us all if it could be cast aside as a relic of the past.

I hope you will not think that I am being naive about this. I know very well that neo-colonialist attitudes and even actions on the part of the outside world have on occasions marred the African scene in the past few years. We for our part know that you will be vigilant to guard against improper interference from outside and vociferous in denouncing it whenever you find it. You would be failing in your duty if you did not.

But, however regrettable these examples of neo-colonialist attitudes by the outside world are, I question how far it would be right to generalize from them. I would urge that you avoid generalizations which might inhibit the work we have to do together. We have, in fact, a continuous, complex, and above all a joint task to do, requiring joint thinking, sometimes joint planning and joint action, to use the scarce resources we have at our disposal to the best possible advantage for the benefit of your countries. I have two particular reasons for introducing neo-colonialism in reverse into this talk.

The long-term need for aid and technical cooperation creates, I know, difficult political and psychological problems for you. It also creates problems for us, one of which is opposition to aid in certain quarters of our own countries. This problem has existed for a long time in the United States, the largest purveyor of aid; it also exists, I believe, in France. It is not yet a serious problem for us in Britain, as recent Parliamentary debates have shown. But it can become one. Part of the cause could, of course, be political, but I do not think that this is the greatest risk to be guarded against. I am more worried about the possible consequences if it were thought that aid voted by our Parliament were not being satisfactorily handled by us, or indeed by you. It could also become a problem if a feeling grew up that there was not sufficient contact, discussion, and joint planning; in other words, if the receiving countries seemed unwilling to deal with us in a relaxed, equal, and completely joint way in the whole process of aid and development.

There is a second, more practical reason why I beg you to avoid what I have called neo-colonialism in reverse. We need to get much closer together in the planning of our aid, particularly if it is, as I am sure it must, to assume a more and more specialized character. Forms of cooperation, links between universities, statutory corporations, cooperative movements, government departments, must be organized well in advance—must be built soundly for relatively long periods. The supply of skilled men and women from our country must be planned, not for months but for years ahead. Training arrangements in highly specialized subjects must be planned and organized. None of these things can be done quickly; all take time.

In some fields—for example, agricultural and industrial development—your governments and ours, through their chosen instruments, may have to go into partnership for particular operations. In agricultural extension services, in development projects, in agriculture, forestry, and fisheries, in industry and mining, projects may have to be planned and run jointly, subject to whatever control your governments wish to lay down, and of course providing for training of local people in the planning, execution, and management of the business.

In this the Commonwealth Development Corporation can make a valuable contribution, and indeed has done so. As a commercially run organization financed by the British Government, it has established a special position in a number of countries and can provide the finance management and training which one needed for these kinds of projects. Often it does so in partnership with a local development corporation. I know that both the United States and France have done these things as well. And they have been encouraged and stimulated by international organizations, including the International Bank, the International Development Association (IDA), and the UN Special Fund. I hope that you will ask us to develop and extend this kind of activity in partnership with you.

To do these things effectively we must plan ahead, preferably for periods of up to five years. We must plan jointly, and the process must be continuous. We have close links already through the staffs of our High Commissions and in our Embassies in foreign countries. We come out here on visits and you come to London on visits, which are most welcome. But this, I believe, is not enough. We ought to think in terms of periodic conferences between those who plan our aid and those who plan your development, preferably here in your countries, to look ahead together and work out what we are going to do and how we are going to do it. We in the ODM are organizing ourselves for our side of this.

This then is my final plea. Let us all accept that we have a long uphill haul together to what Churchill called the sunlit uplands. Let us recognize that we all stand to gain from joint action. Let us bend our brains and harness our skills to establish the best methods of cooperating together, and let us make sure that these methods work. Let us do these things as good internationalists and members of the UN, as well as in our country-to-country bilateral cooperation. The two are not competitive but complementary. Here is a task which deserves to command the energies, the brains, and the idealism of ourselves and our children. It is a task that together we are well fitted to carry out—well fitted by our past associations and our large common stock of ideas.

POLITICAL AND ECONOMIC PROBLEMS OF AFRICA

MAITAMA SULE

Minister of Mines and Power, Nigeria

One of the most remarkable developments in international politics in recent years is the growing interest of the rest of the world in Africa. This is the result of international political movements in the postwar period, particularly the progress toward national self-government. At the end of the war there were just four independent states in Africa; today there are 35. The emerging nations of Africa have asserted themselves more and more in international political cooperation, especially in the United Nations and its specialized agencies, where they are playing an increasingly important role. On the domestic front, the yeast of newly-won political independence has been a motivating force, encouraging governments to introduce new ways of increasing the standard of living of their people. In almost all parts of Africa, there is a new realization of the possibility and desirability of economic progress.

Africa is a continent of great diversity. In the tropical zone, its lands and peoples are a mosaic of many small pieces, largely without the unifying influences of even a common language, common religion, or shared historical experience. There is diversity in the stage of economic development reached. In some countries, like South Africa, industrialization has broken the teeth of poverty. But in a large part of Africa, poverty reigns in its malevolent supremacy. If we apply the income-per-capita yardstick, the low standard of living can easily be quantified. Using $300 average annual per capita income as the dividing line between developed and underdeveloped countries, all African countries, except South Africa, are in a sense underdeveloped. Income is as low as $30 in Ethiopia, and as high as $232 in Mauritius. In between these levels lie a large number of African countries with income of less than $100. This compares with the annual average per capita income of between $1000 and $2000 enjoyed by the United States, Canada, and several European countries.

Politically, too, there are considerable differences in the independent African countries. Some countries have successfully maintained the Westminster model of parliamentary democracy, while a large number have had to resort to a one-party system of government. Yet in spite of political and economic differences, all African governments are confronted with the problems of political stability and raising the standard of living of their people.

Why have African countries remained poor in spite of nearly a century of economic penetration? This has sometimes been ascribed to the climate and physical features of Africa. Also, the social institutions and mental attitudes of Africans are said to be inimical to economic progress. Nevertheless, the major reason for the poor standard of living is probably to be found in the fragmentary impact of European investments. Until recently, economic development in Africa was based on the outdated schema of international division of labor. Under this, Africa constitutes a periphery of the world economic system; its task was the production of food and raw materials for export to industrialized countries. There was no room within this pattern of international division of labor for the industrialization of Africa.

It has been estimated that private investment in African economic development totaled about $16 million during the first half of the twentieth century. But despite this huge sum, the benefits of development failed to spread out very far from the mines and plantations. Europeans came to Africa to obtain raw materials and minerals for export; they were not interested in developing the local economy. This concentration on the exploitation of raw materials and minerals to the neglect of industrialization has had two main effects:

1. It accounts for the marked unevenness of development; some sectors have achieved rapid progress, while others have continued to stagnate or to advance very slowly. The unevenness is revealed, for example, in the limited extent to which the market economy has spread in African countries. It is estimated that in tropical Africa between 65 and 75 per cent of the total area under indigenous cultivation is devoted to subsistence production, engaging about 60 per cent of African males. With such a high proportion of the population living outside the cash economy, or at best around its edges, it is not difficult to explain the cause of low agricultural output, and therefore the low level of per capita income. Production is geared to achieving mere subsistence, rather than to raising surplus for the market.

2. It has made African economies peculiarly susceptible to the vagaries of world markets. Primary production is the major commodity sector, as well as a field for employment for the majority of African people. It is also the main source of government revenue and foreign exchange earnings. Although agriculture accounts for a substantial part of the gross national product, owing to the low level of productivity per worker, its contribution to the national income of African countries is significantly lower than its share of total employment. In terms of foreign currency earnings, export of primary products provided nearly 80 per cent of total foreign receipts.

This heavy reliance on primary production is a source of many difficulties. Because of violent fluctuations in the prices of their export products, African countries are faced with great instability of income levels. They are unable to calculate their export income and thus their ability to pay for imports. Their opportunities for pursuing long-term economic plans are restricted; capital is wasted on projects which must be discontinued; political stability is undermined by financial crises; and the attitude of the people toward economic development can readily become one of distrust and resignation.

These difficulties have been intensified of late by the emergence of other factors. The development of new synthetic processes and alternative sources of supply, along with the trend toward inward-looking trade policies in Europe, may henceforth tend to make industrialized countries become less dependent on imports of various raw materials.

In view of these uncertainties, African governments must turn to, actually have turned to, industrialization as the principal means of obtaining a share of the benefits of technical progress and of progressively raising their standard of living. A program of industrialization offers the special advantage of relatively speedy results. But because of the large share of the rural sector in the economies of African countries, the first step toward industrialization is more efficient methods of production, processing, storage, and marketing of existing agricultural products and raw materials. Such judicious combination of industrialization and agriculture forms the basis of the solution to the problems of unemployment and the low standard of living.

One school of thought believes in what may be called the "natural" solution to these problems, arguing that the present industrialized countries attained their position through several generations of thrift, diligence, and hard work, without international help. The underdeveloped countries of today should likewise pursue the same path, by creating conditions for economic development through their own efforts, albeit the process may be long and painful.

There is no doubt that African countries must first seek to solve the political-cum-economic problems of underdevelopment themselves. But it would be unrealistic for many reasons to think that the nineteenth-century process of economic development will repeat itself in the twentieth century. In the past, when people were ignorant of the living standards in other parts of the world, it was possible to exist in need and misery without giving the matter too much thought. Today, better communication has created a greater awareness of the gulf between the rich and poor countries and what is often called "the revolution of rising expectations." The masses of Africa are now conscious of the need to improve their living standards. Economic development has become not only a political catch phrase, but a positive goal for which African political leaders must strive if they wish to maintain power. Moreover, political stability cannot be achieved in Africa if the slow and painful process of developing through the "natural" route is followed. More complicated is the threat of overpopulation, which makes it probable that any rise in the standard of living may be overtaken by a population increase.

Granted the need for self-help, African countries still need access to capital and know-how in order to translate their political and economic aspirations into reality. In varying degrees, their dilemma is a poverty so pressing that they must consume practically everything they produce. It is difficult to generate a large volume of savings to make the needed capital investments because income is so low. Yet economic progress cannot take place without investment.

This dilemma can be resolved in only one of two ways: through forced savings of the Communist type, or through foreign assistance in the form of capital, expertise, and managerial enterprise. The first alternative poses a political as well as a practical problem. It does not appear practicable to restrict individual consumption of the bulk of the population, which on the whole is too low. The problem of limited resources cannot be resolved by bureaucratic decision within a democratic political framework. Nehru once remarked that the difficulty lies always between the needs of today and the demands of tomorrow. If you want a surplus, you have to be strict with yourself in the present generation—and democracy does not like stinting the present.

An enduring political stability can be ensured if foreign assistance is available to supplement domestic resources, but this raises fundamental economic and political problems. No one, as a rule, invests his capital for charitable or patriotic reasons. A foreign investment is worth-while if it is profitable, and if the profits accruing to the investor can be repatriated.

Without reference to figures, one can argue in principle that Africa should provide a profitable outlet for proper investment. With plenty of labor and natural resources, but little capital, the return on each unit of capital invested is likely to be relatively high. However, the small size of the market, as a result of small population or low purchasing power or both, limits the profitability of investment in most African countries. The flow of foreign capital also depends on a host of more or less intangible factors. The term "climate of investment" covers the many factors and attitudes in the capital-importing countries which make the investor either feel sure of, or fear for, the safety of his investment. Perhaps the most important of these factors is the attitude toward foreign enterprise.

This raises an important political issue. African countries, having just emerged from their colonial past, resent foreign economic domination. Their brand of nationalism has found expression in policies which are detrimental to the flow of foreign capital. In some countries it has been reflected in nationalization of foreign companies, bans on foreign investors in such sectors as retail trade, requirements that domestic capital must participate with foreign capital, restrictions on employment of foreigners, and many other ways. Such measures, however politically desirable, tend to restrict the field in which foreigners can operate.

Certain government pronouncements may also inhibit the flow of foreign capital. Some African leaders have made statements that have created uncertainty about their orientation in world affairs. A striking crop of socialist ideologies has been springing up in Africa. "Socialism," whatever its brand and however vaguely defined, has become a political catch phrase. For these reasons, the achievement of independence has created an unfavorable climate for private foreign investment in Africa, and has in general been accompanied by a slowdown in the flow of capital to the continent.

Intergovernmental assistance, especially in bilateral form, is sometimes influenced not by the economic performance of the receiving country, but by political considerations. This form of assistance has become an expensive instrument for bribing African countries in the ideological conflict which separates the East and the West. African countries, like other underdeveloped countries unwilling to be involved in the Cold War, would prefer assistance channeled through world agencies. However, since the advanced countries still prefer to regard economic aid as an instrument for winning friends, bilateral aid will probably continue to bulk larger than multilateral aid. At present it is estimated that 85 per cent of total intergovernmental assistance to all underdeveloped countries is bilateral, while less than 15 per cent is channeled through UN Agencies.

Does it follow that a poor country in need of foreign capital would have to order her economic and political fate to suit the whims and caprices of foreign powers? This is a problem of development diplomacy which can best be solved through international cooperation and better understanding of the needs and aspirations of poor countries.

Another long-run obstacle to development is the dire shortage of trained personnel in all branches of a modern economy. This lack of the knowledge and skills required to set about raising productivity is as important as the lack of capital. The shortage of entrepreneurial skill and skilled labor is evident in high illiteracy rates and in the concentration of the small class of potential business leaders in market-place bargaining. The absence of skilled labor limits the types of economic projects that can successfully be undertaken. Lack of technical knowledge and managerial skills is also a major reason why investors stick to traditional forms of investment. If the pace of development is to be rapid, the labor force has to be brought together, possibly from remote areas, and trained in the necessary disciplines and routines. A cadre of supervisory staffs and management teams possessed of necessary technical knowledge must be created.

How can the existing system of international cooperation be geared to the requirements and aspirations of African countries? The industrialized countries have come to realize that they have a stake in the political stability and economic progress of Africa. This awakening is not surprising. Economic development which leads to an equalization of economic conditions has become a condition for peaceful coexistence; otherwise, the industrialized countries run the risk of a head-on clash with the African countries.

In spite of the progress made by international and national organizations, considerable scope still exists for furthering economic progress through international cooperation. At present there are many different organizations through which development work is carried out. In addition to the United Nations, there are financial institutions such as the World Bank, the International Finance Corporation (IFC), the International Development Association (IDA), the Organization for Economic Cooperation and Development (OECD), the European Investment Bank, and the Development Fund of the Six. There are also various national organizations.

All these organizations, in one way or another, provide capital and technical know-how. All have different objectives and different operational clauses. Their diverse natures and requirements create a major problem to countries seeking assistance from them. There is without doubt scope here for rationalization and coordination. It is wasteful for poor countries to build up a large administrative apparatus for planning and preparing aid projects. In order to make an effective contribution to development work, the planning and preparation of aid projects should be concentrated in one body, preferably under the aegis of the United Nations.

A more complicated problem in relation to foreign aid is that arising from *tied* aid. Most of the bilateral loans and grants available to African countries are tied to particular projects, or to the goods and services of the donor country. The recipient country cannot use the loan or grant for any project apart from that specifically agreed upon. The danger of this is that a project which appeals to the donor country may not be one which is accorded high priority in the development plan of the recipient country, with a result that the plan priority may be altered. When aid is tied to goods of the donor country, the recipient country is barred from purchasing the capital goods required at international competitive prices. The cost of development projects may therefore be raised beyond the estimate, thus making the realization of targets difficult.

It is because of these dangers that aid-receiving countries have shown a preference for a shift in the direction of multilateral cooperation. Aid distributed through multilateral organizations offers better coordination, a more rational allocation, and less politics.

There has been a tendency for foreign private enterprises to judge the feasibility of investing in developing African countries on the criteria of a developed and smoothly functioning market economy where central direction is regarded as objectionable. Obviously, the situation in Africa is bound to be different. Here sensible planning and direction of development are essential conditions for the healthy growth of private enterprise. In this respect, foreign private enterprise ought to make an effort to become familiar with the political situation and the national ambitions of African countries. The governments of industrialized countries can also stimulate private foreign investment through various support measures, particularly those which aim to reduce the major political risks connected with investment in Africa.

Other areas of international cooperation can be developed to meet the requirements of African countries. In the field of human resource development, the United States Peace Corps and similar programs of other countries could be extended to the industrial sector by the establishment of an "industrial peace corps program." This may be another way of alleviating the shortage of skilled manpower and improving the quality of the labor supply. Foreign assistance to education should include the training of entrepreneurially promising employees in factories and business offices abroad.

Africa has the material bases for economic development and an almost unlimited supply of labor, but inadequate capital and know-how have hindered the utilization of these resources. Furthermore, independence has brought to the surface a myriad of sectional, ethnic, and tribal interests which had long been submerged in the common struggle for freedom. This is a powerful hindrance to national unity and to a rational process of planning.

Many African countries are now at the delicate stage where they have just gained their independence and become conscious of the urgent problems of development. They are, at present, groping for the routes to follow. Because of the urgency of their problems, they are receptive to new ideas and are willing to learn. Through international cooperation, their political and economic aspirations can be channeled in the right way. Now is the time when the rest of the world has the opportunity to establish contacts and forge bonds which can be decisive for world peace and future relations with Africa.

THE ROLE OF
THE UNITED NATIONS
IN AFRICAN COOPERATION
AND DEVELOPMENT

GERSHON COLLIER

*Ambassador of Sierra Leone
to the United Nations*

Without doubt, the existence of the United Nations has done much in our time to lower world tensions and contribute to the stabilization of world peace. This paper attempts to explore the advantages that may accrue to and the dangers that could result for the UN from the existence of regional organizations—with particular reference to the Organization of African Unity (OAU).

In the seventh decade of the twentieth century, when the existence and potentials of nuclear weapons are recognized, the importance of peaceful methods to solve outstanding international problems cannot be overstated. The greater the strength of rival countries in terms of nuclear power, the greater becomes the awareness of the risk and the attendant consequences of a nuclear war. The eyeball-to-eyeball confrontation of President Kennedy and Chairman Khrushchev in 1962 was a remarkable example of this danger.

The only forum today in which the necessary international atmosphere exists for cool discussion and objective assessment of world problems is the UN. With all its imperfections, it has

93

played a tremendous role in preventing war and maintaining the peace, however uneasy that peace may have been in some cases. There is every reason to believe that if the functions of the UN are strengthened and preserved, it can play a more vital role in the years ahead.

Thus the awareness of the existence of the UN has helped in no uncertain measure to reduce world tensions. Men have come to see in it an organization dedicated to the pursuit of peace, in which the small nations as well as the large can hope to find a standard of international morality clearly reflecting the conscience of the world. This hope in itself provides a promise of peace and stability without which the lot of man in these nuclear days would have been tenuous and hazardous indeed.

For the African nations, as members of this world organization, and for the peoples of Africa, the UN has provided not only the greatest hope for peace, but also security for their independence and international recognition and respect for that independence. There is in Africa, therefore, a widespread determination to preserve and improve its effectiveness as a force for peace. But despite this enthusiastic support for the UN, and an overwhelming desire to strengthen its functions, the nations of Africa are not ready at this stage to surrender their independence and sovereignty to any supranational authority in terms of a world government. They believe that unity must be achieved within their continent before this dream of world government can be realized.

There is, of course, the ultimate hope of all humanity—a hope in which the African nations also join—that one day there will emerge a world government, a government of which the UN may well be the forerunner. But at this stage of international understanding, the African nations do not have any illusions as to the distance of such a dream. In proper perspective they recognize the UN for what it truly is today—an organization in which the members, though dedicated to an over-all objective of peace, are anxious to preserve their national sovereignties and are most reluctant to surrender any part of national authority to any international organization. Besides, and this is important, many African nations, flushed from recent victories in their struggles for independence, are naturally anxious to consolidate their authority and press on with their administrative and development programs.

It was this awareness and conviction that led the OAU from its inception—though embracing most of the lofty idealisms of the UN Charter and firmly setting its course on the path of peace—to concentrate its energies on promoting unity within the African continent. The OAU has all the necessary ingredients to equip it for the special role of peace-keeping and reducing tensions in Africa. This responsibility is of particular significance in view of the grave and far-reaching problems which exist in Africa today in the immediate aftermath of independence—problems which could deteriorate into situations of tension constituting a threat to world peace.

Whereas the very nature of the UN Charter seems to uphold the independence of nations and their differences, regional organizations are directed toward emphasizing the points that unite various nations within the context of the particular region. For example, there is no counterpart in any regional organization to the power of the veto which is enjoyed by the permanent members of the Security Council. The provision of the veto power in the UN Charter clearly dramatizes the intention of its founders to preserve certain sovereign rights of permanent members, thus ensuring that the Organization should not encroach on national sovereignty.

The UN Charter recognizes the existence of regional organizations and indeed encourages their activities when it states the following in Article 52:

Nothing in the present Charter precludes the existence of regional arrangements or agencies for dealing with such matters relating to the maintenance of international peace and security as are appropriate for regional action, provided that such arrangements or agencies and their activities are consistent with the Purposes and Principles of the United Nations.

The regional organizations likewise fully recognize the existence of the UN. In the Charter of the OAU, the preambular paragraphs state, *inter alia*:

Persuaded the Charter of the United Nations and the Universal Declaration of Human Rights, to the principles of which we reaffirm our adherence, provide a solid foundation for peaceful and positive cooperation among states.

And in the section dealing with the purposes of the Organization:

To promote international cooperation having due regard to the Charter of the United Nations and the Universal Declaration of Human Rights.

It is thus quite evident that regional organizations, including the OAU, are conceived with the definite intention of helping and strengthening the UN. The OAU certainly had this objective in view at the time of its inception, and nothing that has happened since suggests any departure from this principle.

Nonetheless, there are dangers. The very concept of a regional organization poses a challenge to existing international organizations dedicated to similar objectives. In this circumstance, of course, it behooves any competing international organization to inspire superior loyalty among its members. Unfortunately, however, the UN today is hardly in a position to achieve this. When such an international organization fails to receive this loyalty, it is in jeopardy of losing its appeal and importance to those of its members belonging to regional organizations in which they consider their participation more meaningful.

The very nature of a regional organization gives to its members a closer sense of identification. They feel a greater dedication and a sense of common commitment. In the OAU it is generally more possible to recognize a common posture in matters of foreign policy in a way that is certainly not possible within the UN, in the face of the Cold War disputes still unresolved.

The most important objective of the OAU has always been to promote the unity and solidarity of the African states. In pursuance of this objective it has been necessary for these states to adopt common positions in many areas of foreign policy. Most conspicuous here has been their absolute dedication to the total emancipation of the African territories which are still dependent and their determination to eradicate all forms of colonialism from Africa. Inevitably, the pursuit of such policies is bound to bring these African nations into conflict with imperialist and colonial countries which are also members of the UN.

And so we find that there may well be occasions when the avowed objectives of a regional organization will conflict with those of other members of the UN. In such situations the solidarity and effectiveness of the UN will undoubtedly be undermined.

But by far the greatest danger to the UN posed by the existence of an organization like the OAU is the possibility that UN decisions which ought to be more properly debated and taken on the General Assembly level could be taken by the African Group, the representatives of the OAU at the UN, in private caucus meetings beforehand and later forced on the others in the General Assembly level. This, of course, is quite easy to conceive in view of the membership of thirty-five African countries in the UN and the possibility of their influencing the Afro-Asian group, which has a total membership of more than half of the Assembly. Such a majority strength, if used only to further the interests of the African group, may well spell disaster for the General Assembly as a forum where the actions of nations are harmonized in the attainment of common ends. This could happen when African interests conflict with those of others outside the African group.

Mercifully enough, in spite of this strength in numbers, the African group at the UN has never sought to impose any partisan will on the other members of the UN. True, there have been occasions when the African members have come together to get resolutions passed on matters on which they feel strongly—apartheid in South Africa and the situation of Portuguese territories in Africa. But these have been matters in which their individual foreign policies happen to coincide with each other and also with the policies of many non-African members of the UN.

On questions before the General Assembly which cannot properly be regarded as African questions, delegates from member states of the OAU have never voted as a bloc but as individual member states, reflecting the various complexions of international policies of their countries.

There is, of course, the further danger that in these days of uncertainty surrounding the UN, following the many frustrations because of its failure to solve outstanding problems vital to survival, the UN might lose its appeal and prestige, thus forcing members to look elsewhere for the fulfillment of international solidarity. In such an atmosphere of disenchantment, the OAU might well consolidate its strength and pose a real challenge to the UN for the loyalty of its members. This danger should be considered in the context of the objectives of the two organizations. The UN Charter, while calling upon members to unite in the pursuit of peace and the improvement of the lot of the individual, emphasizes the sovereignty and independence of members. The Charter of the OAU, on the other hand, while recognizing the sovereign rights of the members, emphasizes the promotion of the unity and solidarity of the African states.

However, in spite of the dangers to the UN of the existence and growing strength of regional organizations like the OAU, it seems quite clear that the advantages certainly outweigh the dangers. The strength and success of the OAU infuse new vigor into the UN. There is no doubt, as the UN Charter fully recognizes, that such organizations are perhaps better capable of achieving pacific settlement of local disputes before referring them to the Security Council, viz.:

The Security Council shall encourage the development of pacific settlement of local disputes through such arrangements or by such regional agencies either on the initiative of the States concerned or by reference from the Security Council.

In its short life, the OAU has indeed demonstrated quite satisfactorily its determination and ability to tackle and solve regional disputes. The handling of the Algerian-Moroccan border dispute is a shining example of this. That the vexing Congo problem remains unresolved can hardly be attributed to the failure of the OAU when one considers all the facts.

These attempts at peace-keeping of the OAU are obviously of advantage to the UN. There are also many programs of cooperation in the educational, cultural, and economic fields already undertaken by the OAU which are clearly in furtherance of the larger objectives of the UN. Besides, and this is important, the main objectives of the UN as an organization dedicated to the pursuit of peace and the reduction of world tensions are reinforced by the preoccupation of regional organizations with those same objectives.

Thus the UN, far from suffering because of the existence of the OAU, is undoubtedly strengthened in the pursuit of the objectives of its Charter. The OAU, on the other hand, needs the support and endorsement of its activities by the UN. Both organizations are really using similar methods for the achievement of the same ideal in the avoidance of war, the pursuit of peace, the reduction of tensions, and the preservation of fundamental human rights.

THE HUMAN COMMUNITY

BARBARA WARD

Economist, Author, and Lecturer
United Kingdom

The starting point for any discussion of economic assistance and foreign aid ought to be the fact that all of us, as a human community, are involved in the process of changing virtually all our institutions and all our ways of managing our affairs under the impact of science and technology. We cannot avoid it. For one thing, it is much, much too convenient. All through the world, societies at various levels of development and change are undergoing the same process. And one of the interesting things about this process is, of course, that you never know when you are going to turn out to be underdeveloped.

The British had the idea that they were in the vanguard of development, and indeed I shall argue shortly that historically they were. But after the war we suddenly woke up to the fact that we had the smallest percentage of our students in advanced education of virtually all the countries in the Atlantic world. So with considerable difficulties in planning, in finding the personnel and organizing the teaching services, we have been adding universities to Britain at a speed which to us seems vertiginous and which underlines the fact that in this field we are underdeveloped. One reason is that the needs of modern technology and the scientific transformation of our society have made it necessary for us to make very considerable changes in our traditional concept of education for an elite. After all, this problem is not so different from those that face developing countries at every level. This is merely a reminder that today's development may turn out to be tomorrow's underdevelopment. We are all involved in this process of startling change, which began 250 years ago and is carrying us all, from the smallest countries to the greatest power systems, through an unknown and still uncharted phase of technological change. We are all in the same boat.

On the other hand, at this particular phase of development, it is quite clear that the changes brought about by modern science and technology have produced a startling disequilibrium in the world. There are the rich nations above the Tropic of Cancer, and below, in the developing continents, a vast majority of poor nations. What is less realized is that in the last five years of the Decade of Development the situation has grown worse. This is not because there has been an absolute increase in poverty; by and large, the per capita income among the poorest nations has not fallen. Rates of growth have more or less matched rates of growth of population, and there has even been perhaps a 1 per cent increase. But at the top of the scale, between 1960 and 1965, the Atlantic nations, and with them Japan and up to a point Russia, have increased at a much more rapid rate; their per capita gross national product has grown on an average by about 3½ per cent a year. Therefore, the gap has in fact widened, because the rich are getting richer quicker. This fact is of great relevance to the problem of foreign aid, because clearly when a nation is increasing its per capita GNP by over 3 per cent a year, the much reiterated plea that 1 per cent of its GNP might be consecrated as a matter of juridical commitment to foreign aid hardly looks like a burden or a sacrifice for it amounts merely to asking people to grow richer a little more slowly between Christmas and Easter—a time which for Christians includes the sacrificial season of Lent.

Is this vast gap in income, opportunity, and hope between the nations of this small planetary society a matter for pessimism? Do we have to feel that this is an ineluctable law of nature and that the biblical phrase "To him who hath shall be given," which tends to be so true in unreconstructed economics, is true of the world at large?

Here I want to return to the idea of my own country as a pioneer, because it is both an awesome and an encouraging thought that only a hundred years ago Benjamin Disraeli, who was on the point of becoming Prime Minister, had published a book about Britain which at that time was in its hundredth year of industrialization. The most vivid phrase in this book, which caught on and had a considerable social effect, was the description of Britain as two nations: the Nation of the Rich and the Nation of the Poor. Disraeli regarded this as the chief consequence of nearly a hundred years of modernization, and the descriptions that he gives of the differences between the two nations apply strikingly to the worldwide cleavage today between rich nations and poor.

Today, as then, we see the same differences in per capita income. At this point I have to recall a story once told of Scott Fitzgerald. He was having a cozy drink with Ernest Hemingway, and he looked across at Hemingway and said, "Do you know, Ernest, there's something quite different about the rich?" "Yes," said Hemingway, "they've got more money." In our comparison with Victorian society, we have to begin with the fact that the rich have more money. But in addition to this, there was the crowding of a vast proletarian mass into the cities, ill-prepared to receive them from every point of amenity; there were gross disparities in education, in health (the last cholera epidemic in London was in the 1860's), in housing, in opportunity—in short, in all those characteristics on which we now predicate the division between the rich nations and the poor nations.

Another factor was extreme pessimism, because very few people thought anything decisive could be done about the gap. The economists profoundly believed that the poor would always breed up to the limit, would lower their standards of living, and would therefore never provide a market sufficient to absorb the vast productivity of the growing machine. At the same time, the moral reformers, the administrators of the Poor Law, thought that the poor were essentially idle, and that if you did anything to raise their standards of living, they would cease to work. We now call that "the background-leaning supply curve." Consequently there was no hope for the poor, and a certain pessimism extended over a lot of the social comment in mid-Victorian Britain.

Now, only a hundred years later, these miserable, downcast, irresponsible, and lazy proletarians have become the fine upstanding consumers of today. The gap has been crossed—a gap about which people felt just as pessimistic as they do about the gap today. So it is interesting to ask ourselves why it is that the proletarians of yesterday in the first British version of the developed economy have turned into the consuming citizens of today. Is there any key here to what one might call a world-wide strategy in our world economy?

I suggest that three crucial changes occurred which made it possible for the society to bridge the gap, to create a nation of consumers where, even if property distribution still leaves much to be desired, income distribution is tolerable. The first change was the self-defense of the proletarians themselves (called *proletarians*, incidentally, because of their propensity to produce *proles* or children). The second was the ability, through these means of self-defense, to get a larger share of the product of the economy. And the third was the growth of a liberal, humane, and often Christian conscience which, confronting the fact of great riches and great poverty, recalled that one of the unique elements of this society has been, from its origins in the Old Testament, a sense of outrage at social injustice. This factor developed into a policy of the transfer of resources from the rich to the poor—the third element in this triple strategy—which in Britain, then increasingly in Western Europe and in the developed market economies of the West, ended the vast disproportion and gap between rich and poor.

Let us look at these three factors and see if they apply today.

The trade union movement, the foundation of political parties, the evolution and elaboration of socialist theory, the cooperative self-help movements among the workers themselves, the foundation by workers of mechanics' institutes, the drive for self-education—all these were factors by which the working class, far from being a helpless proletarian mass, became an active, responsible, and, fortunately, tough-minded set of citizens. And this formation of quite adequate and perfectly directed pressure was one of the big factors in the change. I should add that it was a help that in the constitution of Britain the right of people to assembly and to association was safeguarded; nonetheless, these rights would not have had the same effect if there had not been this strong, dedicated movement of self-help on the part of the proletarians.

One of the consequences of this was the second point of the strategy: to secure a larger part of the production of the economy. Early pessimism had been based partly on the belief that if you put wages up and if labor, as a cost, became more expensive, profits would be squeezed out, and with that the engine of growth would stop. Why did this supposed fatality prove an illusion?

On the one hand, the early economists gravely underestimated the scale of productivity which the new machines would make possible, and therefore the degree to which both wages and profits could move up within a framework of increasing productivity— and certainly today, as our technological revolution continues, we should never lose sight of this matter of productivity. But on the other hand, there were enlightened managers to respond to the pressure of responsible elements in the labor movement. Here I have in mind that great genius, though in a somewhat restricted sphere, Henry Ford, who was the first to see that if you paid your workers five dollars a day they might actually buy the cars on which they were working. In other words, if you pay your workers enough to become consumers, you are on the way to creating a mass market. This was one of those profoundly simple insights of genius which can transform an economy.

Then, with the help of war-time invention, we enormously increased the range of possible consumer durable goods. This breakthrough, coupled with the capacity of the new productivity to absorb higher wages, created the reciprocal relation between mass production and mass consumption upon which the modern economy is based. This relation has reached such a pitch that even in Russia two things have happened recently. One is the restoration of the market approach to a large range of consumer goods, and the other is the decision to make private cars for everybody. They may not know what they have started! But the consumer economy is taking over. So the second factor is the creation of a market by the simple expedient of allowing the vast mass of producers to get a larger share of the output of the economy.

The third point, the sense of social justice, is the beginning of progressive taxation, which had the duchesses protesting in Albert Hall when it was only a shilling in the pound. Fortunately, we in the West, who were rather unwilling socialists in the past, were forced into these collective habits by two world wars which made us used to taxes of about ten shillings six pence in the pound; so we were happy when it went down to seven shillings again. There is a Turkish proverb which says that when Allah wants to make a poor man happy, first he takes away his donkey and then he gives it back. Well, this is on the whole how progressive taxation has come to be an acceptable feature of the Western way of life. But in addition, there has always been behind it the sense of moral obligation within a social community in which the rich quite simply must help the poor. And from Disraeli and Bismarck onwards, the way in which this tax money was used has a very direct relevance to the problems of technical assistance, because a large part of that money was spent upon housing, health, better education, better skills, and the gradual upgrading of the mass of workers. And this increase in skill reminds us of the fact that a very large part of the gains in the modern economy came not so much from the introduction of machines as from the training of brains to use those machines.

These three ways in which, within the first developed economy of the world, a startling gap between rich and poor was overcome, suggest the possibilities of a similar strategy today.

First, defense and self-help. One encouraging action from the point of view of the long-term bridging of this gap was the formation of the front of 77 nations at the UN Conference on World Trade and Development at Geneva in the summer of 1964. There the poor nations established their solidarity and began to put pressure on the rich nations on specific points—which could not be dealt with in generalities—about the essential structure of the world economic system. They got down to practical things like the level and the fluctuation in primary prices, the lack of organization in the primary market, the degree to which middleman profits remain entirely in the hands of the rich. Ninety-four per cent of the world's shipping is owned by the developed countries, and all of the insurance is in their hands. This means draining off the middleman profits from the entire world economy to those who are already rich.

Again, the lack of compensatory finance and the tariff structure of the Western world are further reminders that the entire structure is biased against the poor and in favor of the rich. Raw materials come in with zero tariffs; for semiprocessed materials, tariffs can go up to 5 to 10 per cent; for manufactured goods, they probably rise to 15 to 20 per cent. And if materials still get in, on goes a quota! This kind of graded bias in favor of the rich nations became clear in the world dialogue in Geneva, because for the first time specific confrontation on these issues was taking place. In the present situation it would be a tragedy if this front were broken up.

And so I would say, hold the front of 77 together, remain specific, remain absolutely directed toward your objectives, not only because of immediate self-interest, but also because you will be helping to create that second strategy to which I now turn.

With our present system of "demand management" in the Western economies, the degree to which we can probably go on expanding our own internal domestic market is very large indeed.

Once you realize that the decisive element in the economy is not the shortage of supplies but the maintenance of demand, a lot can be done. You can go to the moon and do other extravagant and expensive things. There is really no shortage of ways in which you can use—and waste—your resources. Any group of nations that spends 120 billion dollars a year on arms and gets more miserably insecure in the process probably deserves a planetary prize from the entire solar system for consistent idiocy. I do not know whether any other planet has reached this pitch, but it will be interesting to find out.

The point is that the possibilities of "demand creation" inside the Western economies are very high. Nonetheless, it is a matter of common sense, and of direct analogy to the earlier experience of the developed economies, if part of this demand creation takes the form of mobilizing the consumers in the developing world. In other words, we have to see to it that, like Mr. Ford's workers, the proletarian nations get a larger share of the increasing productivity of the world economy. They will get this, first, through the kind of policies proposed at Geneva, which demanded systematically some slight redistribution of the gains from trade in favor of the poor. The proposal is certainly modest enough. For instance, the aim of the Decade of Development is that the terms of trade, which slipped by about 15 per cent against the poor nations between 1951 and 1961, should be redressed by 8 per cent. In other words, the poor nations are asking only to be 7 per cent worse off than they were in 1950. The second proposal was that the developing nations' share in world trade should go up from 26 to 28 per cent —not, I must say, a shatteringly ambitious goal.

But the modesty of the aims should not for one moment lead the poor nations to be modest in the pressure they put to get these aims. It is by enlarging the share of the developing countries in the world economy that they will begin to create a greater capacity to consume—a greater capacity, therefore, to enter in a systematic way into the market economy on a world-wide scale. Never forget, for instance, that between 1950 and 1960 all the flow of capital aid into Latin America was canceled by the fall in prices of their major exports. You could therefore argue that during that period foreign aid was a very handsome subsidy to the exporters of machinery from the United States and Europe, for without it their trade would have ceased because of the absence of consuming power in the developing continent. Let us remember that any policies which increase the share of the developing countries in the flow of trade at the same time increase their consuming power.

I consider it equally important—and this concerns the wide field of private enterprise—that a larger share in the profits from local investment should stay in the local economy. This is another way in which the consuming power of the local people can be built up. We have to face the fact that on many counts the record was pretty dismal up to the Second World War. The French have a delicious term *le trouisme* (from *trou*, meaning "hole") to describe a foreign investment which comes in to develop a mineral resource. The company is foreign, the amortization (which is sometimes done ten times over) is foreign, the transfer of profits is foreign, the salaries of all the major technicians are foreign. What the local underdeveloped economy receives is, first, the wages of the unskilled labor and, second, the import duties which often go to pay the costs of colonial administration that was there in any case. Lastly, when the mineral reserve is depleted, the country is left with one big hole—*le trouisme*.

This is the extreme, and this is, in fact, an area in which a good deal of consistent progress has taken place. If you compare the treaties made with Persia in the original days of the Anglo-Iranian Oil Company and the treatment enjoyed by Nigeria today, you will see that there has been considerable progress. The 50–50 basis of the Liberian American Minerals Company's arrangement with Liberia and Kaiser Aluminum in its taxation, profit sharing and social fund arrangement with Ghana are examples of much more legitimate methods of private investment which, where possible, should be considered as the norm. What I plead is that both developed and developing peoples may see this aim of leaving more of the take from investment in the developing economy as in the interests of *both* parties because in the long run there is nothing more profitable for private investment than growing consumer markets in the vast penumbra of developing continents. And it is only if these continents do not prosper that the prospects of foreign enterprise and foreign investment will begin to grow dim. How much you can go on investment inside the Atlantic arena I do not know, but there must come a moment when, with television in the drawing room, in the bathroom, and in the kitchen, with three cars and four swimming pools (we are not there yet), consumer demand being so satisfied, satiety will set in. Then where are the new markets? They must be in developing countries.

Now I come to the third strategy—foreign aid. In the last few years this aid has not, except in France, even reached the 1 per cent of GNP which people like me have been pleading for and will continue to plead for. This percentage receives enormous lip service; it was even stipulated in a recommendation passed at the Geneva Conference. But owing to the fact that the GNP in the Atlantic world is going up, appropriations for foreign aid as a percentage of the GNP are actually falling. The reasons given for this are many. One is the claim that the absorptive capacity of the various continents is such that even if we should reach 1 per cent, the developing countries could not use it. This is particularly relevant in the case of Africa, but it is important everywhere.

There are two things I want to say on that. First, let us consider the largest of aid programs, that of Pakistan and India. I would wager that if the per capita aid to India were doubled, the output of that economy could be tripled, for the output is held back partly because of a trade situation in which it is virtually impossible for India to increase export earnings. This is where trade and aid begin to mesh.

If India enjoyed the same level of per capita assistance as Pakistan, we would see there the kind of change that has occurred in Pakistan in the last five years. This has resulted in an industrial rate of growth of between 9 and 10 per cent a year, and an agricultural rate of growth that has suddenly jumped up to nearly 4 per cent a year, giving an annual rate of increase in this economy of 5 per cent and moving toward 6 per cent in the last two years of the plan. Now these are startling figures of growth, and one of the key elements has been massive aid. So when people talk about this problem of absorbability, I accept that a good deal more assistance is needed in the form of feasibility studies and the provision of key technicians, but I think that, with a little more imagination, the absorbability would be found to be not so low. One example of what I mean is Kenya, a country created by a railway. The people building it did not ask whether the railway would pay its way; they were trying first to get rid of slavery, and second, to make sure the Germans did not get there first—both not particularly economic reasons. Out of the construction of that railway came, in part, the creation of East Africa.

If, over the next ten years, the Western powers, or better, the developed powers—hopefully under the auspices of the World Bank and the UN Special Fund—decided to put into Africa a grid of communications and a grid of transport which would increase considerably the range of absorbability, would the results be any less startling than the effects of the railway put in for strategic and humane reasons sixty or seventy years ago? Were people more imaginative, more courageous, then than now? With so many fewer resources, did they go bankrupt? No! Is it not possible that the impediments to absorbability about which we constantly hear are not a lack of technicians, but something much more dire—a lack of imagination and a lack of guts?

So let us not fall short of our proposed aid of 1 per cent of GNP because of intricacies which are so often used as excuses. Let us rather accept that, in a world community, this is an obligation that has to be channeled into constructive growth, into technical assistance, into the provision in the developing continents of all those services and all those capacities and opportunities which taxation has made possible *inside* the developed communities, and which have transformed the people of these nations from rich and poor into citizens with an enormous apparatus of skills, with self-respect, with a capacity for self-help, and therefore with the capacity to live in community.

The fundamental point in all this is that we must accept community, and of course many of us do not. We still imagine that we live in a vast universe. But the fact is that we are all voyagers in a rather small space ship. It is quite efficient, it carries us through infinity, we can live on it. But on its narrow envelope of soil and its little envelope of air, the entire survival of the human experiment depends. I think a space ship is a better analogy than a planet, because even now a planet gives one a sense of space. In fact, there is very little space, and how we conduct our affairs on this ship is obviously the *only* crucial fact before us.

We can continue to conduct our operations in the way that has already, in this century, produced two disastrous wars which, if repeated, would finish us off. If, on the other hand, we can create a real community, the world is not at all a pessimistic place, because a number of changes would occur.

First, mankind would reach a technological condition in which shortage was not the dominant feature, and in which therefore the grab for resources, which has lain behind conquest ever since prehistoric man began inventing weapons, would have no more meaning. That blind need for conquest which lies in scarcity, would, for the first time, be banished from the face of the earth. This is the great hopeful fact about technology. We would have the first chance that precisely those processes which underlie scientific endeavor and indeed industrial endeavor—the processes of cooperation, of systematic search for common solutions—might be the condition of survival, and rid us of the blind urges of conquest.

Second, I believe that if we could extend this concept to our world community, we would little by little see the death of ideology. Some of the more extreme formulations of ideology are what I would call the infantile diseases of early industrialism. In other words, at some stage in the transformation of our technological economy, those who started from the side of the market obviously would find that they have more and more need to plan and direct, and those who start from planning and direction would discover that in the interests of the consumer, of higher standards of living, they have more need of the market. If this convergence of the two systems which dominate the world in this ideological deadlock of the Cold War continues, it may be, as so often in human debate, that the problem will not be solved; it will be found not to be there. We in Europe engulfed the world in the most recent of the bloody ideological struggles—the war between Protestants and Catholics, which alas, erupted even in your own country of Uganda. But look at us now—look at the ecumenical spirit! May it not be that a hundred years from now people will look back in the same way on Capitalists and Communists?

My last point is that if we can have this kind of organized sense or obligation of unity, we will take the essential steps in the creation of a world community. The space ship cannot survive if the only institutions are those based on forces and drives of fear internationalized through arms and warfare, or those of cupidity organized through an unreconstructed economic market. Surely we must institutionalize the drives of cooperation and good will as well. Our community is interdependent economically and interdependent in the risk of annihilation. How can we survive without adding the institutions of shared responsibility and moral obligation?

We have done it, we had to do it inside our domestic societies. The growth of the welfare state represents the acceptance, however unwillingly on the part of some, of a shared moral obligation which then becomes the web of community. We can do no less in the world at large—though the world at large is not a good phrase because it is really very small. If we do not create those common obligations and common responsibilities, our survival itself is at stake. I think we can. One of the things that has been to me enormously encouraging, and indeed moving, about this conference week is that when people meet as we have met, this underlying sense of our common humanity, of our belonging together, comes through, not with effort but really with great enjoyment. Brotherhood is revealed not as a gloomy obligation but as a liberation of the spirit.

III. The African Economy

ASPECTS OF ECONOMIC DEVELOPMENT

SIR ARTHUR LEWIS

Professor of Economics and International Affairs
Woodrow Wilson School, Princeton University

What follows is not a systematic survey of African economies, but a set of notes on some factors which currently limit the rate of economic growth in Africa.

I. NATURAL RESOURCES

1. Not enough is spent on discovery, or on studying ways of improving the use of natural resources.

2. Hitherto, the wealth of the continent has derived almost entirely from minerals, except for a brief post-Korean period of windfall prices for a few crops, since Africa does not have any special advantage over other continents in agricultural production.

3. Geological departments and mineral surveys have yielded several times their cost. Further exploratory work should have the highest priority.

4. Current methods of land use lag behind those of Asia and other continents. Very little has been spent on agricultural research, and that mainly on crops for export, although the bulk of

agricultural production is for home consumption. Too little is known of African soils, or of the best means of cultivating them in the African climates. Plant breeding, fertilization, crop rotation, and pest control are still in their infancy. Agricultural officers have some ideas to pass on to the farmers, but the solid research on which such ideas should be based has been starved of funds.

5. The most striking cause of the prosperity of the developed world has been the progress of science and technology over the past century and a half. Africa cannot simply borrow this technology; she must adapt it to African conditions. In agriculture this means starting almost from first principles, and waiting years before results are ready for application. Scientific and technological research must therefore have the highest priority.

6. Such words as *big*, *small*, or *high* have no meaning until quantified. There is no basis for deciding how much Africa should spend on scientific research. It is estimated that about 3 per cent of the national income of the United States is spent on public and private research and development (excluding space travel). A similar proportion of African national incomes would be equivalent to 20 to 33 per cent of what African governments now raise in taxes.

II. SKILLS

1. Development programs cannot be executed without skilled manpower. The amount of skill required depends on the current level of development, being lowest where the majority of people are still engaged in subsistence agriculture. At current levels of development, Africa needs to have about 1 per cent of the corresponding age group in universities, and about 10 per cent of the corresponding group in secondary schools. This is more urgent than trying to get 100 per cent of children into primary schools.

2. About half of African children today should prepare to take up farming, and the other half to take jobs off the farms. Most of the children who complete primary school are reluctant to enter farming, so in those African countries where the primary school intake is already up to 70 per cent, rural children are pouring out

of schools into the towns, where there are not enough jobs for them.

3. The lack of jobs is often attributed to the inappropriate curriculum of rural schools. But the chief reason is that subsistence farming, as now conducted, cannot give a primary-school graduate the kind of income which he has come to expect. Agriculture has to be modernized if it is to attract and hold modern people. If the rate of modernization of agriculture and the rate of expansion of rural schools are out of step, increased juvenile unemployment in the towns is inevitable.

4. Some countries have schemes for settling primary-school graduates on the land, with modern equipment and technology. The degree of supervision varies—whether they work on individual plots, on large state farms, in brigades, or in cooperatives. This is a hopeful development, if empty fertile land is available, and if the capital and managerial costs of settlement can be kept in reasonable bounds.

5. The main task in the countryside is to bring new ideas to adult farmers. Some interesting experiments are in progress in agricultural education, especially those which involve taking young farmers to training centers for courses of about three months' duration. The main need is to multiply several-fold the sums now devoted to agricultural extension training.

6. It is tempting to think that the small farmer can be bypassed by opening up huge new mechanized farms in empty lands. Most such experiments have failed in the past, mainly for three reasons: (1) Empty lands are usually empty because farmers have learned over the centuries that they are difficult to cultivate, whether through infertility or uncertain rainfall; this should first be checked in small pilot schemes. (2) To keep tractors going requires a highly skilled organization which is difficult to create and maintain far from the main urban centers. (3) Assembling and supervising the work of large numbers of people, including agricultural specialists, also requires organizational skills which are scarce. Opening up empty lands for mechanized agriculture as yet can be

only marginal; the main emphasis must be on improving the work on existing small farms.

7. Modernizing small-scale agriculture is a slow process, but good results are already being achieved in many parts of Africa. Higher priority, more money, and more skilled manpower are the chief requirements.

III. MARKETS

1. Africa produces both for her own consumption and for export. Although home consumption greatly exceeds exports, development has been propelled by the rapid growth of exports, rather than by home demand, because so much of home production is in the stagnant subsistence sector.

2. Exports have great growth potential. World trade in the products of the developing countries, taken as a whole, grows by only about 3½ per cent per year, but in most cases (cocoa is the notable exception) Africa's output is such a small part of world trade that it can expand very sharply with negligible effect on world prices. The old ways of raising the standard of living in Africa are still likely to be the quickest ways: to discover new minerals, and to introduce to the farmers profitable new export crops.

3. Exports not only provide incomes; they also create a home market which is a challenge to domestic production. This challenge has in the past been neglected, partly because the traders who managed the export trade had an equal interest in distributing consumer imports. Africa therefore imports an excessive amount of consumer goods, both industrial (e.g., textiles) and agricultural (e.g., livestock products), which she could profitably learn to produce at home. The word *learn* is emphasized. In many cases, current costs are high, and they will fall only as experience is gained and as the economies of large-scale production materialize. Hence special effort is required to initiate and support production. Rising standards bring changes in food consumption (fewer roots, more cereals, meat, milk, vegetables, and fruit) with which African agriculture is not keeping pace. The possibilities for import

substitution are not confined to manufacturing industries.

4. Import substitution still has some way to go, but the limits of import substitution are soon reached in an economy where more than half the people are subsistence farmers, since the effect of their poverty is that the home market is small. It is right to put into industrial development such resources as it can absorb, but it will not absorb much until the market is widened. Hence efforts to increase agricultural productivity require equal priority. Industrialization and modernization of agriculture go hand in hand. If a country industrializes while its agriculture remains stagnant, the demand of its industrial population for food and raw materials cannot be met; and, beyond the stage of import substitution, its factories will be forced to close unless they can compete in world markets. Similarly, if the farmers produce more food while the industrial population remains the same, the farmers will go bankrupt unless they find world markets. In production aimed at the home market, industry and agriculture must advance together.

5. Regional economic agreements do not bypass the need for agricultural improvement. Putting two countries behind the same tariff may double the market, and so make it possible for one large factory to produce economically where two small factories would fail. But the process doubles the population available for employment as well as doubling the market, so, taking the two countries together, the ratio of industrial to agricultural demand is not changed, and the constraint imposed by agricultural stagnation remains the same. The doubling of the population along with the market is of course the reason why regional economic agreements are difficult to make and keep: the countries have difficulty in agreeing how to share the potential new industries. Given the current political situation, industrialization will proceed more rapidly through each country's expanding its own home market than through regional integration, desirable as that is for many reasons.

6. The most promising areas for regional cooperation are:
   the building of through trunk roads;
   simplification of customs and immigration procedures;

elimination of duties on food and raw materials;
elimination of duties on traffic in transit.

Also needed are measures to facilitate conversion of one currency into another. This is not difficult for those currencies which are convertible into sterling or francs, which are themselves convertible into each other, but it is difficult for the other currencies. Agreement on the location of manufacturing industries is the hardest to achieve. It is also unlikely that progress can be made on any of these issues on a continent-wide basis. A start might be made in West Africa. The time seems ripe for a ministerial committee, with permanent secretariat, to take up and follow through with each of these issues, starting with the easiest. Such a committee should include all the West African countries; English- and French-speaking should come together on these matters. The group could function as a standing subcommittee of the UN Economic Commission for Africa.

7. In colonial times, production for export was assisted in some cases by receiving preferential treatment in metropolitan markets. Such arrangements have been changing during the past five years and are still in flux. Some African states want preferential arrangements to end, and are supported in this by Asian and Latin American states, which object to preferential treatment of African products. Differences between the African states on this issue reflect differences of economic interest, since some have benefited much more than others, and some may even have lost. Unanimity on this issue is therefore unlikely.

8. These preferential arrangements concern trade with Western Europe. Much more important is the failure of Eastern Europe to buy adequate amounts of African or other tropical products. This market should be pursued vigorously, now that Africa and the Communist powers are in direct relations with each other. The African economy would be greatly advanced if the per capita consumption of African products in Eastern Europe approached closer to that of Western Europe.

9. Primary producing countries have been seeking for forty years

to institute international control of commodity prices, both to reduce fluctuations and to raise the average level of prices. They have had only meager success. Prices can be controlled only by controlling output, and control of output is difficult because the number of producers and potential producers is so large. When leading producers control their output, minor producers seize the opportunity to expand, and countries which were not even in the market before now start production. Discussion of these schemes will no doubt continue, but there is no reason to expect more success in the near future.

10. In any case, control of fluctuations does not depend on international agreement, since any country can erect a buffer between world prices and its own domestic prices—whether through marketing boards or through export taxes which fluctuate with prices. The average level of prices matters more than the fluctuations, and it is on control over the average level that the dispute centers.

IV. MONEY

1. Most of the national income is consumed by private persons; part is used by the government to provide public services; and the rest is devoted to capital formation.

2. Economic development requires that about 30 per cent of gross domestic product be used for government services and capital formation, leaving 70 per cent for personal consumption. In Africa, personal consumption takes about 80 per cent, leaving only 20 per cent for public services and capital formation. The financial problem is therefore to decrease personal consumption from 80 to 70 per cent. This takes time, but self-sustaining growth and economic independence will not be attained until this change has been effected.

3. The public service needs are obvious. African states, for a minimum framework, need to spend about 6 per cent of national income on general and economic administration, 3 per cent on education (nearer 5 per cent if there is compulsory education),

2 per cent on health, and 2 per cent miscellaneous (welfare, defense, public debt), making a minimum of 13 per cent on current expenditure only. In addition, governments require money for capital formation.

4. A rate of economic growth of between 4 and 5 per cent a year would involve private and public capital formation (including depreciation) of about 20 per cent of gross domestic product. The biggest share of capital goes into public utilities and public services (especially communications and power) and into residential housing. The amount of capital required to produce a unit of output is probably higher in Africa at present than in other continents, because the cost of supplying a sparsely populated continent with roads, electric power, water supplies, and other infrastructure is always high in relation to national income.

5. Much of this capital has to be provided by the public authorities. Normally agriculture, mining, and manufacturing absorb less than half the total of capital formation, so even in economies where these sectors are left entirely to private enterprise it is not unusual for the public sector (including public utilities) to take half of the total capital formation—especially if the government finances a lot of residential housing. Adding current and capital expenditures together, most African governments should be able to spend at least 20 per cent of the national income, financed from taxes, grants, and loans. This means that they need to raise at least 15 per cent of national income in taxes, but there are still many countries where taxes do not yet amount to 10 per cent of national income.

6. African public finances greatly need reform. There is shocking waste of expenditure, especially on prestige projects, ministerial extravagance, and corrupt practices. This could equally be said of many countries in Europe and North America. The differences are, first, that rich countries can afford waste more easily than poor countries; and, second, that European and American political systems encourage public criticism of abuses, whereas the political systems of some African states discourage the general public from

criticizing government acts.

7. More fundamental than waste is the burden cast on the budget by excessive expectations. All public servants have excessive income expectations, in relation to the incomes of those who are taxed to pay their salaries. The biggest group of taxpayers are the farmers, who produce the exports which directly (export taxes) or indirectly (import duties) yield the biggest revenue. Yet even an unskilled laborer in the government service demands an income twice as high as the average farmer's income, and the whole hierarchy of public service wages and salaries stands like a mountain on the farmer's back. Thus it would take a minimum of 13 per cent of national income to produce in Africa a level of public services which any European country could provide for 6 per cent of its national income or less. This disparity seems not to be diminishing but to be widening, since trade unions in the public service are pressuring the African governments continuously for increases in income, without regard to what the farmers can bear. Nor is the anomaly confined to wage earners or civil servants. The top 2 per cent of Africans demand a standard of living higher than that of their professional counterparts in Europe, while the base on which this rests gives the majority of their countrymen less than one-fifth the income of European workers.

8. Expectations for free public services are also excessive. African governments are expected to provide, out of the central budget, not only free roads, free schools, and free medical services, but sometimes even free water, free electricity, and heavily subsidized housing. This is partly due to excessive centralization of government functions, inherited from the colonial powers. Services which should be performed by municipal, county, or provincial authorities tend instead to be vested in the center. Now one of the maxims of public finance is that where the consumer is getting free service, or highly subsidized service, financial responsibility should be decentralized and brought as close to him as possible, so that he can see the connection between the amounts of the service he uses and of the taxes he has to pay to the village or municipality or

county to defray its costs. When the service is financed by the central budget, the connection between demand and taxes is tenuous. Nobody wants to pay taxes to a distant central government, whose use of them is neither known nor approved, but the demand for installation of services is unlimited. Governments are then saddled with an insoluble problem: if 10,000 villages need a service, but there is money only for 1000, which 9000 shall be excluded? If the service is decentralized, and every village can install it that is willing to pay for it, the obvious connection between demand and cost checks excessive demands and also makes people more willing to pay more taxes in order to have services which they value. Educating the people to pay more taxes is Africa's principal financial problem; so far they have learned only to want unlimited amounts of public service. Decentralization from central to subordinate public authorities is an important part of the educational process. If the subordinate authorities had more to offer in services, they would find it easier to raise additional taxes. Farmers who produce for export tend to be more than adequately taxed, but the 60 per cent or so of agricultural output for the home market is lightly taxed, though these farmers also demand a lot of public service.

9. Another group which does not pay its fair share of taxes is the middle-income group. In many African countries, corporations and individuals earning in excess of $4000 a year are now taxed as heavily as in Western Europe; however, these incomes account for a small part of gross domestic product. People living in towns, earning $1000 or $2000 a year, put the heaviest burden on the public services (secondary schools, hospitals, water, subsidized rents), but commonly pay a smaller proportion of their incomes in taxes than the farmers, who are much poorer and receive much less service. This group also tends to save proportionately least. In inegalitarian societies, where rich landlords and capitalists cream off 30 to 40 per cent of the national income, it is possible to raise large sums in taxation while exempting the poor. This is not possible in most African countries, because there are very few rich people (also very few poor, measuring by Asian standards). If governments are to

raise 15 to 20 per cent in taxes, everybody must pay his share.

10. To gain economic independence, Africa must be able to raise out of her own resources all the finance required for her development. This, as stated above, means reducing the share of consumption in gross domestic product from about 80 to 70 per cent. Such a reduction cannot be achieved overnight. Also, it cannot be achieved by reducing the absolute level of consumption; the most that is practicable is to have consumption grow less rapidly than output. Consumption cannot be reduced because growth needs incentives, which means the opportunity to consume more. There must be incentives to encourage people to change their jobs, or acquire new skills, or invest money or time in new endeavors. Since consumption must grow if output is to grow, widening the gap takes time; to fall from 80 to 70 per cent must take at least two or three decades at the present rate. Africa can have economic independence today if she is satisfied with the low level of growth which is all that its own 20 per cent on public services and capital formation will give. But if Africa wants faster economic growth now, it must have help from outside. The best way to make progress toward economic independence is not to dispense with foreign aid now, but to adopt measures—steady increases in savings and taxes—which reduce the share of personal consumption in national income. How much progress is made can then be read off in the national income figures every year. The two key measures of progress toward economic maturity are thus the annual rate of growth of national income and the rate of fall of the share of personal consumption in gross domestic product.

11. Meanwhile, Africa needs massive foreign aid to sustain a growth rate of between 4 and 5 per cent per annum. Most of this is aid to the public sector, partly because the greatest need for capital is in public utilities and services, and partly because, even inside the private sector, the scope for foreign investment is confined to large-scale manufacturing and mining. African governments have come to terms with the fact that their countries need foreign investment in large-scale enterprises and are adjusting their laws

and practices accordingly. Finding aid for the public sector is likely
to be the tougher problem. Over the past decade African governments have tended to concentrate on international political rather
than economic questions. In this period the net flow of aid to underdeveloped countries has risen from about 2 to 8 billions a year.
But the future is uncertain. The United States is increasingly dis-
enchanted with foreign aid, and France desires to reduce its commitment to Africa. The Soviet Union is also learning that foreign
aid pays small dividends. A continuing supply of adequate aid is
likely to be a problem that will tax the full resources of African
statesmanship.

12. In the absence of adequate aid, countries trying to do more
than they have the resources for are involved in inflation, and in
the maze of restrictive licenses which inflation breeds. So far, most
African countries (but not all) have kept their plans within the
limits of available resources. There are arguments for inflation in
countries which would otherwise have idle resources, but it is clear
that African countries do not at present have adequate administrative structures for coping with the very serious problems which inflation creates. The major effort should be to secure adequate financial aid.

V. UNEMPLOYMENT

1. Unemployment is growing rapidly. Some towns are exploding
in size faster than jobs, houses, water, or other amenities can be
provided. Hence slums, juvenile delinquency, and crime are multi-
plying. On the one hand, the outflow from the countryside is excessive; and on the other hand, the number of jobs created in the
towns is too small.

2. The excessive outflow is stimulated by:
   the relatively high wage rates in urban centers;
   the maldistribution of development expenditure;
   disequilibrium between the rate of modernization of agricul-
      ture and the rate of expansion of rural schools.

3. The growing disparity between wage rates in towns and

farmers' incomes encourages migration to the towns in search of work. The towns offer many opportunities for casual work—in the docks, transport, building, domestic service, etc. Great numbers attach themselves to these occupations and survive with only two or three days' work per week. The effect is cumulative, since the fewer the number of days, the greater the pressure for higher hourly wages, and therefore the more attractive the wage rate seems to country folk. Furthermore, the higher hourly wage increases the incentive to employers to use labor-saving methods.

4. Wages apart, the capital city also attracts because governments tend to concentrate here an abnormal proportion of their expenditures on housing, water supplies, schools, hospital services, transportation, etc. The best way to keep people in the countryside would be to develop a large number of small country towns, so that every villager has easy access to nearby amenities. Reference has already been made to excessive centralization of public finance; decentralization of development is also important. The belief that successful industrialization requires concentration on one or two large towns is fallacious.

5. The influx of primary-school graduates into the towns results from the stagnation of agriculture. Large investments of time and money need to be made in modernizing agriculture if it is to attract, as it should, about half the rising generation. Expansion of rural education and modernization of agriculture should march in step.

6. Nonagricultural employment is also failing to absorb its fair share of workers. This is caused partly by inadequate investment, but even more by the excessive capital-intensity of much of the investment which is taking place. In several countries large sums have been invested in recent years, with little to show by way of additional employment. This is due to several factors:

excessive concern with prestige;
choosing capital-intensive projects;
rising wage levels.

7. Since Africa is rightly desirous of being accorded an equal

place in the world's esteem, some element of prestige enters into every new achievement there. However, while it costs little to gain prestige through intellectual or artistic achievement, through commercial or industrial success, or through wise statesmanship, acquiring prestige through building lavish structures is both difficult and expensive. A large proportion of the money spent on structures in the past decade has been wasted, in the sense either that what was done was unnecessary at this time, or that what was necessary could have been done at substantially lower cost. This means that capital formation leads to less continuing employment and income than would be possible if less attention were paid to prestige.

8. Prestige apart, a large proportion of the projects chosen for development are of the sort which involve heavy expenditures on plant and equipment while employing little labor. Much of this is inevitable, especially in mining or hydroelectric power. But African planners also tend to look in capital-intensive directions, and to neglect the development potential in small-scale enterprise, light industry, and other unspectacular but labor-intensive possibilities. It is easier to plan one large capitalized project than to act as midwife to a hundred small undertakings. And there is more kudos in achieving the spectacular.

9. When choosing between capital-intensive and labor-intensive ways of achieving a given objective, wages are an important element. African wages have been rising much faster than the prices of machines. Hence decision-makers increasingly choose machines to do jobs that labor could do.

10. Several governments have become concerned about the growing disparity between urban and rural incomes (salaries and profits, as well as wages), partly because of the heavy tax burden which this imposes on the farmers, because it eats into the funds for development, because this disequilibrium creates unemployment, and because it is obviously unfair that most of the gains of development accrue to the relatively few people who live and work

in towns. Hence, as in other continents, some governments are trying to win acceptance for an "incomes policy."

VI. ENTERPRISE

1. During the 1950's, development planning concentrated on infrastructure. There was a tremendous backlog. Between 1930 and 1950 very little had been spent on public services and utilities, first because of the Depression of the thirties, then because of World War II. In 1950, infrastructure was certainly inadequate to support any considerable rate of economic growth. Much progress has been made in the past fifteen years, particularly in those countries where tax revenues have been increased by favorable terms of trade for cocoa, coffee, rubber, and cotton, or for mining (especially copper, iron ore).

2. Africa will continue for some time to depend on foreign capital for large-scale investment in mining and manufacturing. Since her people do not yet have the necessary expertise in managing this type of business, concessions to foreign enterprise (with or without association with African private or public capital) will prove more profitable than costly and inefficient attempts at public operation. On the other hand, there is no shortage of small-scale enterprise, out of which managerial experience grows. Africans seize every opportunity to invest in new commercial crops, trade, trucking, power-milling, or other small-scale industry. The chief menace to the development of African enterprise is the maze of restrictive licensing into which some countries get themselves through bad planning. Economic growth depends not primarily on government effort, but on hundreds of thousands of Africans seeing and seizing opportunities to better their lot. The government's major contribution is not to restrict but to widen such opportunities.

3. Government initiative is required in the private sector to promote commodity production, especially by supplying information, carrying some risks, and helping to create a good institutional

framework. As infrastructure has improved, governments have paid increasing attention to their promotional role. The major emphasis has been placed on the manufacturing industry, with moderate success. Mining has been held up by inadequate expenditures on geological services, and agriculture has been almost completely neglected, except for experiments in marketing.

4. Many African governments are not yet in a position to execute development plans, as distinguished from publishing statements of intention, because their administrative structure is in disarray. They have not drawn the line between politics and administration, or decided what is appropriate for politicians and what for civil servants. In consequence, when it is uncertain where responsibility for decision-making lies, economic decisions are apt to be overinfluenced by political and personal considerations. Attractive plans are made which cannot be carried out effectively. Efforts to establish administration on a sound basis are essential to progress in executing development plans.

5. Execution is more important than forecasting. At this stage, development planning in Africa does not require elaborate statistical exercises. The main problem is to identify the development potentialities—unexploited minerals, fertile soils, water supplies, commercial crops, technological improvements, and opportunities for import substitution. Mathematical models are needed by countries where the growth of internal demand is the engine of development, since full identification of the possibilities then requires demand projections and input-output analysis of inter-industry transactions. In Africa, development planning is primarily an exercise in detecting new opportunities; its tool is not mathematics, but lavish expenditure on surveys and research. Thus the highest priorities in Africa are science and skill.

PLANNING IN AN AFRICAN ECONOMY, WITH PARTICULAR REFERENCE TO KENYA

TOM J. MBOYA

Minister of Economic Planning
Kenya

Planning is essentially an exercise in the allocation and use of resources. To plan effectively, it is necessary for a government to have not only the power and ability to plan, but also the power and ability to implement a plan. Planning is not a purely economic function. It must deal with physical, social, and financial problems, as well as economics. Physical planning is required for land use and layout, transport and design, for problems in both rural and urban areas. Social planning must deal with welfare, cultural development, the modification of traditional attitudes, self-help, and community development. Financial planning involves the projection of government revenues, recurrent expenditure, and capital budgeting.

Planning is therefore a discipline which requires the participation and support of every department of a government and every individual in the country. If planning is not to be a waste of resources, this discipline must be firmly enforced, in both the public and the private sectors. Only in this way can the best use be made of the limited resources available for developing African economies.

To plan effectively, it is essential to have a clear and generally accepted national strategy for development. In Kenya the main lines of this strategy are:

1. To attack directly the two principal limitations on growth, i.e., shortages of domestic capital and skilled manpower, in order to increase the growth potential of the nation.

2. To revolutionize agriculture by developing unused and underutilized land through consolidation, development credit, extension services and training, and the introduction of modern methods of farming and marketing. Higher incomes in agriculture will stimulate the development of commerce and industry by

   (a) increasing the domestic demand for consumer goods and services and agricultural supplies, and

   (b) providing raw materials for agricultural processing industries.

3. To develop industry as rapidly as opportunities are created—first, by processing agricultural, livestock, and forestry products, as well as natural resources, for domestic use and export; second, by production for domestic demand in a progressively more fully integrated manner. Tourism—our means of "processing" our wild-life resources—must have a high priority.

4. To develop transport, power, marketing facilities, and other infrastructure in order to draw the entire nation into the market economy and to lay the basis for a rapid acceleration of industrial growth.

5. To provide for a more equitable distribution of the benefits achieved by this program.

The execution of this strategy must also be carried out in relation to the general objectives of our society and the social traditions and political structures which we have inherited. We are therefore planning within the framework of an African Socialist society, the principles and operating characteristics of which have recently been fully set out in a Kenya Sessional Paper. Social objectives, to be meaningful, must be realistic. The first task of the planner is therefore to appraise the resources which may be available in terms of skilled and unskilled manpower, domestic and overseas capital, and foreign exchange. This appraisal provides the hard, cold facts against which the planner has to frame his critical issues and make his choices. Such issues and choices are essentially organizational and institutional and in turn will lead to decisions on priorities. In Kenya, for example, the main issues are:

Under what circumstances and to what extent should we nationalize means of production?

What means should be used to promote Africanization of the economy?

In present circumstances, how much of our development budget should be devoted to expanding welfare services?

What means should be used to promote domestic saving and retain it for investment in Kenya?

What should be the role of the tax structure in increasing revenue, establishing incentives, distributing income, and diffusing economic power?

What part should self-help play in development?

What agricultural and land-tenure policies should be adopted to promote growth and prevent concentrations of economic power?

What means should be used to reverse the trend in many parts of the country toward depleting natural resources—land degradation, destruction of watersheds, and encroachment of desert?

What priorities should be adopted in building educational facilities and providing training programs?

How should public utilities be owned, regulated, and managed?

What methods should be used to develop industry, commerce,

and tourism?

What should be the role of trade unions in promoting development?

What means should be used to protect the interests of consumers?

How much should be spent, and for what purposes, to help the less developed parts of the country?

Once decisions have been taken and policies formulated on the main issues, the planner can begin to determine his priorities for resource allocation in terms of manpower and of finance, as well as his growth targets. Thus the shape of the plan begins to emerge.

At this point, if the plan is to succeed, it is essential to consider implementation procedures and machinery, within the framework of such government and political institutions as are already available or can be devised. In African countries today this poses an exciting challenge. To my mind, there is an inevitable tendency to devote too much attention to problems of plan preparation, and insufficient attention to the problems of plan implementation.

Effective implementation requires both a vertical and a horizontal integration of the planning machinery. Vertical integration requires effective and harmonious machinery for implementation through the sectors of the economy and the individual Ministries of the Government. Horizontal integration requires coordination on a geographical basis which is effective in terms of lesser geographical units than the Central Government, such as provinces and districts.

The concept and machinery of vertical integration are for the most part well understood and relatively easy to implement. But the concept and machinery of horizontal integration require very careful thought in relation to the political institutions and forms of government which are developing in African countries. Problems of horizontal integration are, of course, not confined to African countries, but in a one-party African state they offer a particular challenge, since there are unrivaled opportunities to integrate both the party and the civil service into the national planning organization. Indeed, unless both these institutions can be effectively integrated into the planning organization, it is inevitable that political friction will arise. The problem, therefore, is to devise a form of horizontal planning organization which will enable these institutions to play an effective role, and which will ensure that they cooperate with the Central Government.

In Kenya we hope to achieve this cooperation through a provincial and district planning structure that will provide an executive machine for the implementation of the Plan through the Civil Service, while at the same time enlisting the advice and support of party officials at provincial and district levels to ensure, on the one hand, that the civil service is well acquainted with the thinking and views of party officials, and on the other hand, that the party officials are well acquainted with the practical problems which confront the civil service in implementing the National Plan.

In planning for agricultural and industrial development, our first concern is to identify and expand those areas and projects which will lead to early growth, to provide additional employment for the rapidly expanding labor force, and to Africanize the economy. The next steps are to set targets for particular sectors and districts and to review the institutional framework for implementing the planning policy. Both in agriculture and in industry we regard the provision of the necessary extension services and institutions, particularly financial institutions, as of vital importance to successful planning, and much of our planning effort is directed to the creation and maintenance of such a structure.

In considering general priorities for development, a number of criteria have to be applied. The prime criterion is, of course, the contribution which a project will make to the rapid growth of the economy. Other important factors are the employment potential, direct and indirect, of a project; the contribution which it will make to the Africanization of the economy; the opportunity cost in terms of other development to be foregone (it may be possible, for example, to finance a project from external resources which otherwise would not be available to us); the effect of the project on the balance of payments; the social value of the project and the contribution it will make to general welfare; and other values such as the maintenance of law and order. Applying such criteria, well-conceived agricultural and industrial development projects for the most part acquire a high priority.

The distribution of the benefits of development must be considered in terms of distribution both as between individuals and as between different parts of the country. Distribution between individuals will in Kenya be primarily a function of the national incomes policy and the taxation system, both of which we intend to apply to create an equitable distribution of income and wealth.

Our incomes policy is directed primarily toward the establishment of a minimum level of urban and rural wages which will avoid exploitation, while not setting the level so high that it merely leads to a widespread increase in unemployment through the substitution of machinery for labor.

Our taxation policy will be designed to assist in the creation of an equitable distribution of income and wealth, as well as to provide a sufficient surplus on the recurrent budget to meet part of the cost of the development budget. To arrive at these objectives we are considering the following:

A full pay-as-you-earn system of collecting income taxes.

Reduction in personal tax allowances.

Progressive inheritance taxes and review of death duties.

Excise duties on selected commodities.

Sales and entertainment taxes that exclude basic necessities.

Extension of the list of commodities subject to export duties and revision of existing rates.

Expansion of property taxes.

A capital gains tax.

Elimination of foreign gambling pools and the like from Kenya, and collection by the Government of a larger share of such gains.

Full taxation of dividends without credit for company taxes.

Charging for some services now rendered free by the Government, e.g., charging tolls on major highways.

In considering the distribution of benefits among different areas of the country, we naturally have to balance the special needs of less developed areas with the effect which diversion of resources into less directly productive channels will have on the over-all rate of growth. Individual cases can be considered only in relation to the circumstances. In general, we seek to give special consideration to the less developed areas within the limits imposed by our total resources. In the main, however, we are concerned with the development of people rather than resources, and our policies must be decided by the criterion of what will be best for the people of the country as a whole.

PROGRESS THROUGH COOPERATION

FRANÇOIS A. N'LIBA-N'GUIMBOUS

Deputy Executive Secretary
Economic Commission for Africa

Those of us who are closely concerned with the problems of African development have an overriding preoccupation with economic cooperation. It may be said by some that there is something mealy-mouthed about the term *cooperation* in this context: "If you mean foreign aid," I can hear them say, "why don't you say so?" But I think it is no accident that the word *cooperation* has begun to gain currency. It is an encouraging sign that the world is outgrowing the epoch in which aid transactions between the richer and the poorer countries were considered to be on the same level as the transaction between the wealthy stockbroker getting into his limousine and the ragged man standing hat in hand in the rain. That is charity, and charity is precisely what Africa does not need and should not want. Charity is too risky a business for all concerned, and more particularly for the recipient, who is in danger of coming to believe that his well-being demands no more effort on his part than that of keeping his receiving hand rigid, palm turned upward.

So we are dealing with cooperation, and at a time when a commentator so knowledgeable and disabused as Margery Perham can state that the young African nations have been born into a world

138

which "offers, for the first time, an acknowledged claim upon the help of the more advanced nations." We are talking soon after the publication in *The New York Times* of an article by Senator J. W. Fulbright in which he says: "The continuing need for the rich countries to assist the poor countries is a matter of both political and moral compulsion. . . . It is difficult to see how the rich countries can expect to survive in their affluence as islands in a global sea of misery. But beyond the social and economic and political and strategic reasons for the rich aiding the poor is the simple motive of humanitarian conscience."

I shall deal also with cooperation within Africa itself, something for which the need is as obvious as the lack is great.

Starting with cooperation between Africa and the wealthier nations, I do not share the pessimism which I have heard in some quarters—and which is echoed by Professor Lewis in his background paper for this Conference—about future prospects of obtaining foreign aid for Africa and other developing areas. Senator Fulbright's statement was followed within a matter of weeks by President Johnson's dramatic offer of aid to Southeast Asia—an offer admittedly provoked by the rather special circumstances that exist in that area.

It may be said that we have still to hear from their counterparts in Russia and elsewhere in the Eastern bloc, but here I can speak from recent experience. In 1963 and 1964 an ECA team headed by Robert Gardiner, Executive Secretary of the Economic Commission for Africa, visited a number of Eastern and Western European countries with the aim of learning what kind of climate existed so far as aid to Africa was concerned. We were, in general, very reassured by the reactions to our mission.

I do not wish to enter into a discussion of the ideological motivations behind aid-giving. Suffice it to say that many developing countries have been able to assert their desire for ideological nonalignment while continuing to receive aid. In cases such as this, questions of ideology seem comparatively irrelevant; and in certain circumstances they can be totally irrelevant.

If we accept the evidence that aid is potentially available internationally to help in the development of regions such as our own continent, there are still a number of questions to be answered: What form should such aid take? To what specific ends should it be directed? How should it be administered? The answer to the first question is easy enough in Africa, once you have determined what the recipients need. In Africa we need everything we can get: hard cash and soft loans, scholarships and scholars, techniques and technicians. In short, we need all the aid that can be spared in any form it can conveniently take.

While we, as recipients, have no control over this aspect of international cooperation in the sense that we can get only what others are prepared to offer, the other two questions involve African initiatives, and African decisions on African priorities. It is Africans who must decide which are the best methods of administering the assistance we receive.

As far as the priorities for African development are concerned, we can scarcely go far beyond the admirable analysis that Professor Lewis has provided in his paper. Let us take first, as he has done, the question of natural resources. Since the end of World War II we have seen a remarkable expansion of African agricultural production for export, carried out, for the most part, with only the slightest modifications of traditional techniques of production. At the same time, the output of food per head of population in Africa has been steadily falling; and we are simultaneously faced with a rising bill—in hard currency—for imports of food from the more advanced regions, much of which could easily be produced within the continent. In addition, we have the daunting prognosis of the demographers that the continent's population, estimated in 1960 at about 273 million, will be in the region of 440 million in 1980, and possibly over 700 million by the end of the century. Even if we accept the argument that our continent is—in ideal terms—underpopulated, and by comparison with other regions we certainly have no "population problem" in the orthodox sense of that expression, it is still obvious that something must be done urgently to stop the imbalanced trend if the periodic mass famine is to remain a stranger to Africa.

But we also have to think beyond the problem of merely staving off hunger. How can our agriculture be adapted to our need for economic growth? It is not setting our sights too high to look to what the scientists call our renewable natural resources for a large part of the answer. If we could import—and adequately adapt—the knowledge that the advanced countries have acquired in this field and apply it to our own agriculture, we could, for a start, vastly increase our production for export. By increasing our facilities for processing our own raw materials, we could dramatically cut down our present expenditure on imports of finished goods based on African raw materials.

Taking the continent as a whole, and confining ourselves to food products for the moment, we find that Africa produces a truly Gargantuan variety of food. This is the continent of the strawberry and the sugar cane, of wheat and maize, of the melon and the watermelon, of the grape and the grapefruit, a continent where in some places the cattle outnumber the people, a continent bounded by two oceans and crisscrossed by rivers full of fish, a continent literally abounding in milk and honey. Yet it is also a continent that imports English strawberries and Hawaiian sugar; American wheat flour and canned corn; we import, in tins, tuna fish caught in West African waters; we import beef from the Antipodes, milk from Holland, and honey from Greece. Surely this is the very hallmark of underdevelopment.

I am not suggesting that in the effort to correct this we should be starting from scratch. Some progress has already been made in a number of areas, with and without external aid. But our horizons must be altered now. What we need in Africa is nothing less than an economic revolution, a radical transformation of the structures of our economies. In agriculture this means that we must mount a large-scale rescue operation and bring into the market economy, both as producer and consumer, the subsistence farmer whose methods are tragically wasteful and unproductive both for himself and for society as a whole. If we can teach him to improve and increase his output, we shall go some way toward recapturing the ground lost since World War II in production per capita. The other part of this revolution, the stepping-up of the industrial processing of our own raw materials, must take place *pari passu*, so that the emancipated farmer will have something to spend his money on and be able to take his proper place in the development of the economy.

The process that is called for here is essentially one of training and retraining. This costs money and takes time. It costs money to train the vast numbers of extension workers that will be needed; it costs money to maintain the services once they are brought into existence; it costs money to carry out the research on soils and fertilizers and seeds which is essential to a program of this kind.

To be sure, some of this is already being done with the resources available, and being done successfully. But if we are to envisage a continental attack—as we must, since the objectives are, in the last analysis, continental—we need very large infusions of aid at the continental level. Why? Because most of the problems in revolutionizing African agriculture are not confined within the national borders; the ecological, climatic, and biological factors—and very often the sociological factors as well—that govern agricultural production in Africa follow their own rules; and the rational approach, which is the only approach by which we can justify an appeal for aid of the proportions I am speaking about, must equally transcend the political borders.

Apart from agriculture, what about the need to improve the knowledge and techniques of those who fish our numerous inland waters and our seacoasts? What about the food potential of the continent's wild life? And our mineral resources, underexplored and underexploited? And the power that lies unharnessed within our rivers? In all this, a first priority for development and, therefore, a first priority for aid will be research. What is vitally needed is research of an inventorial nature, to tell us what is there, to be followed by exploitation research to tell us how to make the best use of what is there. Again, we do not have to start from scratch, for a not inconsiderable amount of such research was carried out in colonial times; but, incredible as it may seem, many of the results of these studies are simply not available to African countries, having been retained by the colonizing powers after independence. This, indeed, was the subject of a special resolution passed at the seventh session of the ECA earlier this year.

I have been dealing with *Africa*, as if Africa were already an integrated economic unit, internally linked by adequate communications and telecommunications, turning to the rest of the world the assured visage of a monolith. This is, of course, the opposite of the truth. One might say, on the contrary, that all the dynamic forces of history and politics have conspired to divide rather than unite this continent. Independent African states have just begun, however tentatively, to think in continental—or, at least, in larger than purely national—terms. This is, politically, revolutionary; economically it is far less so. African unity makes considerable economic sense, although common sense sees it as a very long-term perspective.

In the shorter term, there seems no alternative to the approach that has been adopted by the ECA, the attack by groups of neighboring countries that could, broadly speaking, constitute viable economic units. This is a pragmatic approach; it does not deny the desirability of pan-African projects—it is, indeed, a partisan of the immediate feasibility of some such projects. It accepts the fact that if a start is to be made, it has to be made at the most practical level. More important, it corresponds to what might be called certain local unities. When we think, for example, of a future African telecommunications network, a project which is among the most important on our list at ECA, we see that we must start by filling the gaps. And the immediate gaps are to be found at the subregional level, as with the telex line which in February linked the ECA secretariat of the seventh session in Nairobi to our headquarters in Addis Ababa. Needless to say, it went by the most direct route—via London.

It seems to me that this is where cooperation in Africa should start, at the level where geography—and sometimes even politics and sociology—are on our side. Indeed, the process has already started; in North Africa during 1964 the Maghreb countries set up the institutional framework for economic cooperation within that subregion, at both ministerial and civil service levels. The East African Common Services Organization has long been an African byword, and the recent discussions that have taken place between the countries of this group and Zambia are a good omen. The countries of eastern Africa are meeting to work out the broad lines for future coordination of their industrial development programs; in West Africa the first hurdle on the way to industrial coordination was cleared in 1964 when a substantial subregional enterprise for steel production, as well as a number of other joint projects, was agreed on. That year also saw the establishment of the Central and Equatorial African Customs Union, and a study is being carried out on the prospects for a common approach to industrial development in that subregion. At the 1965 session of ECA, member states voted for the establishment of permanent working groups of experts in each of the four subregions who would be a sort of integration task force, responsible for the negotiations and initiatives necessary to bring about integrated action in practically the whole range of economic development problems.

All this represents progress, but it is still not enough. There are two essential elements missing, both covered by the term international cooperation. Put simply, one would like to see, on the one hand, an end to the disjointed doling out of aid under bilateral agreements; and, on the other hand, greater organization by the recipients for using the aid that is available. One feels that the time has now come for those countries which are interested in supplying development aid to Africa to consider forming a kind of "aid consortium"—and we need look no further than the Colombo Plan for a precedent.

The advantages of this approach are obvious, both for the aid-giving countries and for the recipients. One outstanding advantage would be that recipient countries would be better able to under-take long-term planning, because they would be relatively certain of the amount and character of aid that could be expected. Obvi-ously, this would not mean the end of all bilateral aid; for one thing, such an arrangement would be exclusive of the various highly specialized forms of cooperation between countries such as military pacts and the like. But it would, hopefully, account for the bulk of aid.

For the recipients one would envisage something in the nature of a Council of African Ministers of Economic Affairs—such an organ as exists already within the Organization of African Unity —which would have its own permanent secretariat and would be the sovereign body responsible for apportioning aid according to pan-African criteria. Apart from the studies prepared for it by its own Secretariat, the Council, as representing Member States of the ECA, would also have access to the technical services and stud-ies of the ECA secretariat and to outside consultants as well.

Clearly the first step should come from the African states them-selves. Were they to set up machinery of this kind, aid-giving countries would, one feels certain, be more inclined to think of acting together in the way I have suggested. After all, what have been the main grievances of such countries over the question of the aid they give? Primarily, if we are to be frank, that the recipi-ent countries have not invariably shown the proper degree of grati-tude; the second major complaint, I think, would be that aid funds have not always been used in the best ways. Now, if aid-giving countries acted internationally, the first complaint would become irrelevant, and there would be fewer of the occasional lit-tle contretemps that occur, with country X threatening to with-draw its aid if country Y does not do this or that, and country Y making rather impolite suggestions as to what country X can do with its aid.

The second complaint would continue to be heard, since it is impossible to please all the people all the time, but I submit that it would be heard with decreasing frequency. More and more the

Council of Ministers would take on the character of an African development forum, with the built-in impartiality of a democratic organ backed by technicians and consultants with international loyalties. Our experience at ECA is unambiguous on this point: representatives of countries in East and West which are already supplying aid to African countries either bilaterally, or multilaterally through United Nations agencies, have made it clear that they are only too ready to increase the volume of their aid, provided that they can be assured of its being handled through competent channels and directed to adequately prepared projects.

I may be accused of being somewhat starry-eyed in putting forward these suggestions, for their implementation will clearly call for tremendous selflessness on the part of the many nations involved on both the African and the non-African sides. Selflessness is not precisely the most characteristic quality of international relations. But several developments lead me to believe that an action of this kind is feasible. I referred earlier to the article by Senator Fulbright, and I should like to point out that that article is essentially a call for the internationalization of American foreign aid. Mr. Fulbright says: "The fundamental difference between bilateralism and multilateralism in foreign aid is psychological. The one carries a connotation of charity, of patron and ward, of arrogance and humiliation; the other has the more dignified connotation of community organized to meet its common *and rightful* responsibilities toward its less fortunate members. The one is appropriate to a world of nation-states with unlimited sovereignty, the other to a world that is at least groping towards a broader community." The argument could scarcely be better put.

If I were to be asked when such a development should begin, my answer would be "immediately." Frankly, Africa cannot afford to wait. After what has been called our "revolution of rising expectations," we are moving closer and closer to another revolution which could well be produced by the frustration of those expectations.

Already the first signs are visible of the advent of the Cold War on our continent. We really have no use for it. The welcome wind of change that has almost entirely swept colonialism out of Africa was long overdue; it would be only too tragic if the continent were now caught up in the hurricanes of East-West conflict—a conflict which, however it may be justified elsewhere, is utterly irrelevant to a region that is only now struggling out of many decades of second-class citizenship.

Perhaps the African challenge to East and to West is this: that all should cooperate, and even compete, in helping to bring about a better life for the peoples of this continent. It is a contest in which everyone would be the winner.

PRIVATE CAPITAL AND ECONOMIC DEVELOPMENT

LEO MODEL

Economist and Investment Banker
New York

The urge for economic development is not new. After all, the whole world has been engaged in economic development since the beginning of the industrial revolution in England nearly two hundred years ago. What is new is that the underdeveloped countries are making this their primary economic objective.

I think we must start by recognizing that accelerated economic development is the proper policy for underdeveloped countries, where such development is an urgent necessity, not only for economic reasons, but for social and political reasons. The task that confronts them is exceptionally difficult. Some countries have an inadequate base for development, low productive efficiency, scarce employment opportunities, and they cannot provide the capital and technical knowledge necessary for industrial development.

Most underdeveloped countries have development plans prepared by their national authorities, sometimes with the aid of international institutions. Development plans can be very useful if they show the order of priorities for investment, if they match investment with available capital, and if they take account of technical as well as financial needs. To put it plainly, a development plan is useful only to the extent that it is realistic. Much harm can be done by a development plan that ignores the need for capital and for technical knowledge. Such a plan may waste resources in enterprises for which the economy is not ready, and which require excessive capital and sophisticated technical knowledge that are not available.

Nearly all development plans place great stress on the public sector—that is, investment to be undertaken by the government and its agencies. As a practical matter, such investment is the indispensable prelude to development in many countries. A country cannot develop an economy using modern methods of industrial production unless it has transport and communication facilities, power, and other basic requirements for industrial development. Furthermore, we must not underestimate the importance of human resources in development, which means that a considerable investment must be made in facilities for education and public health. All this requires public investment.

Nevertheless, it is not enough to provide power and transportation to have an educated and healthy labor force. Unless these resources, material and human, are applied in the production of goods and services, there will be little progress in the economy; unless they can be applied in production, the investment absorbs scarce capital without having an effect on output. Therefore, apart from the public investment in basic facilities, there must be investment in enterprises that will utilize these facilities in producing goods and services.

Needless to say, the principal scarcities for economic development are capital and technical knowledge. Fortunately, a considerable amount of resources is available in aid from the developed countries and from international institutions. Even so, because of their own limited savings, the underdeveloped countries do not have enough capital for their needs—for the investment in basic facilities and for enterprises that will produce the goods and services required for the country and for export.

It seems to me that this is a need that, to a large extent, private foreign investment can and must meet. There are three characteristics of private foreign investment that make its contribution to development unique. First, in productive enterprises it complements public investment in basic facilities. It is the type of investment that utilizes power and transport in the production of goods and services for use within the economy and for export. Second, private foreign investment brings in capital that would not otherwise be available either from foreign aid or from foreign credits. Thus it supplements domestic savings and intergovernmental grants and credits. Third, such investment brings with it technical knowledge in the organization of production and marketing. A new foreign enterprise is almost certain to be successful because it is usually made by very successful companies. For this reason, private foreign investment makes a substantial contribution to production, employment, and income.

In my opinion, foreign investment is equally productive whether it engages in agriculture, mineral production, or manufacturing. What is important is that the investment should be suited to the economic potential of the country and that it should be successful. It is understandable that the underdeveloped countries should be impatient for the development of manufacturing industries. But manufacturing requires a market at home which can support an efficient industry. This market sometimes depends on developing the agricultural and mineral resources of a country, so that incomes and demands for manufactured goods are increased in these fields and thus the development of manufacturing is possible.

I do not say that manufacturing development should be postponed until there is sufficient development in other sectors of the economy to provide a domestic market for manufactured goods. As a practical matter, development requires the balanced growth of the economy. It means that investment in basic facilities for power and transport should not run ahead of investment in enterprises using these facilities for producing goods and services. It means that the development of agriculture and mining should not be neglected for manufacturing. It means that all sectors of the economy should grow in a way that avoids inflation and minimizes balance-of-payments difficulties.

Some underdeveloped countries seem to think it unimportant to develop their agricultural and resource industries, that only manufacturing contributes to development. This is a serious mistake. The purpose of development is to have efficient production that brings better incomes to the whole economy. Some of the most advanced countries in the world have highly efficient agricultural and mining industries that provide a rich domestic market on which they have built their manufacturing. This is true of Australia and Canada—leading producers and exporters of agricultural and mineral products. It is true of Mexico and Venezuela—among the large producers and exporters of mineral products. These countries have rapid economic growth precisely because they have not neglected their agriculture and mining while simultaneously developing their manufacturing.

There is one other point I wish to stress. Nearly all of the underdeveloped countries have serious balance-of-payments difficulties. In part this is a reflection of their need for real resources from abroad—that is, foreign capital—to finance their accelerated economic development. Nevertheless, it would be destructive to their domestic economy if the payments difficulties were allowed to get out of hand. That is why it is a mistake for underdeveloped countries to neglect the growth of their export industries by concentrating too much on their industries designed for domestic consumption.

Private foreign investment is especially important in connection with the balance of payments. In the first instance, it brings in capital from abroad and thus relieves some of the pressure on the balance of payments. More important, private foreign enterprises put great stress on designing their output for exports as well as for the domestic market. In fact, many foreign enterprises come to a country because they want an assured source of supply for their own imports and for their enterprises in other countries. It is not surprising that the largest growth of exports in the underdeveloped countries is in those sectors in which private foreign investment is concentrated. Only a very small part of these export proceeds is used to remit profits to the foreign investors. By far the largest part goes to meet production costs and taxes. Even of the net earnings, more than half is usually reinvested and thus further increases production.

Private foreign investors need assurances that they will be fairly treated. This has been emphasized again and again. It is a fact that private foreign investment will not come to countries where it is under threat of expropriation and where it is subject to serious restrictions on the transfer of part of its earnings. At the same time, private foreign investors should recognize that their enterprises are part of the national economy, and that their function is to help the development of the countries in which they operate. That means that the growth of the foreign enterprise should be identified with the growth of the domestic economy. It means that the foreign enterprise must be concerned with training a domestic labor force that can perform every kind of work, from unskilled labor to management.

No international problem is of greater long-run importance than the accelerated development of the low-income countries. That is why it is tragic that the vast amount of private foreign investment during the past ten years is overwhelmingly concentrated in the high-income countries. Clearly, if foreign investment is helpful to the economies of Canada and the United Kingdom, it can be even more helpful to the underdeveloped countries. The underdeveloped countries, as well as foreign enterprises, must do their utmost to see that private foreign investment is channeled and managed in such a way that it makes the fullest possible contribution to their development.

IV. Problems of Social Development, Education, and Culture

SOCIAL PROBLEMS OF DEVELOPING COUNTRIES

PUMLA E. KISOSONKOLE

Community Development Officer
Uganda

By my standards, the developing countries—with all their problems crying out for solutions—are the most exciting in which to live. In the midst of so many problems, no one is allowed to sit back and atrophy.

When independence was first granted to the developing countries of Africa, some were convinced that these countries did not have citizens mature enough to carry out the responsibilities that independence would bring. Certainly these responsibilities are borne by men and women whose shoulders are young, by the standards of older countries. But nature has taken over and compensated for their lack of experience by giving them the bouncing energy and impulsiveness of youth. The rate at which higher education has been stepped up in each newly independent country is but one example of how the young nations refuse to be fettered to the comparatively conservative and slow methods of the colonial governments, which always had one eye on the metropolitan country to watch its reactions.

The first big step that every new nation has had to take has been to speed up education, especially in the higher cadres. These train the young people on whom new governments depend to reassess the problems inherited from past regimes, to examine new ones, and to try to produce a solution for all such problems in as short a while as possible. This job has to be done to the constant tune of: "Let us do away with ignorance, disease, poverty, and hunger."

Some of the problems thus tackled have their roots, and possibly their solution, in the historical units of the family, the clan, or the tribe, all of which have lately been pushed under the umbrella of the new nation, which cannot afford to be preoccupied only with itself but has a part to play in relation to its immediate neighbors, as well as to the world community.

ROLE OF THE FAMILY

The family is still the basis of humankind. It is some time since the social anthropologists came up with the term *extended family* to describe the sometimes complicated ramifications of a family. In a way, the social anthropologists saved the African family from disappearing under the onslaught of a culture which was brought from outside of Africa through Christianity, and which was puzzled at the idea of so many people surviving under what must have seemed an obsolete system. For the outsider from Western countries suffering under fast developing economic pressures, and the large families of the Victorian era, the idea of so many fathers, mothers, children, and grandparents living together was nothing short of sin, so the African had to be taught a better way of life. He had to be put under pressure to embrace monogamy, along with his acceptance of the Christian religion, regardless of the sufferings and inconvenience that might be caused to other members of the family, who through no fault of their own, already existed. Describing such a family as an extended family brought it into the realm of decency, and hostility against it became less active as its advantages were praised to the skies.

The idea of the extended family has come to be associated with growing nations. A young mother, sent to represent her country at an international meeting, is often brushed off by the older women from older countries with the remark, "Of course, you can afford to leave your young family behind because of your system of extended families." However, more often than not, this young mother is making a great sacrifice to serve her community and country; and her husband is perhaps left at home to look after the children, including a young baby.

Is the extended family all advantage or disadvantage? Why does the young graduate not take his bride back to the extended family so that he and she can live in the bosom of the family as did his forebears? Since they go to live near their place of work, which is in the city or some big center, who is left to carry out his duties as a member of the extended family? The social reformers are preoccupied with the problem of the drift to the cities; very often, in their minds, this is connected with delinquency. How delinquent is the young graduate whose place of work is in the city as a government official, or at the university as a lecturer? These young people are important members of their extended family, or clan, and they have become even more important as the proud bearers of a university degree, which is a key that opens most doors hitherto closed to the people of the clan or the tribe.

The doors are literally opened when the young graduate is given a house in the city which was previously open only to citizens of the colonial power. The house now belongs to the clan, by reason of being occupied by a member of the clan. The expectation is, therefore, that the extended family will move in. This young man and young woman are loyal to their two families, and they do not wish to disconnect themselves from their own people. But how are they going to decide which members of the clan will be accommodated, and for how long? The house was built for a couple and two or three children. There is not room for expansion, and the rules of the municipality are against an extra building, even if there were space.

The problems arising from such a situation are:

1. Valuable members of the clan or the extended family are lost to their group without replacement.
2. The rural areas are denuded of young men and women who, because of their educational opportunities, should be serving as local leaders of their own people.
3. Members of the extended family, or the clan, following their relatives who have been given an official house in the city, crowd the house—or they must find some other dwelling in the city and add to the city's already existing problems of housing, health, etc.

THE TRIBE

The tribe has played a significant role in the past and, in my opinion, is still playing an important part in keeping individuals together. But to men anxious to build a nation, the significance of the binding influence of the tribe may be lost. They had the experience of forming loyalties to other groups at school or college, to associations and clubs, and therefore to think nationally is no great strain. Most people who have lived only in the rural areas all their lives know the tribe as the body to which they owe their greatest allegiance, whereas the larger concepts of the nation and of independence have grown among the leaders. These concepts took root as a result of outside circumstances which created dissatisfaction with the status quo. Slowly, through careful planning, and again aided by outside conditions, a country becomes independent and a nation is born.

The nation still has to be nursed through growing pains until it reaches its full stature. During this process, the members of a tribe are learning that they can belong to the tribe as well as to the nation. Yet loyalty to the tribe cannot be superseded straightaway by the nation; the tribe is a unit that cannot be supplanted overnight.

As one of the nation-builders myself, I am sometimes struck by a puzzled look on the face of a senior citizen of the tribe when he or she watches a political rally or a conference of women. He thinks, "What a group of noisy young men," and she thinks, "Have these women no husbands and families to look after?"

For more than half a century, people have been referring to the disintegration of the tribe; yet the tribe comes to the fore in almost all countries that become independent. Groups become more affiliated with the tribe than ever before, partly due to the instinct for survival. Individuals, puzzled by the onslaught of a new force of nationalism, unleashed through the fighting for independence, cling to something that for them is older and more secure. The tendency is to exclude any stranger who happens to find himself within the ranks of the tribe and call for an unquestioning solidarity, inward-looking rather than outward-looking. This behavior may be described as one of mass fear, where individuals jealously cling to each other in an attempt to prove how superior they are to other groups.

Where there has been an intermixture of tribes, as has been happening in most groups, this effort to cling together may bring hardships to those who are not members of the original tribe. As they probably cannot get back to their own tribal groups, are they to remain outcasts? What reaction will result from this treatment of them? Thus another problem is added to the long list for the nation-builder.

Is it possible to transfer tribal loyalty to national loyalty? This would be the ideal, but how quickly can this process take place? If some of the older countries are to be taken as examples, tribal groups are still to be found in them; for them, too, the outsider is still the foreigner, regardless of the length of time he has lived with the host group. To say that in Africa the old tribal structures are actually crumbling is only partly true.

In the effort to build a nation, the most highly educated members of each tribe are drawn to the center where the seat of government is. On the outside, this picture appears to show that the nation cuts across the tribal structure. In point of fact, a few individuals are drawn from each tribe, and their educational background and experience in working with other groups put them in the best position to get along with each other. But bringing them together does not forge whole groups into one nation. The imbalance is aggravated by the fact that the few educated individuals who are pulled out of their tribal group leave no one to act as leader in their place, to influence the tribe to be outward-looking and to work toward national loyalties.

Before independence, countries which had a thriving industry found themselves with a large population drifting toward the seats of industry, regardless of the poor housing and health conditions to which many of them were exposed. From the industrial center there was little or no return to the rural areas and the tribes. This had the effect of creating a new type of individual whose outlook became slanted toward city life, which is more individualistic than the communal life of the tribe. The difficulty of trying to create a sense of community solidarity under these circumstances is well known. Politicians found even more difficult the task of trying to build political awareness or a sense of nationhood in the rural areas.

The tribe, thus denuded of its potential leadership, came to consist of old men, women, and children, creating a grave social situation. As the politicians were pressed by the colonial authorities to show reason why their country should be granted independence, they had to justify their claim that the whole country was behind them—not only the so-called "vocal minority" in the cities. Arousing political enthusiasm in a rural community depressed through failure of crops, through uncontrollable diseases, and the lack of a stimulating way of life is a difficult task, complicated by having no one who can be entrusted to carry out reforms. Thus it became necessary that some young politicians should sacrifice their comparative comfort of life in a city and go back and spend some months with the tribe, trying to fire its members with political awareness. That they succeeded is shown by the fact that such countries have become and are becoming independent.

THE PLACE OF COMMUNITY DEVELOPMENT

The politician, therefore, has inadvertently laid the stage for community development, which basically is the motivating of communities to do things for themselves. Once established, this is a continuing program with many exciting possibilities, one which stimulates hope in communities which, for generations, have seen little or no change, thus exposing them to exploitation of every kind.

Many developing countries are carrying out programs in community development, which have proved to be of great value in the broad sense of adult education. Starting from the satisfaction of a few "felt needs," such programs are capable of developing into a vast network of educational schemes for adults. Different colonial powers had different ideas on community development, but since the nationals of newly independent states have taken over the direction of these programs, they have started taking a similar pattern. They aim at involving communities in the process of thinking out and planning projects and activities suitable and desirable for themselves. They often involve an attempt at eliminating illiteracy; improvement of the household, which includes the dwelling and all its appurtenances, and buildings for animals in rural areas; community action to protect local water springs; and upkeep of the road feeding the village. They may also extend to improving farming in order to realize better yields, child care, better nutrition and health programs, as well as citizenship.

The adult is an avid student. When he gets into the habit of learning, there is no knowing what heights he may attain. Some community development programs have started from humble beginnings and have blossomed into full-scale courses, sometimes at the level of university extramural studies. Although there are no formal tests of ability, the adult gets pleasure out of discovering his capability and success in new skills. When he tries his hand at learning a foreign language, which has hitherto been a closed book to him, he finds new possibilities. He will now understand the language in which his children are taught at school; he can even understand the foreigner who comes to visit him.

Community development should be seen as an instrument for lifting adults deprived of the opportunity to continue their formal education to a level where they notice where things need improving. They notice that their homes could be more attractive, that their diets could be bettered by introducing other foods or by learning the values in the food materials they use every day. They notice that their children's welfare could be improved, and they learn how this can be done. In community development language, this is referred to as "dissatisfaction with what you have." This dissatisfaction leads people to find a solution for their felt needs.

Community development is also a means of diminishing the gulf between those who have received formal education and those who have not. It increases the channels of communication between these two groups within the nation, as well as with the outside world. In many developing countries literacy is considered an adjunct to community development programs. At the beginning of the program, adults often wish to start learning the other skills first, but later the desire for communicating with others creeps in, and they learn to read and write.

Leading statesmen in the developing countries see, in community development programs, an ideal way to involve everyone in the process of developing the country. These are continuing programs and can be adapted to include whatever is the topmost problem at the time. They are a practical means of combating hunger, disease, poverty, and ignorance.

THE ROLE OF WOMEN

The greatest value of community development programs, however, lies in the fact that they have released women from a state of unconcern and lassitude. Where women had been regarded as, at most, second class citizens, they had grown to believe that they had nothing to offer to their families, their communities, or the world. Community development and political activity together have brought about a realization of the latent power that they possess. In older countries, women have long recognized the vote as a strong instrument of bargaining for their status. The younger developing countries are experimenting with it.

Going out to take part in community activities has offered women a release from the old way of life where they were shackled to the home, with no prospects of anything better in the future. Marriage was the one thing which gave a girl something to hope for, in that it brought about a change in status; but marriage was also the end of the road. Political activities and community development programs not only give women a release from the monotony of their lives; they go beyond this, enabling them to discover and realize their worth as mothers, as members of their communities, and as individuals within the world context. The transformation that takes place where these programs are successful has to be seen to be believed.

It used to be said that educational programs should be directed toward women, because they were conservative and kept the pace back. People holding this view are surprised that after a while the women go so far beyond the outlook of their men-folk that a pause has to be made to enable the men to catch up. This problem is being solved by programs in which men and women take part side by side, learning together to be good parents, good citizens, and to look beyond the nation into the puzzling but exciting citizenship of the world. This is an ideal way for developing countries to learn to avoid the problems of one-sided development which has been their legacy from the past. One result of this legacy has been the shortage of educated women to carry out the duties required of them by an independent country. Some developed countries engage in arguments as to whether it is a good thing or not for married women to go out of their homes to work. For most of the developing countries, this is only an academic exercise. Educated women are in such great demand that they *have* to work, even after marriage. For these women, the solution is to find ways of having their young families looked after while they go back to their posts; it is not a matter of persuading them to go out and work.

The role of the educated woman in the development of her country is colossal. If unmarried, she is holding a job, taking part in various local committees, perhaps having to do many jobs which require going from one place to another—because she is single her fellows as well as her government expect her to carry more of this kind of responsibility. She also has a house or a flat which means that she must keep house as well. Often she has to take time off to represent her country at international meetings. If she is married, life is still more complicated. She must do all the traditional duties expected of her: see that her home runs smoothly, care for her husband and her family, be a good hostess. She is also expected to go to her place of work, take part in local and national activities, and still find time to go out and represent her country, within or outside its borders.

One can imagine the conflicts and strains that go with the decisions these women have to make to reconcile their different loyalties. The world is dictating the pace for their countries, and the women must move at the same pace. That they are able to perform all these numerous and heavy tasks is due to their understanding husbands.

In spite of the many demands on their time, women are not complaining. They see their role as vital in helping to develop their country. For them, cooperation begins in the home and is carried out into the world.

HEALTH AND WELFARE SERVICES IN DEVELOPMENT PLANNING

JOHN KAREFA-SMART

Associate Director of International Health
School of Public Health and Administrative Medicine
Columbia University

Nearly all developing countries pay a severe penalty for the lack of adequate health and welfare services, in terms not only of very high death rates but also of reduced capacity for a full output of work, low rates of production, diminished energy, and a general lowering of the body's power to fight against illness and disease. Accurate statistics are not available, but it is generally accepted that more than half of the entire population in the majority of developing countries do not survive beyond the early adolescent years. Worse still, about half of all the children born die before reaching the age of five.

It would be useful if a means were available to give an economic value to this tragic loss of human life and to the later effects of continuing ill-health on the surviving adults. But economists have not yet agreed on the financial value of a human life, nor do we have a reliable estimate of the average cash value of the work of a healthy adult human being for one hour.

The definition of *health* adopted by the World Health Organization is "not merely the absence of disease or infirmity, but a state of complete physical. mental, and social well-being." Accepting this definition, therefore, we naturally include in planning for health all those educational and cultural facilities which contribute to maximum welfare of the human body and mind and to the achievement of a *mens sana in corpore sano.*

There is an unresolved ideological argument as to whether the poor health which exists in the developing countries is the result of the underdeveloped economy and environment, or whether it is because the population is in such a poor state of mental and physical health that it has not been able to develop its economy and control the physical environment. No doubt poor health and lack of development interact on each other, each being both cause and effect. In order to persuade development planners to give sufficiently high priority to the provision of health and welfare services, it is useful to examine how the important factors involved in poor health are related to other factors that hinder development.

1. Foremost is the high incidence of disease, with the consequent high mortality rate. To relieve the suffering caused by illness and to restore ill people as soon as possible to a state of health which will enable them to play their part in production, medical services in the form of clinics, health centers, hospitals, and sanitaria are required, and an adequate number of doctors, nurses, and laboratory workers to man these facilities. Both the physical facilities, in the form of buildings, and the training of the medical and para-medical staffs cost money which has to be provided from the common pool of the national income, for which there are many competing claims.

But the high incidence of disease in developing countries is also due to lack of sanitation, the presence of insects and other forms of animal life (e.g., mosquitoes and snails) which carry and transmit disease, poor facilities for the disposal of human excreta and other forms of waste through which parasitic diseases and infections are spread, and the lack of unpolluted drinking water. The correction of these deficiencies in the environment is costly and requires trained sanitarians and engineers.

2. Next, the low nutritional status of the majority of the popu-

lation contributes—together with infections and parasitic diseases —not only to the death of half the children during their early years, as has been noted, but also to much ill-health among adults. Conditions such as intense protein malnutrition (kwashiorkor) in childhood may lead to chronic debility throughout life. In addition, there are various diseases due to deficiencies in specific vitamins (e.g., beriberi) or in elements like iodine (e.g., goiter). Even when there is no specific illness, diets below the accepted optimal standards in both quantity and quality contribute to a state of chronic undernourishment, which not only lowers resistance to disease but leads to lethargy, laziness, and inefficiency.

The means through which malnutrition can be eradicated are, first, making available adequate quantities of the right kinds of food at reasonable prices through increased production and better distribution; second, increasing the purchasing power of the population so that every family is able to buy available foods; and third, conducting the right kind of nutrition education. Those responsible for development planning must decide what relative importance is to be given to these means of providing better nutrition. But any combination of methods chosen depends on other development programs for success. For example, the cost of food depends not only on production methods, but also on related costs of distribution. And whatever the cost, this is important only insofar as it represents a percentage of the total family income. Political considerations also become important in this area. There are probably sufficient quantities of surplus food available in the world to meet the basic needs of countries where malnutrition is a problem. But most of these countries have only recently gained their independence, and for one reason or another they have decided that self-sufficiency in as many areas as possible should be the national goal. It takes time to attain self-sufficiency in food production, with enough food at a low cost for all the people. In the meantime, surplus foods from other countries, which could be useful as a means of releasing funds and manpower for other areas of development, are not requested or accepted for political reasons.

3. A further factor contributing to slow progress in development is that too many people are occupied in food production. In a highly developed country like the United States, approximately 15 per cent of available labor is engaged in food production, yet more than enough for national consumption is produced, with huge surpluses. In developing countries, the percentage may be as high as 90 in some cases. Successful planning for economic development therefore depends on the release of a large number of persons at present engaged only in agriculture, so that they can be employed in other sectors of the economy. This is possible only if agricultural production is made more efficient or if arrangements are made to obtain food from outside sources.

4. Another major hindrance is the lack of adequate educational facilities. Percentages of illiteracy, which are often higher than 60, together with the very low standard of achievement of the majority of those who do go to school, characterize most developing countries. The vicious circle in education is that there are not enough children in school because there are not enough schools, and there are not enough schools because there are not enough teachers . . . because there are not enough teacher-training schools . . . because there are not enough children in school in the first place to provide enough schooled persons to go into teaching.

This lack of educational facilities and of teachers is a serious handicap to efforts to spread knowledge of the basic principles of personal cleanliness and nutrition, and of public sanitation, which is necessary if the general level of public health is to be raised.

5. A fifth group of factors which contribute to underdevelopment includes a variety of economic determinants. These vary from low per capita income (only $50–$100 in some countries, while in the developed countries per capita income is from $1000–$2000), to low levels of industrial production, or gross national product, and poor facilities for transportation and communication. Poor communication is a handicap in much the same way as poor education because it severely restricts the two-way flow of ideas from the leaders to the masses, and vice versa. Communication

and transport facilities often are much better between a developing and the distant developed country that was recently the metropolitan authority, than between developing countries which are near neighbors.

6. A final factor is the rate of increase in population. Most of the developing countries are not threatened just now with overpopulation, and therefore there is not the same immediate concern as in the developed countries about the dangers of a population explosion. Nevertheless, given the present economic and social conditions, the chain of events which begins with high birth rates will naturally lead to overcrowding in substandard houses, a major factor in the spread of disease. The resulting poor health leads to low economic production, with consequent low income, low purchasing power, and little or no savings for capital development.

Attention may now be turned to an examination of priorities in planning for health. The main objectives of planning for better health should be: to reduce the high incidence of disease; to achieve an improved nutritional status for the whole population; and to make available to all people a knowledge of the basic elements of sound health.

Very often hospitals are given the highest priority. Apart, however, from the humanitarian motive of bringing relief to those who suffer and, in the case of infectious diseases, the prevention of contagion, the claims of hospitals for such high priority should be reexamined. It is doubtful whether the provision of more hospital beds has any significant effect on the residual pool of illness in the community.

To begin with, a high standard in the practice of modern medi-cine and surgery in hospitals depends on the availability of well-trained physicians, surgeons, medical specialists and nurses, labora-tory workers, and other para-medical personnel. The colonial-type one-doctor hospital, with major emphasis on curative medicine for a privileged few while the sources of disease are not being attacked, may have political justification for the money spent on it, but little justification in the economics of public health.

Further, until the time comes when the resources of the country can provide enough schools to produce enough potential medical students, while meeting the needs of the other services, there will not be enough national doctors and other medical personnel to staff adequately a significant number of hospitals. Sufficient consideration should, moreover, be given to the enormous capital requirements and recurrent expenses in establishing and running a national medical school before a decision is taken to establish one.

More rapid and substantial gains can be achieved by placing greater emphasis on control of the sources of the major diseases, which, in most developing countries, particularly in Africa, are malaria, tuberculosis, and other communicable diseases, such as venereal disease, yaws, leprosy, and various parasitic diseases. The medical profession has enough knowledge of the causes of these diseases, the means of their transmission and the methods of controlling them, that, given a basic organization of health services covering the entire population, campaigns could be mounted for mass treatment or for mass inoculation or vaccination. Such campaigns would not only control the diseases, but in some cases even eradicate them.

This is a matter in which an ounce of prevention is worth a pound of cure. The level of training necessary for efficient workers in such mass campaigns does not involve more than a basic understanding of certain principles and procedures; it can be reached after a few months of instruction, as compared with the seven or more years needed for full medical training. It is therefore important to give high priority in health planning to the organization of community-oriented preventive centers at the village, clan, district, regional, and national levels. Such curative services can also be given in these centers as is consistent with their major functions of prevention and control of communicable diseases and epidemics.

The role of environmental sanitation in the reduction of disease is of the greatest importance. Wherever pure drinking water has been made available to everyone in the community, and safe and sanitary methods are employed for the disposal of human and animal wastes and refuse, a marked drop in the incidence of infections and parasitic diseases has followed. Usually these services are the result of a general rise in the standard of living of the population, following increases in per capita income and in productivity rather than the direct result of planning for health. However, it is generally accepted that it is the responsibility of the health authorities to set and maintain the standards of sanitation.

Similarly, the provision of adequate housing, by lessening overcrowding with its possibilities for the rapid spread of disease, has often been accompanied by lower incidence of illness. Again, while medical and health authorities do not have the principal responsibility for providing adequate housing, they often share responsibility in setting acceptable standards.

The second major objective, namely, the improvement of nutrition, calls for close cooperation among the authorities responsible for agricultural production, for internal and international commerce, and for education. Health workers can identify the specific problems of malnutrition and they can prescribe the remedies for actual clinical cases under their care. But only nationally integrated programs involving the provision of adequate quantities of food of the right quality, at a cost not beyond the means of any families, can bring about a change in the nutritional status of the whole population.

Finally, there is the objective of imparting useful knowledge about all aspects of health to the entire community, which again calls for interdepartmental and interprogram cooperation. The Department of Education, through its schools and colleges, has a major responsibility to provide instruction in health, as in other subjects. The agency responsibile for adult and mass education should include health facts and ideas in all its programs, beginning early with literacy. Of course, the medical and health authorities should assume full responsibility for the content of health education materials.

The constitution of the World Health Organization recognizes in its preamble that "the health of all peoples is fundamental to the attainment of peace and security and is dependent upon the fullest cooperation of individuals and states, and the achievement of any state in the promotion and protection of health is of value to all." For this reason, those responsible for planning for national health have an obligation to cooperate fully with other nations, especially in the control of communicable disease. They also have the right and responsibility to participate in all international efforts—such as those of the World Health Organization and other agencies in the United Nations family—to promote and protect the health of their own and of all peoples.

PRIORITIES IN INVESTMENT IN EDUCATION

W. SENTEZA KAJUBI

Director, Institute of Education
Makerere University College, Kampala, Uganda

In 1963, the Uganda Education Commission, in describing the task which faced the country in the field of education, posed the following problem: "When over half the nation is illiterate and the people rightly clamor for education, when teachers are in short supply and inadequately trained, when government and industry demand trained recruits, when unemployment is widespread and increasing, when the nation is poor—what policy should the government pursue?"

The problems of the East African countries—Uganda, Kenya, and Tanzania—illustrate similar dilemmas which exist in varying degrees in the new nations of Africa, and elsewhere in the developing world. The demand for education is so great, and the means to satisfy it so limited, that some people would argue that it is not possible or wise to establish priorities for educational development —on the grounds that what these countries need is more of everything, at all levels.

The importance of education as a basis of social and economic growth is almost universally accepted. Parents desire education for their children, and students look at schooling as a means of emancipating themselves from the poverty of subsistence production, from the restrictions of the rural environment and the traditional way of life.

Both before and after independence, governments have regarded investment in education as a high priority. In Uganda, for example, the number of children in secondary schools has increased more than eight times in the last decade, while the elementary-school enrollment has more than doubled. In 1952 the Uganda government spent $3.1 million on education. By 1964 this expenditure had risen to $17.6 million, representing more than 20 per cent of the total budget, or about 5 per cent of the GNP, which is one of the highest quotas devoted to education anywhere in the world. Future plans call for more ambitious programs, with recurrent expenditure on education in Uganda to rise to $33.6 million in 1970, and the capital investment required for this expansion to be in the order of $36.6 million. Even this proportionately high expenditure on education can do little more than scratch the surface, and only a small proportion of the population will be able to go to school.

Under such circumstances, the questions must arise: When the people demand education, and the means to supply it are limited, who should receive it? And of those who are privileged to go to school, what kind of education should they receive, and at what level? These indicate the need to set goals and to identify priorities at all levels.

The production of high-level and middle-level trained manpower is recognized as an indispensable condition in the process of economic and social development. It is also a crucial factor in establishing and maintaining effective political institutions and a sound system of government. African countries are, therefore, faced with the problem of devising educational programs to meet these manpower requirements, at the same time taking into consideration the aspirations of all their people and their demand for education and other services at all levels.

Priorities

1. *Expansion of Secondary Education*

During the pre-independence period, high-school and higher education were unduly neglected compared to elementary education. In 1960, for example, it is estimated that 90 per cent of the boys and 50 per cent of the girls aged seven to eleven in Kenya received some kind of elementary education,[1] but only about 12 per cent of the elementary-school leavers found places in secondary schools. In Uganda, 50 per cent of the primary-school age group are at school, but secondary-school enrollments represent only 1.5 percent of that age group. There is thus a very narrow bottleneck between the end of the six- or seven-year elementary school and entrance to the secondary school.

The meeting of African States on the development of education in Africa, held in Addis Ababa in May 1961, established the expansion of high-school education as one of the top priorities. Plans for economic and social development very much depend upon high-school graduates for an adequate supply of technicians, agricultural assistants, clerks, bookkeepers, nurses, medical technologists, and other middle-level skilled workers. Universities depend upon these graduates for their growth. Secondary-school expansion is also urgently needed to increase the supply of teachers at all levels. Following the surveys and recommendations of the Missions of the International Bank for Reconstruction and Development, all East African countries have placed the greatest emphasis on the development and expansion of secondary education.

Governments are trying to accomplish this in a number of ways: by building new schools; by upgrading elementary and junior high schools to secondary-school level; by adding extra sessions in existing high schools; and by consolidating teachers' colleges into larger units, making the buildings thus freed available for conversion into

---

[1] These numbers are inflated owing to the fact that children both above and below this age group are attending Classes I to IV. (Government of Kenya Education Department Triennial Survey, 1958/60, p. 26.)

high schools. The number of pupils per class has been raised to at least 35 to make more efficient use of the teachers, and the proportion of day high schools to boarding schools has also been increased. All these measures are aimed at minimizing the capital requirements involved in the expansion of secondary education.

There has been a great deal of international cooperation and assistance in this field in East Africa. Assistance from the US Agency for International Development has been a *sine qua non* in the creation of additional streams in Uganda, and a three-stream girls' secondary boarding school at Tororo, Uganda, has been opened this year through grants. Similar assistance has been received by all East African countries from the Department of Technical Cooperation, and later the Ministry of Overseas Development of the United Kingdom, for the purpose of expanding secondary education.

On the other hand, although lack of capital is an important factor in restricting the expansion of high-school facilities, it must be pointed out that the most formidable obstacle is the recurrent cost of running new schools once they have been completed. Receiving countries are particularly gratified by projects such as the Tororo Girls' Secondary School, the secondary school proposed for Korongwe, and the Nordic Centre at Kibaha (the last two in Tanzania), in which donors have provided for recurrent costs during the initial period. There is no doubt that it would assist greatly if an increasing number of donors followed this practice.

2. *Supply of Teachers*

A crucial obstacle to the expansion of education is the critical shortage of secondary-school teachers. Greater and improved facilities for the education and training of teachers are essential if there is to be any significant increase in the quantity and quality of education in East Africa. In fact, without the services of expatriate teachers (through the TEA Project,[1] Peace Corps, and other

[1] Teachers for East Africa—a tripartite project whereby teachers supplied by the USA and UK undergo a period of training at Makerere, then go out to

agencies), there would be very few secondary schools in East Africa. To illustrate the limitations imposed by the shortage of teachers, it is estimated that the demand for new teachers in Kenya from 1964 to 1970 for Forms I to IV will be 1573, of whom only 416 will be available in Kenya.[1] The total teacher needs for secondary schools in Uganda are estimated at 850 in 1965 and 1770 in 1970, of whom 100 and 800 respectively are to be Ugandans.[2]

The staffing of secondary schools will thus, for a long time to come, continue to depend on the flow of expatriate teachers into East Africa. This will again hinge on the extent to which external sources of funds will continue to be available for passage-money and for supplementing local salary rates.

These two priorities—the expansion of high-school enrollments, and the expansion and improvement of facilities for the education and training of teachers—stand out as the most pressing needs. They are connected and interacting. For the lack of local teachers, the expansion of secondary and higher education is impeded; and because there are few secondary-school graduates, teachers' colleges face a critical shortage of recruits.

Providing secondary-school teachers, and teacher trainers, therefore, offers one of widest fields for international cooperation in East Africa. Expatriate teachers, however, stay for a very short time and have to go on leave during part of their short contracts of usually two years. This means a lack of continuity in the schools; and provision must be made for an average of 1.5 teachers per class in order to meet shortages created by absence through leave and delays in replacement. The problem of lack of continuity is likely to become even more serious as the experienced missionary teachers, who stayed many years, are gradually replaced by government-sponsored teachers on short-term contracts. Meas-

teach in the secondary schools under the direction of the Ministries of Education in East Africa.
[1] Government of Kenya: Development Plan 1964–1970, p. 103.
[2] Unpublished figures by Ministry of Education, Uganda Government.

ures aimed at lengthening the time which teachers spend abroad would be of great assistance.

3. Training of Local Teachers

Despite the vital contribution of expatriate teachers to African education, the prospect of relying so heavily on external sources of teachers is naturally disturbing to East African educators. The teaching profession was the largest reservoir of educated people that could be drawn upon for parliamentarians and for the rapid localization of the senior posts in the public service and private institutions. But at a time when the reins of political power are in the hands of East Africans, the civil services are localized, and it is most urgent to nurture the spirit of national consciousness and to project the "African personality" in every aspect of life, it is paradoxical that the educational institutions, which are "most powerfully formative of the national mind and outlook," [1] should be staffed almost entirely by non-nationals.

Most African countries are passing through a critical stage of contradictions and conflicts. They are, on the one hand, greatly dependent on external support for their development plans, and at the same time they are anxious to build up their national prestige and project the African image. Politicians are very sensitive to any form of cultural or political arrogance—no matter how justified from the point of view of donor countries—which seems to undermine the newly won national prestige. The lack of guidance and encouragement which senior East African members of staff might give is a critical problem, and at times a serious threat to the morale of expatriates in the schools.

Yet there is no need to be unduly pessimistic. As the Kenya Education Commission has rightly pointed out, the atmosphere of a school is created, not only by the staff, but by the pupils. It is possible for a sensitive expatriate headmaster and staff to go a long way toward building up and preserving within the school the ideals and spirit of African nationalism. What is needed in expatriate

[1] Kenya Education Commission Report, 1964, Part I, p. 79.

teachers is adequate sensitivity and humility to understand the problems and aspirations of African nationalism today.

In the last analysis, however, the fundamental need is to provide more and better indigenous teachers. A potential source is the large body of East Africans who are studying abroad, particularly in America, and who have no funds either to complete their courses or to return home. East African governments would welcome a crash training program, either abroad or in East Africa, aimed at attracting and assisting East Africans abroad to enter teaching and other fields considered important in terms of East Africa's manpower needs. It is understood that Teachers College, Columbia University, would be prepared to organize such a project.

A BROADER VIEW OF PRIORITIES

The problem of determining priorities is often examined only in terms of numbers and finance. Planners are concerned with achieving a given level and pattern of manpower supply by a certain target date, and with the financial means of attaining the desired goal. Material needs such as buildings, teachers, and equipment are important for expansion of schools and universities. But the content of education and how it fits the learners into the society in which they are going to live and serve is of paramount importance. It is therefore necessary that priorities be considered in terms of both quantity and quality. Money and manpower must be invested in each.

1. *Improving the Quality of Education in Primary Schools*

At the primary level, the greatest need is to improve the quality of education rather than to increase the number of schools and buildings. Thousands of primary-school children sit on benches and are lectured by teachers who themselves have had little more than a few years of elementary-school education, and in many cases no professional training. In Kenya, for example, 6270 out of

25,791 (or 25 per cent) of the primary teachers in 1963 had only primary education or less.[1] In Uganda, 40 per cent of primary-school teachers were trained a long time ago in their own vernaculars, when entry standards to training colleges were very low and required only about four years of formal education. They are unable, therefore, to keep abreast of modern educational ideas unless they learn English.[2]

The result is that teaching methods at the primary level are often formal and academic, consisting of drill on the part of teachers and learning by rote on the part of children. The firmest emphasis, therefore, should be placed not on expansion, but on raising the standards and improving the quality of teaching in the primary schools. Paradoxically again, the enthusiastic and up-to-date teacher who wishes to use activity methods and visual aids finds that her classroom's old-fashioned benches cannot be rearranged for group work; it has no shutters, doors, or storage space to enable her to lock things away overnight. Provision of better furniture and storage space for classrooms could almost revolutionize the methods of teaching in the primary schools.

All East African governments have projects to reorganize teacher education by consolidating several small teacher-training colleges into a few larger and more efficient ones, and by raising entry standards to these colleges.

2. Role of the Institute of Education

All three East African countries, through the assistance of the Carnegie Corporation of New York, have established Institutes of Education which will play a vital role in the improvement of standards. The Institutes will initiate, promote, and cooperate in the organization of educational conferences, and in-service courses for teachers and others engaged in educational work. They will assist in the preparation of syllabuses and curricula adapted to the needs of East Africa. They will provide advisory services and li-

[1] *Ibid.*, p. 49, Table I.
[2] Uganda Education Commission, 1963, Education in Uganda, p. 44.

brary facilities to schools and teachers' colleges, and they will, in particular, circulate information and advice on new teaching materials, methods, and results of research and experimentation. They will bring teachers nearer to the university and take the university nearer to teachers throughout East Africa; and through them, teachers of all levels will be able to study for a university qualification. The Institutes, in other words, will be the national foci for the study, improvement, and expansion of education in these countries.

There is no lack of enthusiasm for these programs. Teachers of all levels come in great numbers to refresher courses, lectures, book exhibitions, and other activities aimed at giving them an opportunity to discuss their problems and achievements and improve their standards. Any financial and personnel assistance given to expand the work of the Institutes would go a long way toward raising the standards and the quality of education. The TEEA Scheme (Teacher Education for East Africa), by supplying a number of teacher trainers, is meeting part of this need, but the Institutes could do much more if they had larger staff and more financial resources at their disposal.

3. *Adapting Curricula and Teaching Materials to Local Needs*

(a) Agricultural Education. As long ago as 1924, members of the Phelps-Stokes Commission on African Education were shocked by the insignificant role played by agriculture in the educational system of East Africa. They found that Uganda, with all the wealth of agricultural resources in the Protectorate, did not have a single agricultural school to prepare the natives to take advantage of their wealth. The attention given to the subject by a few institutions was negligible.

The situation today is not much different. There is a large and growing number of primary-school leavers who do not find places in secondary schools. Rejected by the education system, "too educated" to go back to the land, but ill-prepared and too young to find work in towns, these children go out into the world almost as displaced persons. There is a serious need for the development of agricultural schools linked to cooperative farms or to land resettlement systems which will enable the farm school leavers to acquire capital and make a decent start on the land.

An agriculturally oriented curriculum in the primary schools is needed. It must be admitted, however, that the education system by itself cannot solve the problem of the rural-urban exodus, unless there is at the same time a concomitant revolution in the economy. The school leaver will not be satisfied with the confines of a rural environment dependent upon a one-acre-one-hoe economy. There is great need for research and thinking on this issue. Is the answer, for example, in the Kibutsim and other agricultural settlement schemes of Israel, the collective farms of the Soviet Union, or the Workers Brigade idea of Ghana?

(b) Cultural Subjects. There are only four indigenous art teachers in the secondary schools of Uganda, and possibly a smaller number in Tanzania and Kenya. Art, music, and crafts are an essential part of culture, without which the children's personalities cannot be fully developed. Yet these areas of education are grossly neglected, mostly because they are not usually included in external examinations. Indigenous art, songs, crafts, folk tales, and riddles are disappearing rapidly.

The Rockefeller Foundation has assisted in promoting research aimed at encouraging the teaching of African music in schools. No small-scale investment is more essential than extra manpower and grants to awaken and maintain interest in these subjects.

(c) Teaching Materials. In order to adapt curricula to local conditions, new instructional materials, particularly textbooks, are needed. At the moment, virtually all books used in East African schools are the products of British authors and publishers, meant for British children. This is not to speak disparagingly of the work of foreign publishers in producing books for East Africa. But if truly African nations are going to be fostered and maintained through the schools, the bulk of the books used in these schools must, in the long run, be written and published by responsible citizens of these nations.

We are very concerned that there should be an increasing influx of educational materials developed in terms of the needs and aspirations of the people of East Africa. Furthermore, schoolbooks represent a substantial proportion of East Africa's foreign expenditure. The promotion of indigenous authorship and publishing skills should therefore be a high priority of human investment.

Cooperation in this field could take the form of expatriate experts working with local authors or would-be authors and publishers to adapt existing textbooks, children's stories, etc., and later to write and publish entirely new textbooks in East Africa. It is gratifying to note that a number of British and American publishing houses and foundations are interested in encouraging indigenous authorship in Africa. Franklin Book Programs, for example, has made a study of this problem in West Africa. It is hoped that similar projects for East Africa will receive generous foundation support.

4. *Educational Technology and Investment in Education*

Africa's impatience to develop its human and material resources through more and better education is so great that some governments are spending up to 30 per cent of their annual budgets on education. But even this proportionately high expenditure will do little more than scratch the surface if only the conventional methods of one-teacher-one-class are continued. For a real breakthrough, these countries need to examine some of the latest inventions and discoveries of educational technology. Only drastic departure from conventional practices will break the vicious circle of lack of trained teachers, lack of teacher candidates, and back to the shortage of teachers.

There is another reason why developing countries should look toward educational technology with hope. These countries do not have much investment or vested interests in textbooks, classrooms, teachers, even sentiments based on the traditional approach to teaching. They can afford to jump into the future, and thereby omit many of the steps which Europe and North America, for example, have tried and discarded through a process of trial and error. Here there is great scope for the application of a combination of radio, television, correspondence lessons, and programed instruction to implement the education program.

CONCLUSION

This discussion has not considered university education, universal primary education, or adult literacy—not because they are unimportant, but because they have special problems and priorities. The improvement of elementary education and the expansion of high schools are the foundation on which universities and other forms of education are built. In conclusion, therefore, the problem remains: 50 per cent of East African children fail to find places in primary schools; about 80 per cent of primary leavers "fail" and cannot proceed to post-primary education because there are not enough places.

Such universal failure is a real source of tension and discontent among school leavers and their parents. No stable society can be built on failures. This is why African countries have placed a high premium on investment in education—toward the improvement of the quality of teaching and the expansion of schools. They have discovered that their poverty and apparent backwardness are due not so much to lack of natural resources as to the underdevelopment of human resources. For, as the Kiswahili saying goes: *Kali ya inci ni wantu wa inci*—"The wealth of a country is its people."

EDUCATIONAL PROBLEMS IN
THE DEVELOPING COUNTRIES

ADAM PIERRE ADOSSAMA

Minister of National Education
Togo

Education in all countries, and more particularly in the developing countries, constitutes an essential factor in development. Indeed, to recall the theme of this Conference, neither progress nor cooperation is possible without education.

Educational problems in the developing countries have two major aspects: first, illiteracy, and second, the shortage of qualified personnel. These are the main bottlenecks that hold up development.

Illiteracy is a social scourge similar to poverty and disease. Investment for its eradication would undoubtedly promote the growth of our nations. Education is the basic element in the intellectual and social infrastructure, where its effects on production help to expand the economy of each country. Thus educational expenditure is now recognized in all countries as a productive medium- or long-term investment.

Educational problems of tropical Africa have great complexity and urgency from the points of view of politicians, teachers, intellectuals, and the population as a whole. Certain features of colonial education have become obsolete, in view of the increasing national awareness of the African masses, and the extremely rich political experiences they have lived and are living through in the struggle for national liberation on the African continent.

The achievement of political independence awakened the young African states to the inadequacies of the educational systems inherited from the period of colonial domination. Therefore, efforts are being made to adapt curricula to the realities and needs of each country, and to introduce a general reform of education.

Let us first consider our ancestors' concept of education before the colonial era. As a result of the niggardly development of colonial education, and the economic, social, and cultural stagnation of the African peoples during the period of colonialism, the traditional system of African education has for the most part survived as it was in pre-colonial tropical Africa. In all geographical regions and zones, in all clans, tribes, and ethnic groups, it is characterized by:

Certain common features, illustrating a community of culture among all peoples, and therefore having a very important collective and social content.

Importance of the family framework. Children occupy a central place in African families. Married life (monogamous and polygamous) is to a very large extent conditioned, if not determined, by the ability or inability to have children. Marriage exists to produce children; divorce in order to remarry and have children. A woman without children meets disapproval; she does everything in her power to become fertile, spending her money on consultations, treatment with healers, priests, and witch doctors.

In its basic assumptions, traditional African education makes no distinction between *education*, in the current sense of the word, and *instruction* or teaching—both these aspects being intimately linked. This education includes character-building (attainment of the moral qualities regarded as an inseparable attribute of the state of man), development of physical skills, and acquisition of the knowledge and techniques that everyone needs to allow him to take an active part in the various aspects of social life.

After World War II, as a result of the psychological, social, and political changes in the colonized countries, education underwent a more vigorous development. This was marked by an awareness on the part of the African people of the need to send their children to school, to acquire education beyond the African traditions. An analysis of the development of education in tropical Africa between 1945 and 1960 reveals the following features:

An increase in total school attendance, but little advance in the attendance rate.

Very little development in secondary education, in spite of the possibility of recruiting existing pupils, there being on the average one teacher for 15 to 20 pupils. This delay in secondary education holds up the development of primary education through lack of qualified teachers.

The limited number of higher-grade personnel, the results of which are now evident in economic, social, and political life.

Nothing was done with regard to adult literacy; country districts in Africa seemed doomed to illiteracy.

In 1947, in the French-speaking countries, and no doubt also in the English-speaking, the following ratios prevailed:

Out of 100 children of school age, 4 actually attended school; for 100 primary-school children, there were 3 secondary-school pupils. In other words, out of 10,000 children of school age, an average of 400 actually went to school, of whom approximately 12 proceeded to secondary education and 3 to higher or higher technical education.

In 1957:

Out of 10,000 children of school age, 1,540 actually attended school, of whom 46 proceeded to secondary education, and an average of 7 to higher or technical education. These figures relate to the former Afrique Occidentale Française (AOF).

After 1957, the picture was considerably improved by the inclusion of Togo and Cameroon, which had been United Nations Trusteeship Territories.

In the final report of the Conference of African States on the Development of Education in Africa, held in March 1963, the following details can be found. Taking pupils in primary and sec-

ondary school and students undergoing higher or technical education separately, the percentages they represent within their respective age groups are as follows:

24.2 per cent of the total population aged 6–14;
10 per cent aged 15–19;
7.7 per cent aged 20–24.

Since independence, the African people's awareness of this educational lag, their desire for political, economic, and cultural freedom, their determination to assert themselves and to develop all
their potentialities, have been the chief concern of all African political leaders at every level. In tropical Africa the postwar years
saw a considerable increase in the rate of training of national personnel. Secondary and higher education became accessible to a
relatively low but by no means negligible number of Africans. The
result was the appearance of an intelligentsia and of specialists of
various kinds, in whom the faults inherent in a training system
based on European standards were compensated by a greater
awareness of the African situation.

The political implications of colonial education between 1945
and 1960 are found, first, in the creation of a powerful African student movement—in spite of various attempts to divide the students and the divisionary maneuvers undertaken by some European states and certain African politicians. As a result of the sense
of awareness created by contact with European organizations,
African students were active in their countries' struggles for independence. A further consequence of new educational trends was
the development of a "diploma cult." Many young Africans made
all-out efforts to win diplomas which had previously been regarded
as inaccessible to Negroes. Success brought satisfaction; students
were treated with due respect and pride by other Africans, and
great hopes were placed in them.

As the first graduates from overseas universities returned to their
own countries, signs of esteem or favor by the people, due to the
genuine respect for knowledge shown in tropical Africa, came to

be regarded as a right which some graduates claimed aggressively through an ostentatious display of genuine or false degrees and diplomas. This phenomenon subsequently degenerated into a belief that the diploma should be exploited as a capital resource which bears fruit without particular effort. The result has been political opportunism, careerism, and above all a lack of productivity on the part of many of the African intelligentsia. Engineers sit in offices, perfectly happy to be directors or heads of services, doing only paper work; magistrates dispense justice according to European civil law or customary law as codified by colonial administrators and lawyers. The lax attitude of African intellectuals toward their responsibilities is one of the greatest obstacles to rapid progress in culture and education in many sectors of African political, economic, and social life.

This state of affairs was recognized and tolerated by the colonial authorities, and subsequently by the majority of African governments after independence. But now the harmful results of the absence of a coherent educational philosophy and policy, the inadaptation of school systems and curricula to African realities and national needs, the overcrowding in classrooms, the lack of financial resources, and the shortage of employment for the young people who do receive training, are forcing the developing countries to change their ideas and to look for solutions to the problems of training and utilizing personnel.

African political leaders are now aware of the need to reform education systems. National, regional, and even international conferences, seminars, and symposia have been organized in an attempt to find new directions. Important decisions were taken by the historic Addis Ababa Conference in March 1962, and a program was adopted by the UNESCO General Conference at its thirteenth session in 1964.

At Addis Ababa, it was recognized that every state must draw up an education plan, projecting the progress of school attendance up to 1980. Generally speaking, in view of the lack of financial resources and adequate technicial personnel, the objectives laid down in the plans can be achieved only through effort and sacrifice on the part of all African governments and through international co-operation. The efforts made by the African peoples to reform their educational systems must be supplemented by greater understanding on the part of the better equipped countries and by assistance of all kinds: resources for the building of schools and the study and expansion of curricula, for equipment, teaching materials, regional training centers, teaching staff, research technicians, and so on.

In all this, we must not overlook the need to integrate educational planning in the over-all development plan of each country. Often school attendance has not kept pace with demographic growth, and national education budgets lag behind the actual needs. In such countries as Togo and Dahomey, this has created a catastrophic situation: lack of premises, shortage of teachers owing to limited financial resources, ineptitude of curricula. The same situation exists in many other countries.

THE SITUATION IN TOGO

I should like to discuss Togo as an example, since I am better informed of the situation there. Moreover, Togo and Dahomey, which have very high school attendance rates and more trained personnel than other West or East African countries, have special problems.

After independence, the overwhelming need was felt to adapt the educational system to Togo's realities. A reform committee has been set up to work out a more effective and realistic system that would not sacrifice the traditional principles of our education. The aim of the new system is to train, in the short and long term, useful and responsible citizens.

Studies have been carried out with a view to humanizing the educational system, freeing it from purely budgetary criteria and, without any major upheaval, bringing about a creative reform that would be economically and socially beneficial to the whole country. In applying the plan, emphasis will be placed on the need for a change in outlook and attitudes on the part of teachers.

The alarming increase in attendance figures (in some southern regions we have reached a rate of 85 per cent, and the current average figure for primary school is approximately 55 per cent) makes it impossible to run classes properly. The attendance total for the year 1954–1955 was 57,000 pupils; by 1964–1965 it had increased to 155,000 pupils—an advance of almost 100,000 in ten years. During the same period, the number of classes rose from 1100 to 2300, and the average number of pupils per class from 52 to 67. This average conceals wide disparities: few preparatory classes have less than 100 pupils, while some have up to 150 or even 200, which explains the high proportion of pupils who repeat classes (60–65 per cent). Under these conditions, however devoted and competent the teacher may be, he cannot give proper atten·tion to every pupil.

The school-age population continues to increase very rapidly. The figure for 1965 is 395,000, and this will rise to 427,000 in 1970, 485,000 in 1980, and 687,000 in 1990. The present population of Togo is 1.5 million and the annual rate of increase 2.6 per cent. If we accept for the future an advance in the school attendance rate similar to that observed over the last five years, the number of primary-school pupils will reach 310,000 by 1970, which means planning for twice the number of pupils over a five-year period, and an annual output of 12,000 primary certificate holders who probably cannot be employed.

In secondary education, the number of pupils has risen from 1000 to 8000 in ten years, and the number of classes from 50 to 220. Between 1965 and 1970, the present rate of development would result in the training of 9000 elementary certificate holders and roughly 1500 additional baccalaureate holders. According to the estimates of the national economic development board, eight-tenths of these students would be unable to find employment in Togo.

This explains why so many young people go abroad. The same problem arises in Dahomey. About 1000 students are enrolled abroad in higher education. On completing their degree course, many of them fail to return, having found employment abroad. For example, about 50 Togolese nationals are teaching in French secondary schools and universities. Others can be found in Germany, the United States, and the USSR.

Thus the number of qualified students has increased out of all proportion to available salaried work. Our educational system, instead of producing people who are making a useful contribution to the country's economic life (based mainly on agricultural production), is forming an army of unemployed city-dwellers, who abandon the rural sector even though it offers the best chances for employment.

Trapped between financial imperatives and the danger of a disruption of their educational system, owing to the relatively high rate of demographic growth, some underdeveloped countries have attempted to escape from this dilemma by introducing a basic policy which ensures:

An increase in school attendance without overcrowding, at the same time maintaining the standards and duration of courses;

The adaptation of the school system to economic needs through the ruralization of education, by introducing elementary economics, sociology, and domestic science into curricula;

A personnel selection system designed to bring the kind of people needed into the technical life of the nation.

In almost all African states it is essential to build up pride in work in the fields and in craftsmanship, and to attempt to inspire in young people a feeling of love, or at least respect for, the things of the earth. Agricultural work and rural crafts must be carefully organized by competent technicians and conducted in the light of local conditions.

Starting with primary schools, teachers should receive special training and preparation for this purpose. Greater emphasis will have to be placed in curricula on the applied sciences, practical skills, drawing, and civics. This new direction for schools in rural areas will succeed only if it is supported by continuing education and public information, both in and out of schools, backed up by press and radio. The training of national and local staff from the primary-school level will strengthen and hasten an awareness of the possibilities for progress that exist in our countries.

We must foster in our schools a "development mystique" in as dynamic and confident an atmosphere as possible. We must create a collective will at every level of society, and a sense among all that they are taking part in developing the tremendous resources of the community to the advantage of our peoples.

In every village and town, teachers must be the spearhead of the spiritual renewal and mobilization of resources desired by all Africans. The success of any kind of creative reform in the education system depends not only on the training of teaching staff, but also on its stability and administrative security, which can be achieved by avoiding the introduction of politics into teaching. But primary schoolmasters, like teachers at the secondary and higher levels, must not stand aloof from the environment or from the community in which they live and work. They must not lock themselves away in their ivory towers, since their activities in country districts and in the towns are of crucial importance.

Who but the schoolmaster can instill a love of the land, and respect for manual work and the importance and grandeur of the family? Who can better prepare the way for the evolution needed in an underdeveloped economy which is too settled in its ways and can survive only by concentrating on production?

The teacher can and must condition the minds of the people by example and persuasion. He must influence peasant opinion by joining without reserve in their lives through out-of-school activities. The most important quality for success in this kind of work, apart from general knowledge and teaching ability, is the moral worth of the teacher, as manifested in his actions. In all social groups the teacher must arouse a conscious desire to go forward, an enlightened determination to meet common needs, to enhance and enrich the national heritage.

Complete dependence on a "welfare state," expecting the government to take responsibility for everything—which is a curse in the underdeveloped ex-colonial countries—must be combated. Primary and secondary education in our countries must provide young children with the means to knowledge and action, and teach them to think and act for themselves, to develop a respect for work. From the primary-school level, foundations can and must be laid for productive pre-craft work, better planned agriculture and stock-raising, and harmonious economic and social development.

At the present stage in the evolution of our young states, schools should no longer exist without an experimental plot, a garden, and a school cooperative, where pupils can learn to live in a society. The operation of a cooperative will give a new and educationally revolutionary meaning to the work carried out.

School must no longer be an obstacle to good relations between the older and younger generations, or an object of suspicion, but rather the common ground between families and nation. Voluntary schools organized by teachers on behalf of adults can inscribe over their doors this fine, realistic, and dynamic motto:

Down with Illiteracy! You Have Learned—
Now Teach Your Neighbor!

The teacher must galvanize his class, creating a new state of mind in all social groups. In the light of the reforms to be introduced, all subjects must help to advertise and popularize country ways and people, giving every citizen a feeling of respect and faith with regard to the background in which he was born and brought up. Lessons must accent the nobility, beauty, and sacred utility of the act of sowing, the solidarity between people at the family, national, and international levels, and the interdependence of states.

The education that we give our young people must be continuing, so that they can proceed with their studies and learning at every stage in life. For this purpose, laboratories, libraries, experimental plots, and the cinema must be used to adapt the training of children to modern techniques and help them to acquire not only basic knowledge, but individual working methods, so that they have well-trained rather than well-packed minds.

To achieve this, we shall have to cast aside old habits and resolutely pursue methods which will allow the pupil to take greater personal initiative through the development of his imagination. Pupils must get into the habit of studying the real problems in their lives, not the artificial ones that exist in textbooks. Book knowledge must be supplemented by the development of skills. We must fight against cramming, whose evil results bear heavily upon the rising generation and are of no assistance to them when they face up to the practical problems of their lives and work.

The need and eagerness of our young states to progress rapidly must bring out our ingenuity. Since our schools lack resources at every level, they can and must become pilot institutions, leading to new ideas and methods, producing citizens prepared for life. Many remarkable innovations, scientific discoveries and inventions came about in industrialized countries through the pressure of economic and financial necessity. Why should the same thing not happen in our countries? Teachers must be pioneers, militant workers in the service of education, children, and the nation. They must make every effort to develop in children a positive concept of and capacity for happiness, for enjoyment of achievement, of work well done, of a sense of humanity.

In training qualified personnel, we should draw attention to the university's role in the young nations. Higher education is no longer the sole concern of specialists, interested only in academic controversy. It has become one of the chief problems of all countries. The training of African students must be strictly coordinated with national development plans. We belong to a society in which most people's minds are still turned toward the past, so we must train men of new ideas capable of deciding about their future and overcoming the serious consequences of colonization.

Politics, as introduced into our countries, has taught us to live for individual, personal interest, instead of teaching us to love one another and to develop a sense of collective values. European individualism has taught us to defend our only interests to the detriment of the common good, and even against the interests of the people. Consequently, a difficult and prolonged task lies ahead: to make an effective over-all joint effort, for which all of us must feel responsible, to meet the aspiration for unity, or at least for the union of all Africans.

In all countries we must promote a system of education firmly rooted in our native soil, fed by the realities and traditions of our countries, adapted to our economic and social needs, but at the same time open to the world and transcending national and continental boundaries to achieve a genuine world outlook and culture. The product of this system will be not only the African, but the responsible man of the twentieth century, and above all, the world citizen.

In this task of education for adult citizenship which must be undertaken in all the underdeveloped countries, we should not overlook the constructive role that can be played, under responsible leadership, by trade unions, community and youth organizations, political parties, and religious societies.

We must combine the whole philosophy of civilization in a universal concept of mankind in order to bring about at last the brotherhood of man. This is the one basic idea which all young independent states, having no past to separate them, hold in common—an idea through which we can join together without hate or bitterness to build a better world.

In a greeting to the Tiers-monde, the poet Aimé Césaire gave a superb picture of Africa:

> I see Africa, many and one,
> Upright in the tumult of fortune,
> With its lumps and swellings,
> Slightly apart, but abreast
> Of the times, like a heart without reserve.

A great effort is required before Africa can combine its own spiritual and moral traditions, which are the pride of Africans, with the foundations on which the great progress to be brought by modern science and technology can be based. We must understand that for mankind satisfaction and happiness are not to be found merely in the material goods necessary to life, but also in moral progress. Above all, our educational system must develop the moral, spiritual, and human values within us. We must seek to develop in our young people a deep sense of justice—economic, social, and moral justice—and of brotherhood among all men, regardless of race, color, or creed. We must transcend ideology, and in all simplicity and honesty we must seek the happiness of all men, whoever they are, and wherever they may be.

V. Intercontinental Views on Cooperation and Development

COOPERATION IN AFRICA AND IN THE UNITED NATIONS

SAMUEL N. ODAKA

Minister of State for Foreign Affairs
Uganda

First among the points discussed here is the question of national unity and the factors which militate against this unity. Real problems arising from uneven development within a country exist in Africa, but are not unique to Africa. Examples can be cited throughout all continents, including the most highly developed. In Italy, for example, the uneven development between north and south has created definite tensions. In the United States, incidences of uneven development are very much in evidence as between the southern and northern states. In the Soviet Union, the west is decidedly far ahead of the east—which, incidentally, coincides with geographical and racial groupings within this large country.

What is the answer to all these problems? It is necessary, I believe, to place special emphasis on central planning, with a view to concentrating on the more backward areas and allocating resources for their upliftment.

In considering this, we must face the question of the merits and demerits of single-party and multiparty systems of government, as well as the role of labor organizations in the promotion of national unity and cooperation. The idea of the people's organizing themselves politically or in trade unions is foreign to Africa, and the African is entitled to experiment with other alternatives in order to discover for himself a form which is appropriate to his special conditions and requirements. This would, inevitably, involve some changes in or rejection of imported institutions.

Mainly because of our historical connections with the West, it has been assumed that the only course open to us in dealing with labor problems would be to continue with the West-oriented concept of labor organization. But is this necessarily the wisest and most practical course for us to take? Or should it be replaced by completely new ideas, in view of the different conditions prevailing in developing countries, such as Uganda, which are predominantly rural? The same questions apply to political parties. And developed countries, in the West or in the East, must make an effort to understand and appreciate Africa's need for modification of non-African patterns.

We need a sympathetic approach. The initiative should not be exclusively in the hands of the developed countries. We, in Africa, should also be free to introduce new ideas, to modify existing or pre-independence institutions, or to reject them as inappropriate and unworkable—without being unduly criticized.

The question of a one-party system of government, for instance, has aroused what I consider to be an unfortunate, unwarranted, and, in many instances, uninformed spate of criticisms. Without attempting to enter into the merits or demerits of a one-party system, I wish to state, quite frankly, that no attempt has been made, so far, to understand the reasons leading to the modification of the Westminster model of government in the case of ex-British colonies. Although it is agreed that one way of ensuring individual liberties and free criticism of the government is the retention of a two-party system, this is not necessarily the only way. Some voices have gone even further to suggest that the existence of a one-party system is undemocratic. I am convinced that those reactions arise, not because modification of institutions originally imported from Western countries is, in itself, a bad thing, but because there has been a tendency to identify any modification with the importation into Africa of monolithic or totalitarian regimes existing elsewhere. One-party governments have, in fact, proved to be a welcome source of unity and strength in a number of countries.

It should not be a crime for Kenya or Tanzania, for instance, to have a one-party system. Experience has shown that there are definite and obvious advantages for certain African countries to take this course. One advantage, which some countries tend to overlook or forget, is the desire to have some neutral institutions to which everyone in an otherwise heterogeneous society could belong, without the risk of losing either his tribal identity or his soul. In Uganda we have a racially mixed society with various religious groupings; and we have many divisions of the Africans into tribal and ethnic groupings. Thus, in an attempt to forge ahead with national unification and economic construction, it may not be altogether a bad thing to have a political institution which cuts across the various tribal, religious, and racial divisions.

At this Conference are persons concerned with the day-to-day political decisions in their various countries, and people who are directly involved in solving problems of economic development in Africa as a whole. I have been privileged to be a member of a Committee which has been dealing mainly with the financing of development, the mobilization of domestic resources, the role of the public and private sectors in national development, and, perhaps of even greater importance for Africa, the question of foreign aid—its sources, values, dangers, and other related factors. We have discovered that in African development, much as we should like to adhere to our several plans, it is painfully clear that everything needs attention, that all aspects of our economic problems are urgent and can only be classified as top priority. This does not mean that there should be no planning. The main problem is that there is so much to do, and so little accomplished, that we need to press ahead as quickly as possible on all fronts.

This immediately raises the problem of finance and foreign aid. From the statistics, one is struck by their magnitude and the apparent generosity of the donors. We must, quite obviously, examine a little more closely what these figures mean to the donors, and particularly their effect on the recipient countries. The Geneva Conference left no doubt in our minds that this aid is negligible in proportion to the donors' gross national products and to the effectiveness of the aid itself.

Except for one donor country, the aid is less than 1 per cent of the GNP. The situation for developing countries is even worse when you look at the unfortunate fluctuations in the imbalance of trade, the effect of which in many respects tends to wipe out the benefits of such aid. Despite suggestions of foreign experts that all efforts should be directed to capital development and such projects as would produce capital, the pattern of aid clearly shows that donor countries are more concerned with prestige projects—with a high import content, projects to benefit the donor countries—than with those directed, as they should be, toward the needs of the recipient countries.

Perhaps worse, there is a great preponderance of massive military aid, the economic value of which is marginal. It is a pity that sometimes this aid appears to be given for no reason other than curtailment of objectionable political ideologies. In Africa there is a definite disappointment that the country most capable of giving such aid has, to date, given a mere token to Africa. Africa needs massive aid, and yet the contribution of those countries which are in the best position to assist the developing countries has been negligible. The United States has given little more than 7 per cent of her total aid to this continent which needs it most. What is even worse, 80 per cent of the flow of capital resources into this continent goes to South Africa.

Turning to the question of trade, it is obvious that the Eastern countries, and especially the Soviet Union, have done absolutely nothing to establish normal trade relationships which could help emerging African countries to develop their national economies. I now turn to the question of African solidarity and international cooperation. We in Uganda believe in and strongly support the Organization of African Unity. The OAU has been in existence for only two years, and although it has had one or two setbacks, its achievements so far are most significant and point to a very bright future. One problem it faces is common to most of the newly independent African states, namely, high expectations of quick results. Some may be disappointed not to see a continental government within two years, but we believe that within the OAU Charter there are broad principles of cooperation on which African states can build. The greatest achievement, however, has been to arouse the hitherto latent desire for personal and continental contact. We must be determined to explore all sources of cooperation. Perhaps the best area of greater inter-African cooperation is that of trade and the establishment of interstate industries.

Both the Economic Commission for Africa and the OAU must examine very closely and recommend to the African governments possible commodities that can be exchanged between their states, and must also find the obstacles that hamper this exchange. East Africa offers a good example. The East African governments, whose interstate trade is considerable, are now examining the possibility of expanding trade with Zambia. There is no reason why this same exercise should not be jointly undertaken with reference to the Congo, Rwanda, and Burundi on the western side, and to Ethiopia and Somalia in the north. This exercise does not need outside financial aid; within our own states we have enough people capable of advising governments on the areas and methods of cooperation, in order to boost the volume of trade between one African state and another. The exercise need not, of course, be confined to eastern Africa; it can and should apply with even greater force to the north and west of the continent. In this way, Africa will reduce her dependence on outside markets and will go a long way toward translating the African solidarity we all talk about from a purely political objective to an economic reality, with all the attendant advantages.

Let me remind you that this is the United Nations Cooperation Year. I have expressed our undying faith in African continental solidarity. With even greater force I now reaffirm our support of the United Nations. We believe that the UN is a powerful force for promoting the advancement of each member state, and that cooperation within it must include peaceful coexistence and economic cooperation within this continent as everywhere else. We believe that the UN is supremely fitted to help in a global attempt to reduce areas of economic tension, and that in the next decade it can overcome many difficulties which hinder full economic cooperation.

STEPS TOWARD UNITY
IN EUROPE AND IN AFRICA

RENÉ FOCH

Director, EURATOM, Brussels

As a specialist in European integration problems and an official of one of the European Communities, and speaking only for myself, the first thing that strikes me is that, in both Africa and Europe, the idea of unity is a driving force that all politicians look up to and none would dare to contest. On both continents it seems obvious that this ideal cannot be attained without going through intermediate stages; in so great a task as the unification of an entire continent, one cannot skip the preliminaries. It is equally obvious that the major problems of the twentieth century—economic, technical, and scientific—are insoluble, in Africa as in Europe, if they are set in the narrow framework of the purely national state, whether ancient or modern.

These two observations have given birth in Europe to a new political concept. Fifteen years ago, when Robert Schuman, the French Foreign Minister, at the instigation of Jean Monnet, launched a solemn appeal for Franco-German reconciliation—not just rhetorically, but in the highly concrete form of a proposal to pool the two basic industries essential to both peace and war, coal and steel—he set in motion a process whose results we are still witnessing, and made a political gesture whose scope transcends the frontiers of Europe. His appeal is undoubtedly one of the most important political texts of this century. The idea that, to prepare the way for political union, which is the goal and purpose of all our efforts, we should first create common interests by tackling together common problems, is an idea that is still bearing fruit. In Africa, as in Europe, it can solve otherwise insoluble problems, and at the same time it can create a growing network of common interests, without which political union would remain a vain hope.

Surely the most promising approach consists in establishing centers of regional development based on the joint exploitation of major natural resources, the construction of dams, the operation of mines and refineries, the integrated use of large river systems on the lines of the Tennessee Valley Authority, the establishment of coordinated transport networks, and, perhaps even more important, the creation of inter-African universities and development institutes. Many African countries will no doubt find it to their advantage not to convert the former administrative frontiers of the colonial period into economic frontiers, but to set up among themselves regional unions, such as the one now being negotiated between the Ivory Coast, Guinea, Liberia, and Sierra Leone, in the form of customs unions or free-trade areas. It would be far simpler to set up even limited unions of this kind now, before the advance of industrialization has crystallized frontiers to the detriment of the economies concerned. Multinational undertakings of this kind could provide employment for the many young trained Africans who do not always find an opportunity of using their knowledge in their own countries. They would also create concrete links of solidarity between countries that would subsequently extend to other fields.

In Europe, this functional approach has already brought governments to the next stage, i.e., economic unification, which is halfway to completion in the European Common Market. The ECM, in turn, is now posing in urgent terms the problem of political unity. There were grounds for suggesting—people have, in fact, suggested—that European unification might tip the political balance in favor of the colonizing as opposed to the colonized peoples, leading to a kind of European neo-colonialism. On the other hand, it has been suggested that the creation of this new market might close certain traditional outlets of the African countries and cause the former metropolitan countries to lose interest in their ex-colonies. These pessimistic forecasts came to nothing, and quite the opposite effect is to be observed. In the field of financial assistance, for instance, the contributions of a united Europe have supplemented French and Belgian financial aid. Compared with the 510 million dollars spent in the first five years of the Association, the Yaoundé Convention now provides for a European contribution of 800 million dollars.

In the field of trade, Associate States are granted free access to the Common Market, an advantage which many developed countries would very much like to enjoy. In return, the Associate States open their markets to the Six, although they can take steps to protect their economies, and in particular their infant industries. In addition, they retain freedom of action in their commercial policy with regard to third parties, since the Convention sets up a free-trade area, not a customs union. The Yaoundé Convention goes even further, referring specifically to the possibility of measures in favor of African integration. This is a fact of considerable political importance. Article 8 provides for the maintenance or establishment between Associate States of customs unions or free-trade areas; Article 9 goes still further, providing for the same possibility between Associate States and third parties. Far from preventing the closer relations with other African states so obviously desirable from the geographical point of view—between certain countries of West Africa, for instance—these texts explicitly provide for such links.

Finally, the Yaoundé Convention provides for institutions based on parity and designed to ensure this cooperation between equals: a council of association, a parliamentary conference, and a court of arbitration. Through these paritary bodies, the African states have their say in the ECM's internal affairs, whenever they are concerned. In drawing up its joint agricultural policy—in respect of fats, for instance—the European Economic Community consults the Associate States and takes their interests into account. In all this, it should be noted, the sovereignty and ideological trend of each signatory have been respected.

It should be pointed out that the Associate States would never have obtained separately what they have obtained jointly, and that the advantages gained by them reflect their collective bargaining power. But it should also be stressed that, for obvious reasons of convenience, the permanent and institutionalized system of consultation set up under the Convention implies an ever-increasing degree of African unity. In any dialogue, the unity of one party implies and stimulates unity in the other, and this applies as much to the Europe-Africa dialogue as to the Atlantic partnership.

All this does not add up to a closed system. The Convention is open to all states whose economic structures and products are comparable with those of the Associate States.

Negotiations are now proceeding between the European Economic Community and Nigeria, and there are grounds for believing that they will be brought to a successful conclusion, once the problems concerning the relations between the Maghreb countries and the EEC have been successfully solved. For it is one of the rules of the EEC game that progress can be bought only by further progress.

Thus more and more points of contact will be established between the African countries—French-speaking and English-speaking, the Africa of the Latin Quarter and the Africa of Oxford, the Africa that drives on the right and the Africa that drives on the left. If it is true that the divisions of Europe are reflected in the divisions of Africa and have survived the colonial period, it is also true that any progress toward European unity is bound to facilitate progress toward African unity. I should like to conclude by suggesting that the African countries, particularly those belonging to the Commonwealth, ponder on the immense advantages that the United Kingdom's membership in the Common Market could bring them, and on the powerful impulse it could give to African unity.

UNIVERSAL PROBLEMS
OF DEVELOPMENT

A. S. DHAWAN

High Commissioner of India in Uganda

The dominant impressions about this Conference are the universality of many of the problems explored here and the validity of these discussions for most developing countries. Poverty, disease, and ignorance, which the continent of Africa is now battling to overcome, are by no means exclusive to Africa. With varying degrees and emphases, their eradication is as urgent for most of the Asian continent and other areas as it is for Africa.

One is struck by the basic humanity which permeates this Conference and which transcends geographical limits. The picture that repeatedly emerges before one's mind is that of a humble man striving desperately to find a place in the sun and willing to cooperate, for the sake of his future, with friends who can possibly help him. There are degrees of underdevelopment; the developed countries of today may be considered somewhat underdeveloped in the future, and vice versa. What stands out is the human side of the picture. One does not find any basic difference between the peasant of Asia and the peasant of Africa. Both have the same problems of modern techniques of agriculture, of better tools, farm implements, fertilizers, seeds, and other prerequisites of progressive farming. Both need help and training for improving their lot by cooperation among themselves. Both have the problem of marketing produce. The fall or rise of prices in primary agricultural products affects the producers in both continents. The difference is hardly more than the question of degree. Further, it is by no means certain that, even though there may be advantages of better knowledge or technology in some areas, a comparatively depressed area should not be able to telescope its progress and even crash ahead.

The frank discussions, with sometimes conflicting points of view put forward in a healthy spirit, have been heart-warming features of these meetings. The deliberations of this Conference will certainly have influence beyond the geographical confines of Africa. I am sure that we in India, and in other parts of Asia, will study the reports with great care and will be enlightened both by the knowledge they throw on the problems of the African continent as it strives for higher development, and by the close correlation of these problems with those in Asia and in other developing parts of the world.

A good deal of emphasis has been placed here on the vital question of aid, or assistance, or collaboration between the developed and the developing countries. Our times, though exciting and stimulating, are certainly pregnant with terrible potentialities for self-destruction. Perhaps never in the history of mankind have science and technology developed to such an extent. As the Prime Minister of Uganda said, "We are now capable of destroying the whole world, perhaps in the course of a single day." Nuclear holocaust is almost too terrible to conceive, yet it cannot be brushed aside as entirely a fanciful conjecture. A hopeful and, according to some, the brightest part of this picture of our times is the growing realization by the developed countries that the more fortunate must give assistance to the developing countries in solving their urgent problems of eradicating poverty, disease, and ignorance.

Whatever may be the reasons for this aid, whether an expression of enlightened self-interest, for political objectives or selfish gains, or a mixture of these, there seems to be no doubt that this concept of aid and collaboration provides germs of hope for humanity.

There is also a growing realization by the developing countries of the need for full cooperation with the developed countries so that such aid is used for fruitful purposes. The colonial era is dying, if not already dead, and a new relationship is in a formative state.

We have some ancient sayings or concepts in India about gifts generally. According to these, assistance, gifts, or donations may be classified under three categories. In the first and noblest classification, the gift, to be really fruitful or blessed, for both donor and receiving country, should be without any selfish motive, i.e., without any strings. The second classification relates to gifts which, though given to deserving persons, are largely motivated by some selfish ends. The third category, of course, is that type of aid which is given with destructive motives, not for the good of the recipient but to satisfy the donor's base, selfish motives at the cost of the receiver. As nations gain greater understanding of each others' problems and needs, we have hopes that the bulk of aid from the developed countries will be generous, will be guided entirely by humanitarian grounds, and will mostly fall in the first category.

SOME NOTES ON SCIENCE
AND TECHNOLOGY

LEONA BAUMGARTNER

Assistant Administrator for
Technical Cooperation and Research, AID, USA

I came, as I am relatively certain most non-Africans came, to this
Conference to learn, to listen, to exchange ideas and feelings, to
think and laugh together. These things we have done; all participants have entered into this exchange. We have learned about:

African solidarity and African diversity;

The problems created by economic fragmentation;

The existence in most countries of dual economies—the traditional
and predominant subsistence economy as contrasted with the small
but growing modern economy;

Tolerances and intolerances;

The deficiencies of skilled manpower on apparently every front;

The beauty of Africa's countryside and a sense of her vastness;

Something of her ancient and modern art and culture;

A great deal of what African hospitality means;

Africa's great dreams and potentials for the future—her eagerness
and ability, as evidenced by her leaders at this Conference, to
jump far ahead despite obstacles.

Each of us has had a different experience. Each of us is carrying home different jewels. One of mine is a phrase used one day by our distinguished educator, Monseigneur Bakole of the Congo, when he said, "In my country, every time an old man dies, it is as if a library has been burned." So it is with all of us as we lose those who know our respective heritages.

In my opinion, however, one facet of the main problem of "Progress Through Cooperation" has not been discussed in a manner commensurate with its importance to the future. That is the contribution science and technology can make to modernization. I say *modernization,* for as a member of one of the most rapidly developing and changing countries in the world, I am uncomfortable with the commonly used phrases, *developed* and *less developed.* I refuse to be thought of as incapable of change and further development.

Sir Arthur Lewis touched on science and technology in his paper, as have others, but there is little evidence that the importance of its adaptation to African problems was widely considered. It is of considerable significance, for example, that the 1964 UN Conference on Trade and Development was discussed often, but that the 1963 UN Conference on the Application of Science and Technology to Development was scarcely mentioned. And it is quite probable that the latter has more to offer the economic and social development of the African people than the former.

A characteristic of modernization is the application of the methods and spirit of science to all problems. The method is essentially one of forming an hypothesis and testing it. The spirit is one of continuing inquiry, of finding new ways to solve old problems, of discarding what does not work, of adventure into the unknown.

In using modern science and technology in the process of modernization, one common experience is important. That is the need to *adapt,* not *adopt,* as there is a transfer from one area to another. Africa may need new strains of maize, but they must be strains adapted to her soils. Her teachers must know the characteristics of African children to select what is best for them. Her doctors must be trained to take care of African health needs. Direct transplants often wither and die. Willows will not live in a desert, but deserts can be made to bloom. The curriculum of a British, French, or American School of Agriculture or Medicine, or of a secondary school, is probably inappropriate to African needs, but their methods of developing curricula may be appropriate.

Now may I speculate on a few examples of what can happen? Africa need never build the miles and miles of telegraph poles that accompanied progress in the Western world. Progress available through modern electronic communication theory and knowledge can displace them. Via the satellites, which are a by-product of that often criticized race to the moon, African students can listen to the best teachers of Paris, London, Princeton, Dakar, or Makerere. Imagine the joys of listening to Barbara Ward or Sir Arthur Lewis whenever they give a major speech anywhere in the world, and watching the audiences they address. Imagine the value of a technician's watching a new machine, with which he is as yet unfamiliar, being used by another technician who knows it well.

Africa worries over the growing number of children for whom education is needed. If modern methods of programed instruction can be adapted to Africa, the burden of educating thousands of teachers will be lessened.

Or take the vast waste lands of Africa where saline soils make agriculture impossible. Will the further development and adaptation of scientific knowledge for desalinization recover new acres for a vastly increased production? Also, as Dr. Karefa-Smart pointed out, one acre of a properly stocked fish pond can supply one ton of fish annually and provide much needed protein. This procedure could save, in Nigeria alone, five million pounds of foreign exchange and customs duty now spent on importing less nutritious fish from northern seas. Similar gains to health and the economy are accruing through the mass vaccination of cattle against rinderpest, already under way in West Africa.

How rapidly will these practices spread? And will the further development of man's knowledge of how the human mind and human emotions operate make it possible to reduce the tensions we now suspect are often the result of fear of the unknown?

Yes, Africa and the world have much to gain from the development and application of science and technology—too much to explore in these remarks. But I make four specific suggestions:

1. This is no time to pile up more studies that accumulate facts of interest only in themselves. Africa needs the practical inventories of soil characteristics that can tell exactly where to resettle people and what can be grown productively there. It needs the inventories of African natural resources which Paul Hoffman advocated. In other words, it needs studies and surveys that lead to action, not to reports for library shelves.

2. Africa needs to expand and extend its scientific research institutes and activities. This entails a vastly increased training of scientists of all kinds—veterinarians, biochemists, soil scientists, epidemiologists, economists, chemical engineers, mathematicians.

Institutes to train scientists and conduct studies in the fields of agriculture, education, social sciences, and diseases prevalent in Africa are of great importance. Better ways of communicating rapidly the results of successful ventures must be an essential part of research. Clearing houses, visiting expert teams, conferences can profitably be used.

3. To encompass all of science and technology is too much of a burden for today's Africa. It would seem wise, therefore, to concentrate on scientific analyses of obstacles to growth, with a willingness to give priority to two kinds of problems: the most important and the easiest to solve with resources readily available.

4. Basic to the future development of science and technology— in fact, to the modernization of Africa—are the awakening and maintenance in old and young alike of a spirit of curiosity, of innovation, of experimentation and a willingness to try the new.

Action along these four lines will undoubtedly point to the need for changes in African development plans. And African leaders must be prepared to reallocate resources, to adopt the more fruitful, the more humanly advantageous, courses of action indicated. This may mean giving up some of the prestigious, visible schemes popular in many countries today.

Most of us have talked much of progress, but less of cooperation. I assure you that cooperation in science and technology is, like cooperation in the arts, easy compared to cooperation in many other fields. The exchange between Western and non-Western scientists, you will recall, has been active even in the darkest days of the Cold War.

THE RATIONALE
OF COOPERATION

WALTER H. WHEELER, JR.

Chairman of the Board
Council on World Tensions, Inc.
New York

In this International Year of Cooperation we are meeting here to pool our experience and backgrounds, to learn from each other. We are paying particular attention to the problems of Africa, but we do so with the understanding that these problems are only the African manifestations of our common human struggle toward a free, dynamic, and abundant society, based on respect for the dignity and rights of every individual.

We all know that men working together can accomplish more than they can working alone. But to work effectively together, for any long-term purpose anywhere, men must have not only a common objective, but—far more—faith in one another. When the objectives of men become antagonistic, they create tensions, to be sure; but these, if kept within limits, can and do become productive. It is only when there is loss of faith that our real trouble starts —trouble so serious that we threaten to destroy ourselves completely in a nuclear holocaust. Yet this very threat may well be the force compelling man to search his soul more deeply for a common faith which is the necessary ingredient for real cooperation.

I hope that we can make a real contribution to this search,

215

meeting on a continent of new nations, where opposing world ideological differences may sometimes appear to be attempting to capitalize on man's most ancient and inbred antagonism—racism. We must find a basis for faith in one another, and I believe we can do so through understanding that, as human beings, we are all fundamentally alike. All of us, as individuals and as nations, develop through the same process of struggle, trial and error, although the time and place may be quite different. The selfishness, the crassness, the prejudices, the mistakes, the cruelties in the evolution of any race or grouping of people can be found in some form in every other. Also the same virtues—courage, sacrifice, kindness, love.

Individual material self-interest, innate in all individuals, has clearly been the great incentive for mankind to lift his standard of living. And yet this material self-interest—unrestrained by conscience—has, in every part of the world in every race of people alike, brought inequity, even hardship and cruelty, to others, usually resulting in some form of revolution.

Our basic challenge today is to have this world evolve with more equity and opportunity for every human being, by using only reason and cooperation, not force or dishonesty. Fortunately, to help us meet the challenge, we all have within us another innate instinct, regardless of race or religion—a God-inspired inborn aspiration. We call this morality. So, in whatever fields we find ourselves working, I believe we must try to uncover morality from the recesses of the individual conscience and the shelter of religion, family, or inner circle. We should bring morality into our lives in terms of decency and fair play. We should give it a really accepted and recognized status. We do not suffer as much from a basic lack of moral instinct as we do from astigmatism in its application.

It seems to me that as we look at history from the dawn of it to yesterday, we can clearly see what life in essence is all about. It is basically and irrevocably a struggle, without which life would be colorless, with no meaning or real satisfaction. For only through something done, something accomplished, can we attain satisfaction, happiness, and meaning. This struggle is essentially one involving not only material and scientific challenges, but man's deepest spiritual nature.

While it is easy and superficially convincing for the sophisticate or cynic to jeer at man's aspiration in the face of man's inhumanity to man, his material selfishness, and his moral degradation, a long look at what has happened over the ages discloses that this aspiration is by all odds the most obvious and impressive force in history. In what other way can one explain how man has lifted himself from a primitive animal to the spiritual and moral level?

Man's spiritual aspiration has won over wars, pestilence, famines, despots, and periods of moral disintegration that have sometimes threatened his very existence. It has made possible most of the things we enjoy today. It has created the ethical standards by which man's conscience measures his actions. Instances of retrogression in ourselves or others only prove its existence. I believe it is the mightiest force on this earth, albeit that we have not yet found a way to really harness it.

Many people believe that whatever spiritual or moral aspirations they feel or see in others stem from religion, and historically this seems to be true. But I would put it the other way around. While respecting every individual's religion, and supporting my own, I believe that the spirit of God is inborn in every man—the capability, the urge for honesty and courage, humility, fairness, tolerance, generosity, mercy and love—all that we put under the heading of morality today, however imperfect their expression may be. But they are the basic tenets of the major religions of the world today, as well as most of them of yesterday. In one form or another they can be found in folklore, if not the scriptures written by the great prophets and teachers of ages gone by. One of the most encouraging manifestations of our time is the coming together of religions for common spiritual and moral purposes—for cooperation.

Again, I say that it is the recognition of this common experience of moral struggle which is the basis of man's community. No man can escape it. One cannot lead his life in two separate compartments: one in public affairs in which he can justify wholly selfish and materialistic actions, and the other in his private and family

life in which his spirit can find expression. We have been successful in splitting the atom, but no one will ever split the man.

It is interesting that most of us actually prize morality so highly
that we are more sensitive about it than any other thing—so sensitive that we shy away from the word itself, although we may talk
all around it. While we may readily admit that others are more
handsome or more competent than we, most of us, no matter how
far we know we fall short of attaining the ideal of a perfectly clear
conscience, are unwilling to admit anyone is more moral, except
perhaps a religious leader.

I wish we could find a way of symbolizing among all men this
community of spiritual struggle, because it is a real bond. There is,
in fact, no greater bond than men struggling together.

We in the USA realize that our society is full of challenging imperfections, contradictions, and shortcomings. For one thing, we
have not yet adequately met the challenge of racism, although we
are at long last on our way. I am sure that most thoughtful Americans realize that, given our experience, our heritage and resources,
any other people would undoubtedly have evolved a similarly free,
dynamic, and abundant society. Americans are, in fact, a con-
glomeration of "other people."

Whatever degree of morality we have attained is primarily based
on the productivity which has given us the time and opportunity
to think about spiritual, moral, and cultural matters. Although
seemingly contradictory, this is the lesson of history. For until man
was assured of his material survival, he had time to think about
little else.

We in America have a great kinship to Africa. Since the development of North America, Africa is the next great new continent
to emerge and struggle for the freedom and advancement of its
people. And in this struggle, the spiritual aspiration and understanding so necessary for cooperation will be strengthened. We
urgently need the success of the new Africa, and we stand by to
aid you in every way we can—not because of "enlightened self-
interest," but because we are people like you.

AFRICAN PROBLEMS: CZECHOSLOVAKIA'S APPROACH

JIRI HAJEK

*Ambassador of Czechoslovakia
to the United Nations*

Enormous technical, social, and political forces have been released which are changing the face of our world at a remarkable speed and to an unexpected degree. The criteria of values are also changing, and so are the economic and legal norms which until recently were considered as cornerstones of order and stability in the world. The situation is ripe for a substantial revision of the existing concepts and rules of international economic relations, in order to promote progress and effect the necessary changes in the international division of labor and trade.

The socio-economic needs of socialist countries and developing countries in Africa do not fit easily into the traditional philosophy of free competition. The drive toward accelerated economic growth calls for a deliberate mobilization of all available resources and a rational determination of priorities. The desire of the masses for a breakthrough from poverty toward a substantial improvement in their living standards creates in African developing countries a socially and politically explosive situation which does not allow its leaders to follow the traditional slow paths of development.

In promoting economic growth, foreign trade has extraordinary significance for African countries. Any plan to expand exports, however, must face the fact that competition in world markets is so keen that it may prove difficult for newcomers to find an appropriate place in the existing pattern of international trade. Therefore, changing this pattern calls for a responsive cooperative attitude on the part of the traditional industrial countries toward the needs of African countries.

It has been reaffirmed on many occasions that if tangible results are to be achieved here, the very core of the problem must be attacked, i.e., the present international division of labor, the mechanism of which tends to petrify and even reinforce the privileged position of several powerful centers of industry. This situation should be counteracted by a consistent policy—national and international—designed to effect structural changes in the international division of labor which would give all countries equitable participation in the achievements of technological progress.

Present technological development provides conditions for the solution of this problem. Powerful forces have been set in motion which bring about profound shifts in the world's economic structures, with the rise of new industries, their greater concentration and specialization. Such a dynamic situation should enable all countries to find a new place in the emerging economic pattern. Countries which deliberately and without delay shape their policies with a view to meeting the needs of African countries will obviously have an advantage over those which, because of the resistance of invested capital, will be forced to change their policies under pressure.

The approach of Czechoslovakia to the problems of African countries is marked by one specific feature: at no stage was Czechoslovakia's industrial development nourished by colonial exploitation, through which other developed countries accumulated capital, riches, and enhanced their own well-being. Czechoslovakia's policy proceeds from the fact that there is no automatic way to ensure that structural adjustments conform to the recognized need of narrowing the discrepancy in economic and social levels of various regions and countries of the world. The centrally planned economy is capable of facilitating and accelerating the process of structural adjustments. It is guided by the interest of the society as a whole, not impeded by the interests of individual entrepreneurs, and is capable of purposely adjusting itself to alterations which have become historically unavoidable or intentional.

It is obvious that measures designed to improve the position of African countries in the pattern of international division of labor and world trade cannot be limited to the field of trade policy. Trade policy generally has to deal with a given set of facts which cannot be easily influenced, and which are bound to offer violent resistance to any attempts to modify them. It is, therefore, indispensable that changes in trade policy be supplemented by appropriate positive measures in the whole range of economic policy.

The nature of the Czechoslovak economic system and the political will and readiness to carry out a positive economic policy toward African countries may be regarded as a broad and flexible basis for particular measures that might be required. In the years to come, Czechoslovakia will be ready and able to continue an economic policy that will produce market opportunities for imported goods, especially for goods from the developing countries. In this way, a systematic expansion of a mutually advantageous trade can be achieved. In the Czechoslovak economic system, trade policy is not an isolated field but an integral part of the general economic policy. This greatly facilitates effective measures to be taken directly in the sphere of production.

Czechoslovakia's contribution to solution of the problems of African countries lies primarily in its positive economic policy. This is based on the conformity and complementation of Czechoslovakia's interests with those of African countries, and her willingness to take into account in the formulation of policy the inevitable changes brought about by the economic progress of the African countries. The decisive factor behind this policy is the growth of her economic potential and her willingness to make it instrumental in solving the economic problems of African countries. These are the dynamic elements which should ultimately establish a broad and lasting basis for promoting economic cooperation and a close interconnection of the economic interests of equal partners.

At the UN Conference on Trade and Development, Czechoslovakia announced her willingness to include in her import plans an increasing quantity of manufactures and semimanufactures, thus meeting the efforts of the developing countries to diversify their exports. The logical outcome of such a policy is the strengthening of more advanced forms of economic cooperation through international division of labor, where the economic system of Czechoslovakia is capable of producing greater and more lasting results. Obviously this is a higher type of economic cooperation, the introduction of which, as a rule, must be preceded by some positive experience concerning the advantages accruing to both parties. On this basis, it is possible to proceed to the creation of a general legal framework—often in the form of comprehensive agreements on economic, scientific, and technical cooperation, including cooperation in the field of investments, credits, technical assistance, trade, etc. The practice of linking technical arrangements with long-term trade agreements, ensuring that the agreed adaptation will be reflected in exports, has proved to be useful. Such agreements introduce the necessary prospects of expanding outlets for exports and achieving stability of trade.

Initiatives for a more intensive economic cooperation emerged primarily from trade negotiations, from the experience of trade missions, or from the participation of the developing countries at Czechoslovak fairs. It has now become necessary to provide for these activities on a more systematic basis. To that effect, permanent joint committees for economic cooperation have been established with Nigeria and the United Arab Republic. Experience so far indicates that these forms of cooperation might usefully stimulate closer interrelation of the economic structures of the respective countries.

The possibilities of economic cooperation depend on and are

limited by a number of factors:

1. The normalization of international political and economic relations constitutes a basic condition for deeper structural adjustments; it is necessary to create an indispensable degree of security in international relations as the basis for economic cooperation.

2. The structural adjustments must meet the criteria of economic rationality; it would be unreasonable to expect that the Czechoslovak economy would absorb all possible disproportions generated by chaotic market machinery or by arbitrary designs of individual investors.

3. Even reasonable structural adjustments can seldom be achieved in a short time; it is necessary to respect national and local interests and, in particular, to create substitute opportunities for employment, to ensure the retraining of labor for new jobs, etc.

4. Balance-of-payment considerations may slow down the process of structural adjustments, since an imbalance may arise between reduced production and increased imports on one hand, and the insufficient increase of exports on the other.

Czechoslovak economic relations with countries of tropical Africa were established only six or seven years ago. Nevertheless, the results are encouraging. Czechoslovakia now has trade agreements with 14 countries, agreements with 11 countries on scientific and technical cooperation and with 5 countries on comprehensive economic cooperation. The credits granted have reached almost 63 million dollars. By the end of 1964, there were 125 Czechoslovak experts in tropical Africa working in various important branches of economics, health, education, etc. The volume of trade has increased by more than one third since 1960.

This is only the initial stage of mutual economic contracts, which do not yet utilize the enormous potential of useful cooperation. Such cooperation could be considerably sped up if there were a deliberate policy on both sides seeking to enlarge the fields in which economic interests may complement each other. There is no doubt that such efforts provide an efficient way of promoting progress and understanding among nations.

Summary of Discussions

AFRICAN PROGRESS
THROUGH COOPERATION

JOHN KAREFA-SMART

Associate Director of International Health
School of Public Health and Administrative Medicine
Columbia University

The reports of the four committees of the African Conference on Progress through Cooperation, the full texts of which follow, incorporate the principal points that emerged during the committee deliberations, as they were reported to the final plenary session of the Conference, as well as suggestions made during the discussion of these reports. The purpose of this introduction is to share with the reader my general impressions of the Conference as the coordinating rapporteur.

The Conference setting on the beautiful hillside campus of Makerere University College, and the smooth way in which the rather full program was run—thanks to the excellent cooperation between the officials of the Council, the Conference secretariat, and the authorities of the College—contributed to the relaxed and friendly atmosphere which pervaded the Conference. It is not easy to convey to those who were not present the stimulating effect of the week's experience. This was largely due to the remarkable group of men and women from nations old and new, industrialized and developing, rich and poor, who met together to share the vast range of their experience, to learn from each other, and to gain new understanding of the development problems of their own and other countries.

Although the participants included cabinet ministers and other officials of governments, diplomats, educators, business executives, and private citizens, frank and free discussions were held with the understanding that all were participating in their private capacities and had been invited by virtue of their knowledge of, and experience in, problems of development. No one was expected to defend an official position, and everyone worked hard to define the problems and to seek acceptable solutions. The fact that the sixty-six participants, although mainly from African nations, included also a number from Europe, Asia, and North America was a practical demonstration of the Conference theme of Progress through Cooperation.

The four committees worked on the following sub-themes: Problems of Cooperation within Nations; African Solidarity and International Cooperation; The African Economy; and Development of Human Resources—Education, Culture, and Social Problems. Despite the separation into these categories, the participants soon realized that because of the interlocking nature of the various development problems, each committee would have to consider internal and external political, economic, and socio-cultural factors.

The Conference met during a period when political problems of a particularly urgent nature confronted the African nations. There was civil war in both the Congo Republic and the Sudan; Southern Rhodesia presented an unsolved crisis; and no agreement was in sight about the timing of the planned conference of heads of state of the member nations of the Organization of African Unity. The committee reports nevertheless reflect the balanced attention given to the economic, social, and cultural components of progress, together with the political factors.

The discussions did not deal merely in generalities, but were strewn with references to specific situations, and all the reports contain recommendations on practical steps toward progress. For example, in Committee I these recommendations specify the prerequisites for unity, cooperation, and stability within each country. Having accepted the need for progress through maximum development of the resources of the continent as quickly as possible, Committees III and IV addressed themselves separately to economic resources and human resources. Priority of importance in economic progress was given to agricultural and rural development, with suitable emphasis on integrated planning for concurrent development in industrialization and mining. In the development of human resources, priority was claimed for education, mainly directly toward the expansion of facilities for secondary education, for the training of teachers, and for research into the content and objectives of elementary education.

Running through the discussions and reports of all four committees is the importance of the role of external assistance. The historical dependence of most African countries on the economy of European metropolitan powers was emphasized. Independence has brought with it tensions in these relationships, yet most African countries have maintained special relations to outside economic groups, such as the European Common Market and the British Commonwealth of Nations. Although increasing importance should be given to multilateral economic assistance, as through the United Nations and its agencies, continuation of the existing special bilateral relationships was accepted as a practical necessity for rapid and efficient economic development in the immediate future.

A special problem, highlighted in discussions in committees and in plenaries, was the difficulty which African countries generally find in financing the local costs involved in most development assistance projects. The hope was expressed by both African and non-African participants that the aid-granting countries will take a fresh look at this matter and see what relief can be offered.

Two recommendations of a general nature deserve special mention. First, in accordance with the UNESCO proposal to stimulate and encourage research toward the publication of a history of Africa in the next ten years, it was suggested that 1965–1975 should be designated "The African History Decade." The second calls for urgent research in education, both in problems relating to the "growth, development, and psychology of African children" and in the "effect of teaching young children in a language different from that used in their homes." Stress was laid on the importance of cooperative efforts among African countries toward these goals, and also on the help needed from external international agencies.

Perhaps the most decisive and far-reaching act of the Conference was the unanimous approval of a proposal which was made during the final plenary session "that the report of this Conference be forwarded to the Secretary-General of the Organization of African Unity with a view to requesting all member states of the Organization to consider the implementation of the findings of the Conference."

The Conference was not expected to produce any dramatic or novel solutions for the many problems discussed there. However, when new or old proposals for improving relations between peoples within countries, or among the nations of the world community, receive the support of a responsible and eminent group of persons such as those who met in Kampala, these proposals are likely to receive serious attention from the general public and from the governments of the countries concerned. It is in the hope that the findings of the Conference will prove useful to governments and will broaden public understanding of the problems of the emerging countries that the full text of the reports is presented in the following pages.

COMMITTEE I—PROBLEMS OF COOPERATION WITHIN NATIONS

This committee was under the chairmanship of Chief H. O. Davies. The following account is based on the report prepared by Whitney M. Young, Jr., serving as rapporteur. The committee first took the position that the degree of unity, stability, and cooperation within each country is fundamental to its own economic and social progress and to its effective cooperation with other countries. It is axiomatic that a country preoccupied with domestic disputes cannot effectively pursue development plans or contribute as a member of the international community.

The discussions were divided into two general parts:

I. Identification of the basic sources and causes of disunity, conflict, and instability within the African countries;

II. Suggested measures and institutions which might effectively be utilized to promote unity, cooperation, and stability.

Recognizing the impossibility of analyzing fully the causes of or remedies for instability, an attempt was made to suggest practical measures which could be taken to improve internal cooperation for economic and social development. All nations face many of the same problems, but they are particularly severe in Africa. Despite the complexity of the situation, there was the conviction that solutions can be found, given the determination and the good will of the people.

I. Basic Sources and Causes of Disunity, Conflict, and Instability

Tensions must be seen in terms of historical factors which may accentuate the present situation. Therefore, attention was given to these factors with reference to five elements in the populations of African nations.

1. Ethnic Groups

Practically all developing countries are composed of several ethnic groups, some small, others large. In Africa, some of these were hostile to each other prior to and during the colonial period. But colonial rule often cut two ways: by creating an idea of a nation and building common institutions, it was a strong influence toward unity; by pitting tribal groups against one another and creating or accentuating uneven development, it often worked toward disunity.

Since independence, politicians in some countries have aroused moribund sentiments of tribal hatred. In other places, the conflicts are embittered by improper exercise of power and discriminatory distribution of resources. Ministers of state have been known to fill posts in public service only with members of their own ethnic group, and to have awarded contracts on a like basis. Such actions result in or tend to perpetuate uneven development and to sharpen ethnic or tribal conflicts. Racial minorities are a significant tension factor in the East African countries, for example. (For comments on certain aspects of this problem, see the Report of Committee III, Section III.)

2. Geographical Areas at Different Levels of Development

Due to concentration of natural and/or human resources and to various historical factors, certain areas within a given country are more developed at the time of independence than other areas. This uneven development creates dissatisfaction and tension.

3. Rural vs. Urban Elements

Tension between urban and rural elements varies among African countries. Where a considerable degree of urbanization has taken place, or where there has been concentration of physical resources and amenities in the urban areas to the exclusion of the rural, problems and tensions have developed. Another cause of difficulty is the frequent lack of effective communication between rural and urban areas. The migration of people to the cities has created problems of congestion, housing, unemployment, poverty, and growing resentments.

4. Religious Differences

Wherever religion is permitted to become the basis of alignment for political parties, rigid positions may obtain and differences between opposing groups are often almost irreconcilable. A factor which has accentuated religious friction in some places is that, during the colonial regime, the religion of the metropolitan power assumed the character of a state religion, even where the bulk of the population embraced another faith. Although concessions were almost invariably made to the popular religion, nationals who were adherents to the metropolitan religion often enjoyed preferential treatment in education, jobs, and other ways. On attainment of independence, the process of adjustment is often fraught with bitterness—for example, in Uganda and the Sudan.

5. Economic Groups

Most African countries are basically agricultural communities, but the growing working class is in a strategic position to further economic development or to be a disruptive force through their organized demands. It was recognized that labor unions in Africa are generally associated with political parties and can be a force for unity or disunity.

Summary

The above list includes only some of the more important and common sources of conflict. Within one country, any or all of these problems may exist—sometimes reinforcing each other and making solutions more difficult. To avoid aggravating the differences which already exist, it is of the highest importance that African governments exercise their power, allocate resources, and plan and promote development with scrupulous fairness and constant regard to the equal participation of all elements in their countries' efforts for and benefits from development.

II. Measures and Institutions for Promoting Unity, Cooperation, and Stability

1. Organization of Political Parties; One-Party vs. Multiparty Systems of Government

The view was expressed that the differences between the one-party and multiparty states can be seen as shades of a spectrum rather than as a dichotomy. One-party systems may differ widely as to the character of their own internal procedures and their general attitudes on policy. Some one-party systems contain mechanisms for considerable political competition, whereas others may be rigid dictatorships.

Recognizing that the large majority of African states are operating under a one-party system, the utility of this system as a unifying force toward economic development was examined at length. Some compelling arguments have been offered in favor of this system in developing states, e.g.:

(a) The necessity for unity, stability, and discipline;

(b) The fact that opposition elements are often irresponsible, exploiting ethnic or religious differences for their own benefit;

(c) The need for maximum use of scarce resources, training, and leadership in promoting rapid economic development.

The claim that one-party systems are justified as the most efficient means of promoting unity and achieving development was not accepted without qualification. It was noted that one-party systems can foster disunity if they become rigid and coercive and suppress legitimate minority opinions.

Nor could the committee accept the claim that rapid economic development is a simple corollary of the one-party system. It has been shown in some places that the give-and-take of a multiparty system and constructive criticism from the opposition have stimulated development.

There was a consensus that in some cases one-party systems can be useful in damping divisive and destructive forces. However, the danger was recognized of repressive measures and abuses which can be taken by a one-party system in the name of unity. It was noted also that this problem is not limited to Africa, and that Western critics of African systems are often unaware of their own history in this regard.

2. Constitutional Arrangements for the Distribution of Power

Here the committee concerned itself mainly with the applicability of the federal or unitary approach to creating a national government in different African states. Whereas undue concessions to parochialism were not favored, it was felt that where there are large and self-conscious groups, either ethnic or geographical, some federal arrangement may be the only workable solution to the problem of creating a stable and functioning nation.

A realistic approach must govern any attitude toward this question. In a country such as the Congo, where communications are difficult, where there is a huge land area and many separate groups have not as yet harmonized their identities within a unitary state, strong centralized institutions of government are not feasible. In Nigeria, with vast areas and large distinctive ethnic groups which are almost nations in themselves, a federal solution is the only realistic approach. Also in Uganda, comprised of kingdoms with long histories and strong local political institutions, a federal government has operated well.

On the other hand, it was felt that when a great many small ethnic groupings exist, a unitary system may be the best way of incorporating them in a new nation.

3. Structure and Administration of the Civil Service

The committee recognized the importance of an efficient, independent, and nonpolitical civil service as an indispensable factor in stability. However, emphasis was put on the importance of achieving, insofar as possible, representation of all elements of the country, even at the risk of what might appear to be a temporary lowering of standards and efficiency. With due regard to that factor, adherence to merit should be strictly followed in the matter of promotion. There was strong feeling that in building up the civil service, emphasis should be placed upon qualifications such as competence, integrity, and morality, as well as academic preparation. The importance of civil servants' remaining sensitive to the people they serve and to their problems was also stressed.

4. The Educational Structure

Both the machinery and content of education can be of great value in promoting national unity. Curricula and textbooks should provide students with a view of common elements in the national background and the shared interest of all groups in national co-operation. By recruiting teachers from all regions of a country, and by creating institutions which are open to students from every region, the objective of unity will be served. Schools which bring together teachers and students of varied origins can also prove valuable in breaking down prejudices born of unfamiliarity.

At the higher education level, mention should be made of the role which Makerere University College plays in East Africa, and also of national universities such as those at Ibadan, Accra, and Dakar, which have been so important as unifying elements within their countries. An important role can be played by universities through adult education programs, extramural teaching, and extension work in the rural areas. Their unifying role can be further strengthened if, in the rural areas, the universities stress the keynote of cooperation and national oneness in the content of such courses. Remedial education in the rural areas can be a major means of overcoming uneven development of regions and peoples.

5. The Military Service

Many African states have inherited from the colonial regime military and police forces whose personnel was recruited almost exclusively from particular regional, tribal, or ethnic groups. The resulting imbalance has always been a source of tension, which should be remedied by broad-base recruitment both at officer levels and in the ranks. Stress was also placed on the value of military establishments as a mechanism for continuing education in practical and technical fields, and in the political problems of a country. Attention was called to the potential use of the military in practical development projects, such as road and bridge building and engineering.

6. Communication Media

Depending upon how they are developed and used, television, the press, and radio can be productive of unity or disunity. How can a country make sure that these media are used only for promoting unity and advancing education? It was generally felt that the press, for example, has proved in some African countries to be the only mass medium which criticizes government foibles or excesses. If this is allowed to fall exclusively into government hands, it may degenerate into a means for the ruling party to perpetuate itself, and thereby become an instrument destructive to balanced national development.

On the other hand, control of the press by private elements interested only in advancing the interests of special groups can be equally damaging. What would appear essential is the control of the press by people who are mindful of the need to promote unity and cooperation.

On the subject of the competence and responsibility of the press, it was stressed that, up to the present, journalism had not been regarded by many people in the developing countries as a worthy profession; sometimes only those who could not get ahead in other professions turned to journalism. However, a rapid change has now begun to take place. In Nigeria, for example, which has a free and vigilant press, journalists are already a very influential group.

Nations should make more conscious use of TV and radio as media of instruction in many fields relative to development, by promoting understanding of development goals and the efforts required of the people.

7. Police

Recruitment to the police force should be as broad-based as possible without major damage to efficiency. If recruitment is from only one section of the country, the effectiveness of the police in dealing with critical situations will be reduced, thus creating a factor of national disunity.

Careful recruitment and thorough in-service training can contribute to national unity. It is not desirable to post police officers or contingents exclusively to their areas of origin; appointments should be to any region without regard to ethnic origin.

It was the consensus of opinion that armed police were not desirable, particularly in the context of the African developing countries.

8. Courts

In searching for solutions to the problems of stability and unity, it was agreed that the two democratic values of independence of the judiciary and freedom of the press are essential from a purely practical viewpoint. Under a one-party system, if the independence of the judiciary and the press are destroyed, the result may well be to create such a deep form of dissension and disunity as to leave large elements of the population with no alternative but violent protest in order to protect their interests.

9. Voluntary and Professional Organizations

It was unanimously agreed that an important way of knitting together the people of a country is by the development of voluntary, unofficial national organizations of persons with a common professional or other interest which cuts across tribal, ethnic, religious, and other sectional boundaries. Such groups might include women's, professional, business, and cultural groups. Though they would meet to advance their common interests, the members would also gain a better understanding of the problems of their country and could do much practical work in support of measures and projects. If such organizations are to promote rather than injure national unity, their membership must be politically nonpartisan and must be open to all relevant elements.

10. Labor Organizations

The subject of the unrestricted right of labor to strike in a developing country committed to rapid economic development was fully discussed. It was generally agreed that this right, being a rather expensive method of resolving industrial disputes, and resulting in every case in loss in the GNP, is an unfortunate legacy which the colonial period has left behind. Some felt that the conflict between labor and management in the form of strikes and lockouts is an example of taking the law into one's hands. It was therefore suggested that, in the context of contemporary African conditions, where the government is particularly concerned with economic development and is often the employer, and where considerable national resources, as well as foreign grants and loans, are at stake, compulsory arbitration and other alternative mechanisms for resolving industrial disputes should not be ruled out. Industrial tribunals could be set up to which labor, management, and the government would appoint members, and these should function in the same manner and spirit as a civil court.

Another viewpoint expressed was that, while sympathetic to the unique position in which Africa finds itself at this stage of development, and aware of the cost and waste which might be occasioned by irresponsible strikes, the elimination of the right to strike was not favored, and such a ban should be restricted to those services which are essential to the national security and interest. At the same time, it was pointed out that, in time of emergency, people of different countries have willingly accepted limitations upon some of their fundamental rights. In this sense, the necessity for rapid economic development in Africa can be viewed as a case of emergency, where the right to strike may have to be temporarily curtailed.

It was agreed, however, that other approaches to dealing with the problem of labor-management relations should be explored. In India, for example, there are strictures or conditions under which strikes are or are not allowed. In Western Germany, relative labor peace has resulted from the system of *Mitbestimmungsrecht*, in which labor representatives are included on the directing boards of companies. In the United States, profit-sharing plans have proved to be of value in encouraging better cooperation between management and labor. In the French-speaking countries of West Africa, governments have sought the cooperation of trade unions by arranging round-table conferences at which unionized labor has been made to realize that it formed a relatively small proportion of the population, and that it could not be permitted to press its demands to the point of injuring the well-being of the majority.

It was also noted that foreign subventions to African labor organizations have sometimes contributed to division and conflict.

11. Youth and Youth Organizations

The achievement of independence in Africa has released great forces of interest and idealism in the younger people. These forces, if permitted effectively to participate in and contribute to the development of the new states, can be of immense value as a factor for unity and progress.

On the other hand, it has also become clear that political agitation by some youth organizations can be not only harmful but divisive and detrimental. Another regrettable tendency has been for political parties and personalities to manipulate organized youth groups for personal or partisan purposes.

The problems of youth in Africa, and particularly in East Africa, are especially important because an unusually high proportion of the total population—in some cases, as much as 50 per cent—is less than sixteen years old.

Their problems divide into two elements:

The political, which relates particularly to the elite educated youth, especially at the university level;

The economic, which relates to the massive number of restless and unemployed youth in both urban and rural areas.

In various countries of Africa and elsewhere, a number of programs have been launched to channel the energies of youth into national development and to check disruptive political activities. Some of these programs reflect a disciplinary approach; others give primary emphasis to providing increasing opportunity for participation and involvement by youth in both the political and the economic life of their nation.

The countries of Africa would be well advised to study carefully the results of the various experiments and programs under way in order to improve their own efforts. As a general principle, the search must be for effective means of channeling the vast and potentially constructive energies of Africa's young people, rather than of repressing them.

Conclusion

The committee reaffirmed its confidence in the potentialities inherent in the African countries for increasing internal cooperation and unity. This potential, it was felt, is reflected in the determination, faith, and optimism evident among many African leaders. In achieving this unity and cooperation, Africa will not only be serving its own interests, but might well provide a model for unity with diversity for the entire world.

All independent African countries are displaying considerable enthusiam for achieving progress in the continent of Africa through the Organization of African Unity, and for achieving world peace through the United Nations. If these desirable objectives are to be attained, however, the whole process must inevitably begin with unity and stability within their own borders. For this reason, the committee reiterates its belief that the subject assigned to it is of fundamental importance, and that solutions to the problems examined here must be constantly and determinedly pursued.

COMMITTEE II—AFRICAN SOLIDARITY AND INTERNATIONAL COOPERATION

Committee II met under the chairmanship of A. Z. Nsilo Swai, with Albert Kervyn serving as rapporteur. It agreed upon the following subjects for discussion:

The accomplishments, problems, and potentialities of the Organization of African Unity as a factor in African solidarity and in intercontinental relations, the role of subregional groups, and regional groupings;

Nationalism, its positive and negative values in aiding or retarding development, integration, and cooperation, its effects on foreign assistance and foreign capital investment, and on interregional cooperation;

The role of the United Nations, advantages and dangers that may accrue to the UN from the existence of regional organizations, with particular reference to the OAU;

National and international effects on Africa of racial conflicts and practices within and outside Africa, and race conflicts as a global problem.

These subjects being closely related, this report is organized in three sections:

    I. A general statement of the principal aims of the international actions of African states;

    II. Brief review of the chief factors making for greater unity or division among African nations;

    III. Assessment of the progress toward solidarity achieved in the first few years after independence.

I. *Principal Aims*

While a certain feeling of solidarity has existed for a long time among African societies, the attainment of national sovereignty has created the need to transmute this feeling into coordinated political action by independent states. Much of the discussion centered around the problems arising from this transition.

The African states wholly subscribed to the principles of the UN Charter. They have unanimously supported strengthening the role of the UN in both peace-keeping and peace-building. The latter involves a substantial increase in financial support for technical assistance and investment activities to create the economic and social conditions that can serve as bases for peace.

Within this framework, the aspirations that were given particular prominence in the discussion are grouped under three headings: greater unity within the African continent; solidarity in African relations with the outside world; and the effective achievement of decolonialization.

In expressing the need for greater unity of action, some speakers envisaged essentially closer cooperation among states which would, at the same time, respect hard-won national sovereignty. Others stressed the need to transcend nationalism in a wider vista of African unity.

African solidarity in its outside relations was viewed as a means both to protect the continent from outside interference and to make the voice of Africa effectively heard in promoting the basic aims of peace and development.

The aims of decolonialization will be secured only when respect for human dignity obtains over the whole area and the intrinsic equality of all people belonging to different races is recognized—not only in legal and political institutions, but in the minds and values of every citizen, inside and outside of Africa. The most important (though far from the only) violation of these principles occurs in South Africa, where the situation was universally recognized as intolerable. Among other dangers, South African policies could create among Africans race hostilities and even hatred, of which there is so far little trace. The committee proposed that the Conference launch one more appeal to arouse the conscience of the world to the need for finding a just solution to this explosive problem, which has wide repercussions on race relations as well as on relations among nations.

II. Factors of Division and Unity

The principal factors affecting the extent to which common action has already proved possible or may increase in the future can be summarized under the headings of language, economics, nationalism, and external relations.

Language and Cultural Differences. As Africa emerged from the colonial era, it found most of its territory divided into two principal language areas—English-speaking and French-speaking. The separation is, in fact, deeper than language alone and involves modes of thought, of procedure, and of action, as well as types of legal and administrative structures. Both languages have served and can serve to establish common ground and facilitate understanding over wide and separated areas. However, they may also carry divisive elements; one language sometimes increases the difficulties of establishing cooperation in countries belonging to the same region, sharing the same social structures and development problems, but using the other language. To overcome this difficulty, wider and more regular contacts than exist at present are needed among people of the different language groups—not only top political personnel, but leaders in all areas of national life.

A plea was made that, although particular groups cherish their own languages and cultures, the practical value of the English and French languages as bonds of unity, as means of communication, and as tools for cooperation should not be ignored, and both should be more widely taught. As cooperation becomes more and more urgent, the English-speaking areas should give more attention to the teaching of French, and vice versa. Simplification or abolition of visas and other formalities which hamper people in crossing borders would be a step toward better communication.

Economics. The fact that African economies were geared first and foremost to those of the former metropolitan areas creates a problem as well as an opportunity. It establishes among African nations a common interest in improving the terms on which primary products can be traded with the industrial world, as well as achieving better general economic and financial relations with these areas. The unity of purpose and action demonstrated by developing countries from all continents at the Geneva Conference on Trade and Development in 1964 appears as a new and most hopeful factor in international life.

On the other hand, the economies and exports of African countries are essentially competitive with one another rather than complementary. Thus conflicts of interest can arise over the sharing of markets, preferential arrangements, and the distribution of aid. This points to the need for efforts to work out coordinated plans for patterns of production and trade.

The splitting up of the continent into separate entities has increased with independence, and administrative dividing lines have been turned into political frontiers which often enclose areas too limited in their resources for effective separate development. The difficulty presented by these manifold divisions and by the need of cooperation to overcome the resulting disadvantages is felt in many fields, from economics to health and education. It is particularly important in economics, as the rapid progress of industrialization will depend partly on trade across these lines, in order to develop sufficiently extensive African markets. However, the impact of this unifying economic need may be limited in the presence of dominant divisive political forces.

It is nevertheless in the field of economic and technical integration, rather than political unity, that the most significant progress may be achieved in the next few years. This practical approach appears more promising than any direct attempt at political unity. While regional economic and technical groupings can provide a most useful stepping stone, the political will to cooperate remains a necessary precondition both for organizing regional institutions and for overcoming the conflicts of interest that occur when decisions must be made collectively regarding the location of economic activities.

Another problem arises from the special relations that exist between certain African states and outside groups, such as the European Common Market and the British Commonwealth of Nations. There is the possibility that aid, either bilateral or channeled through such ties, might limit the political freedom of the recipient countries. Yet, while placing emphasis on the advantages of multilateral assistance, it was pointed out that bilateral relations are still valuable at the present stage, since technical assistance within this framework is made more effective by prior knowledge and experience of procedures and problems as between donor and recipient countries. More importantly, bilateral and special-relation assistance could not be foregone without risking a marked decrease in the sum total of aid available. Since bilateral aid is likely to remain a necessary major factor in cooperation among African countries and the outside world, it is of vital importance that this aid be provided without political strings or objectionable economic conditions.

Donors of aid should coordinate their actions so as to minimize the drawbacks and confusion which African nations experience as a result of multiple sources of assistance. In the same way, African states should coordinate their requests for aid so as to avoid undue competition with one another.

Nationalism. This powerful force presents both positive and negative aspects. North of the Sahara, countries have forged the links of their national unity in the course of long and sometimes violent struggles for independence. Consequently, the sense of nationhood is relatively widespread among them. Elsewhere, nations are only now emerging, and nationalism as a sense of a national entity is often confined to the elite, while tribalism remains a force with the masses. In extreme cases, nationalism has meant little more than the entrenchment of vested interests in local power positions. Young people attracted to perspectives wider than tribal or national interests are often denied their share of reponsibility. Many educated in foreign universities tend to stay abroad; the most dynamic elements among the youth are then lost to the tasks of national development. This results in the impoverishment of African leadership—so greatly needed as the new countries face the necessity of simultaneously establishing their national identities and building a wider African unity; the integration of the educated generation in the political and social structure can contribute positively to avoiding the potential conflict between these two tasks.

Nationalism was built up as a force to fight colonialism, but its purpose now is that of national construction. While the problems of transition have not been fully overcome, nationalism provides an immensely powerful spiritual force—probably the only one that can supply the incentive to put forth the great effort required for economic and social improvement in the African context. If political parties can spread its positive values among the masses and effectively channel them toward these constructive goals, nationalism can help overcome some of the main internal obstacles to development, including local conflicts based on tribal, language, and cultural differences.

External Relations. A common approach to their relations with the outside world is a powerful link among African states. Fostered and symbolized by the concept of nonalignment, it connotes a refusal to join either of the Cold-War military blocs. This is not a passive attitude of neutralism, but an active effort to maintain peace and to prevent large-scale military confrontations. It may have to be reconciled with another objective—noninvolvement in affairs that do not directly concern Africa. When confronted with issues that carry a threat of global conflict, such as Cuba or Viet-Nam, the African states have played an active role in the UN peace effort.

Another feature of nonalignment is the will to bring about decolonialization and to present a common front against possible interference in Africa by outside forces. The solution of regional conflicts must be entrusted to the regional organization of the OAU; and African states simultaneously recognize that they should not interfere in each other's internal affairs. However, collective action through the OAU may be necessary, since in a Cold War even internal conflicts can become the occasion for outside interference. This purely regional approach may in some cases break down because of limited effectiveness. Thus the problem of South Africa must be dealt with through the UN, as united action would be necessary to make sanctions effective.

There was unanimous agreement on the advantages which would accrue through African solidarity on issues of particular interest to the African states. Concern was expressed by certain committee members, however, over the growth of bloc voting in the UN because of the distinct possibility that the real views of the individual members would be obscured.

III. *Assessment of Progress Toward Solidarity*

Two conflicting pictures emerge from an attempt to assess the achievements of African solidarity. There are examples of increasing nationalistic divisions, as well as signs of a trend toward more effective cooperation. The political pattern of African life has shifted rapidly as new countries obtained independence, and it is as yet too early to distinguish what may become the ultimate pattern of cooperation.

Negative elements in some areas include deterioration or even disintegration of machinery built up during the colonial period. One example would be the increasing strain felt in the mechanism common to the three East African states. Some experiments at closer union, such as between Ghana, Guinea, and Mali, have failed. Border problems not only have created ill-feeling between neighboring states, but have led to breaches of relations. Ideological differences, not critical in themselves, have sometimes sharpened to the point where subversive activity has been carried out by one country in another. The general and genuine desire for unity and solidarity has not always been translated into corresponding actions.

With respect to South Africa, some members, while recognizing the severe obstacles to organizing effective international action, felt that, in view of the unanimity of purpose and the strength of feelings that prevail in African states, more purposeful unified efforts should have been initiated.

It was then agreed that this Conference should join in the efforts "to arouse the conscience of the world to the need for determined efforts on the part of peoples and governments everywhere to find a solution for this explosive problem, which has widespread effects on race relations, impedes economic and social development, damages relations among nations, and endangers world peace." The following statement was generally approved by the committee, as well as by the plenary session when reviewing the committee's report:

Exactly twenty years ago the defeat of Nazism rid Europe of a regime based on brutal racial injustice. Since that victory, the principle of racial nondiscrimination has been formally endorsed by the United Nations and, through it, by world society. At the same time, practical measures have been taken to reduce discrimination, notably in North

America, Asia, and large parts of Africa.

In one corner of the African continent, however, this promising trend has been reversed. In the Union of South Africa, inequality has been elevated to a principle of government, and the steps taken to enforce discrimination have grown steadily more severe. While the human family in the world at large attempts to come to grips with racial injustice as a tragic cause of human misery and degradation, one small segment of humanity has cut itself off from the common effort and even defends its delinquency in the name of civilization.

In sponsoring the Conference on Progress through Cooperation in Kampala, the Council on World Tensions has continued its work of bringing together men and women from different backgrounds, nations, and continents, to define the main causes of tension in world society and to discuss possible means of dealing with them. In the African setting, tensions caused by racial discrimination have inevitably taken a high priority in the concern of the Conference. The members do not wish to bring their discussions to an end without putting on record their conviction that racial discrimination, practiced anywhere, is an affront and a menace to civilized life. Practiced against Africans in their own continent, it carries an added charge of humiliation and outrage. It is, in itself, a fundamental denial of human dignity.

Unchecked, such discrimination will involve the African South in the horrors of racial conflict. It will envenom race relations everywhere. It may even precipitate the worst calamity that could overcome mankind—an international race war.

The injustice and the risk are such that the Conference feels impelled to make its appeal to peoples and governments everywhere to join in seeking a just and acceptable settlement based on full racial equality in the south of the African continent, and to use such pressures and measures as may be necessary to bring about such a settlement.

To emphasize elements of disunity would, however, badly distort the picture. Many of the differences which are inevitable in an area as vast and diverse as Africa may yet be described as family quarrels. While occasionally intense, they may quickly become less critical.

The establishment of the OAU, created at Addis Ababa in May 1963, provides tangible evidence of the will to resolve differences within an African framework. Its creation shows that transitional alignments into, for example, the Brazzaville and Casablanca groups, must not be mistaken for permanent divisions within Africa. It is too early to judge the full potential of the OAU, but clearly an important medium has been established, not only to resolve intra-African problems, such as the Congo and the Morocco-Algeria disputes, but also to concert action relating to the outside world. The common pledge to adopt a policy of nonalignment is one example, and other efforts of the OAU in a variety of fields may soon provide others.

Cooperation has manifested itself in other ways. A Free Trade Area is currently being negotiated between Guinea, the Ivory Coast, Liberia, and Sierra Leone, which cuts across the previous ties some of these countries have with outside groupings such as the Common Market or the Commonwealth. The establishment of the African Development Bank and the Development Institute provides other examples of the great potentiality for cooperation.

While it would be idle to maintain that the divisive forces in Africa discussed earlier have been wholly overcome, or that action is always suited to principles and long-term goals of unity, the solid achievements of the first few years since independence justify a cautious optimism for the future. The period of trial and error is not completely over, and more experience must be gained in the conduct of external relations. Yet the new African nations have already proved an effective force for the maintenance of peace. With growing internal solidarity, their weight could increasingly be felt in the world of nations.

COMMITTEE III—THE AFRICAN ECONOMY

Committee III was under the chairmanship of Mohamed Awad. The following account is based on the report prepared by Bernard Chidzero, who served as rapporteur. Five major topics were selected for discussion:

I. Planning for balanced development; expenditure priorities
II. Financing development; domestic resources; foreign aid
III. Roles of the public and private sectors

IV. Prospects for expanded intra-African and world trade

V. The need for technical assistance and the development of skills.

Throughout, special attention was given to the background papers prepared by Sir Arthur Lewis and Tom Mboya. The frank exchange of views also drew heavily on the participants' own knowledge and experience, opinions and convictions, and numerous references were made to the programs and development plans of specific countries.

I. Planning for Balanced Development; Expenditure Priorities

A development plan should be a carefully integrated, balanced, and conscious device for promoting development and growth—not merely an article of faith endowed, as it were, with a magic power of its own, aside from the deliberate and sustained efforts of the people. Implementation of the plan is the crucial element in development. The objectives must be explained to the people and understood by them in order to enlist their efforts and cooperation. Only in this way can genuine support be built up among all ethnic and cultural groups, urban and rural areas, and different economic sectors.

While African development plans must clearly be integrated to secure a dynamic sectorial balance, and while most aspects of economic and social development in developing countries involve questions of equal or competing priorities, agriculture has a particularly vital role to play. Revolutionizing African agriculture is a matter of crucial importance, not only because the export of agricultural and other primary products constitutes the principal means for earning foreign exchange, but also because increased agricultural income can help meet the great need for domestic consumption and for the enlargement of internal markets, which are necessary to stimulate the development of industries producing consumer goods. Planning must, therefore, give top priority to agricultural and rural development. Provision must be made for:

1. Integrated development, with particular reference to industrialization and mining;
2. Research into African agricultural resources and methods of agricultural development, soil chemistry, crop and animal husbandry, etc.;
3. Training of farmers, education of peasant producers and of trained personnel for the supervision and implementation of the plan;
4. Training of extension workers;
5. Dissemination of information to farmers in general and to peasant farmers in particular, by radio, films, and other means;
6. Availability of credit, fertilizers, and extension services;
7. An adequate network of roads and communications, linking rural areas with marketing centers;
8. The necessary administrative and organizational machinery for development.

Agricultural planning and development require a different approach in each country. Methods which may be suitable in other sectors of the economy, such as mining or education, may be quite inappropriate for agriculture. There are fundamental and often stubbornly resistant sociological, psychological, and land-tenure problems in predominantly subsistence-farming economies. For the proper approach, it may be necessary to work through existing local institutions; this is a field for deeper research. Economic planning, always complex, is much more precarious where peasant agriculture needs to be revolutionized, where land-tenure systems are bound up with tradition and restrictive socio-political systems.

Though based on local conditions in its inspiration and objectives, planning nonetheless requires technical assistance because it is a highly technical business. Outside experts are needed up to the point where the government and the people can take over and effectively continue the process. This applies equally to agriculture and other fields of development.

Most, if not all, African development plans depend on external financial assistance for their implementation. Foreign aid has not

hitherto been readily or adequately provided for agricultural development, possibly because of the high recurrent and local costs
often involved, as well as sociological and political factors connected with traditional land-tenure systems. However, participants
from developed nations pointed out that their countries are now
giving highest priority to assisting agricultural development. Likewise, the World Bank and UN Special Fund, the FAO, and a
number of international companies are giving great attention to
effective methods of assistance and cooperation in this field, and
there is hope for more rapid progress. Even so, recipient countries
can never count on the amount or continuity of foreign aid and
thus cannot base their development plans mainly on this source of
finance.

Since diversification of the African economy is absolutely necessary, planning is essential in other fields. Though the discussion
centered mainly on the role of planning in agricultural development, the crucial importance of industrial development and mining was recognized. Constant emphasis was placed on integrated
planning and development, and on the need to determine carefully expenditure priorities among the different sectors of the
economy, which ought to be mutually supporting. Decentralization
of planning and administration is necessary to bring planning
closer to the people and to local conditions and to distribute more
equitably the benefits of development. However, local plans must
be coordinated effectively with the national plan.

Coordination of planning is equally indispensable at another
level—cooperation among neighboring countries in certain regions
within one continent or special areas of the world. The need for
the harmonization of various national development plans was emphasized, lest African countries duplicate each others' efforts by
producing the same things for their limited markets, or for the
near-saturated markets of developed countries. In spite of the difficulties, it is necessary to establish regional economic groupings and
common markets if African countries are to have balanced and
efficient industrialization.

A great deal of technical and scientific information which would be useful to farmers and entrepreneurs already exists, but inadequate dissemination impairs its value. Also, there is still a deplorable lack of statistical data on which to base development plans. Little is known of Africa's agricultural, mineral, and water resources. Systematic and comprehensive research, surveys, and inventories of Africa's resources are necessary for their full exploitation. These can discover new resources, new uses, and better methods of processing resources, thus opening up new or expanding old markets.

The great possibilities presented by studies of afforestation and forestry products, and the scientific development of such industries, were cited. In the Republic of Gabon, considerable work is being done in this field, with bilateral aid and with assistance from the UN Special Fund. There was general agreement that a scientific inventory of Africa's natural resources and comprehensive research into their development and exploitation should be given the fullest support and should receive external assistance.

Knowledge, however, is not enough; it is its application which is decisive in advancing development. Africa's critical limitations may prove to be shortages of capital and skill, especially the latter. The capacity to create wealth is essentially a human factor. Planned development, research, implementation of plans, proper use of capital and foreign aid, exploitation of natural resources—all these are possible only by meeting the all-important need for training personnel, stimulating imagination and creative ability. The problem of intensive investment in human resources seemed to underlie the whole discussion on the role of effective planning. Development plans, it was agreed, must make effective and adequate provision for this all-important human factor.

II. Financing Development; Domestic Resources; Foreign Aid

The vital importance of domestic resources to support economic development plans place more and more reliance on internal resources, over which a developing country can have greater control than over external aid. Various means for mobilizing domestic resources for development were discussed: direct and indirect taxes, import and export duties, revenue from road and bridge tolls, excise taxes, and the like.

Granting that external aid will be necessary for some time, attention was called to the fact that many developing countries, not only in Africa but also in other continents, need to examine their tax systems and improve their tax structures and administration, increase revenue, and ensure tax collection in accordance with ability to pay. This would permit the people to share more equitably in those development costs which countries must inevitably bear themselves.

Development finance can also be supplied effectively by local development banks and insurance firms. But it is clear that foreign earnings from export commodities constitute a crucial element in most if not all African countries. Although external aid in 1963 amounted to over a billion dollars [1] from official bilateral and multilateral sources, 70 per cent of which was grant aid, there was general agreement that the needs of developing countries are far from satisfied, and that more and more foreign aid for development purposes is required.

References were made to various aid programs of some of the countries mentioned in this report. It was further recognized that a number of other countries are also giving valuable aid, but are not mentioned herein.

Some participants felt that development is retarded by a lack of suitable projects; others maintained that the lack of finance was the principal limiting factor. Paradoxically, either there is money but no projects, or there are projects but no money. The fact is that, while the needs of developing countries are undeniably real and multifarious, projects are often not understood or defined clearly enough to enable donor countries or investors to commit

[1] Of this, $938 million and $103 million respectively were from bilateral and multilateral sources. The figures relate to African countries south of the Sahara and do not include private capital flows or assistance by voluntary agencies.

themselves with full knowledge of the duration and level of their involvement. Thorough pre-investment surveys and feasibility studies thus become necessary. The problem has been realized for some time—witness the establishment in 1958 of the UN Special Fund and the pre-investment surveys and projects that it has undertaken. It was predicted that, in five years' time, Africa's capacity to absorb financial and technical aid would be considerably increased as a result of such surveys and studies.

It is clearly necessary for developing countries to define their needs in concrete, precise, and practical terms, and to demonstrate their willingness to help themselves and the degree to which they are able and willing to enter into long-term relationships, on the pattern, for instance, of the Marshall Plan. Donors and investors must know what they are going into and what the costs in the long run are likely to be. But some participants felt that too much emphasis was given by the donor countries to drawing up plans and compiling statistics, which inevitably caused unhealthy delays and undesirable effects on government policy and plans.

The financing of local costs presents difficulties for many developing countries. It is not always possible for poor countries to secure the funds in local currency required to pay their share of launching a project otherwise financed externally. While recognizing that some donor countries are meeting substantial amounts of local costs through their development loans and grants, there was a definite view, particularly among the African participants, that donor countries ought to make greater contributions of this kind in order to speed up development and to ensure quick and effective use of foreign aid. But donor countries or foreign investors have their own balance-of-payments problems and are reluctant to interfere in matters of local budgets. The problem has been met in some cases by the use of surplus commodities donated by developed countries, which are then sold locally by the government of the developing country to obtain currency. A method is being tried by the UN Special Fund, whereby local costs of given projects can be met by a loan from the Fund to the country receiving aid; the repayment of the loan is made in local currency put into a revolving fund to be used to meet local costs of other projects. But the problem still remains difficult.

Discussion turned to the difficulty faced by donor countries in attempting to give or allocate aid equitably to all developing countries. The criteria of need, productivity of aid, and absorptive capacity of the economy must be applied. It is not feasible to operate on the principle of per capita distribution of aid. Although not allocated on this principle, in practice aid received by Africa is relatively high in per capita terms, as it tends to be in smaller and less populated countries. This ratio, however, is not necessarily conducive to productive investment. It might be constructive if African recipient countries came together in groups and agreed on the flow and allocation of aid, as the European countries did during the operation of the Marshall Plan. There are some dangers; the countries concerned might find it difficult to agree among themselves. In Latin America, committees are still working on this problem. But the idea generally accepted was that developing countries should rationalize the type and volume of aid requested by each country and coordinate their demands, in order to confront donors with consolidated requests or projects, It was agreed that there is a need for greater exchange of views between donor and recipient countries, for joint planning, and, in some cases, joint action in working out development projects.

Turning to the relative merits of multilateral and bilateral channels of aid, it was argued that when unnecessary strings are attached to bilateral aid—which is nearly always the case—multilateral channels are safer. It would be desirable to have more aid given, for example, through the United Nations, the World Bank, and the various international development banks. Great importance was attached to international organizations such as the UN Special Fund and the UN Economic Commission for Africa or its new African Development Bank. But in many cases, historical, political, social, and human factors tend to favor bilateral assistance. There are limitations to what can be done by international organizations, and if bilateral aid were ruled out, the volume of aid available would drastically decline. The general conclusion was that both types of aid were complementary and there should be more of both.

This section has dealt with the mobilization of domestic resources and of foreign resources for financing development in the sense of public funds. These sources, important as they are, are far from sufficient; they must be supplemented by private imvestment, both domestic and foreign, and this problem is the subject of the following section.

Another essential source of funds is the export of domestic products, and problems of increasing foreign trade are dealt with in Section IV. However, emphasis must here be placed on the close relationship between foreign aid and trade; on the fact that the sums provided by foreign countries in terms of aid are often nullified because income from exports is reduced by falling prices of the primary products exported; and on the views expressed in the discussion, to the effect that a donor country should not make increased trade in her favor a condition for granting aid.

III. The Public and Private Sectors

Developing countries must be able to draw on both public and private capital resources in order to build up their economies to keep pace with the expanding needs and expectations of their peoples. It was agreed that these countries, with mixed economies, should formulate, as early and precisely as possible, policies governing the roles of the public and private sectors, and that they should adhere faithfully to such policies. An attempt should then be made to allocate certain industries to the public sector, or to both sectors operating jointly.

Certain basic or strategic industries in developing countries, such as steel plants, cannot be left entirely to private enterprise, particularity foreign private enterprise. On the other hand, developing countries often do not have the necessary private capital and experience to operate such large-scale industries. Here a pragmatic approach is necessary. Operations should be carried on in one or the other sector, depending on where they can be conducted most efficiently. Nonetheless, it is clear that the public sector will inevitably be growing, since government has to take the initiative in many cases to exploit resources which private enterprise might not exploit. The government, the public sector, must safeguard the national economy and activate new schemes or projects. Government must also establish national institutions, such as development corporations, marketing boards, and the like, through which it can operate government enterprises and assist people to invest their own resources and market their products effectively. This reinforces the need for governments to improve their tax structures, as indicated above, to provide greater public resources.

As for the merits or demerits of private foreign investment, it was pointed out that some foreign investors tend to be their own consultants, managers, and entrepreneurs and then to repatriate the profits. Thus little is added to the economy of the developing country. On the other hand, nationalization of certain industries, though often necessary, is not in itself a panacea. Several participants drew attention to the fact that indigenous people are not always in a position to provide the efficient administration and management essential for given enterprises. Since most developing countries require foreign capital for investment, as well as technical assistance, private investors must have assurance regarding markets for their products, growth possibility (i.e., possibilities for secure reinvestment in the country), and ability to repatriate at least some portion of the returns. It is also important that reasonable guarantees be given that new private enterprises will not be nationalized for a period of 15 to 20 years and that, if eventually nationalized, fair and adequate compensation will be made. Otherwise, private foreign investment will not be forthcoming. More attention must be given to methods by which the interest of developing countries can be served while private investors, domestic and foreign, are given incentives to supply the necessary capital.

Careful study should therefore be made of the ways in which nationalization, when it is clearly necessary, can best take place without impairing administration, or enterprises can be owned and managed jointly by a government and private investors. Joint enterprises have proven advantageous, especially when private investors are associated with locally based development banks in financing these projects. Experience in West Africa demonstrated the importance of this in the Ivory Coast and in Nigeria, where American, French, British, and other foreign capital and finance are associated with local capital. Similarly, in Nigerian textile mills there is Swiss, Italian, and American, as well as Nigerian, participation in the investment. This joint principle should be further developed.

Even where there is public money available to buy up or nationalize private enterprises, it may be wise to adopt a gradual method in achieving this end. For instance, a government could buy shares on behalf of indigenous people and eventually sell these shares to the people, who thus would own and run the enterprise or participate effectively in it. There is a danger that governments in developing countries may nationalize precipitately and make political appointments not justified on the basis of competence to the boards of nationalized industries. This could result in inefficiency and even in the collapse of the industries concerned, to say nothing of possible corrupt practices and nepotism.

The role of the private sector was fully appreciated as an important source of additional capital and management skill, but this should operate within the framework of, or take account of, the objectives set forth in national development plans. Private enterprises must identify themselves with the national struggle and the common aspirations of the country, while continuing to operate efficiently on business lines and to benefit both the private investors and the public in general. The suggestion was made that foreign investment, greatly needed in Africa, might be attracted by more favorable terms of credit and tax reductions according to the degree of reinvestment in the country and of domestic participation.

A distinction must be made between private enterprises owned by resident foreigners and indigenous private enterprises. In most African countries, for instance, retail trade is predominantly in the hands of foreigners—e.g., Lebanese in West Africa, Asians in East Africa. The same can be said of the transport industry. It is important that African governments study this problem and take appropriate and fair measures to remedy the situation. Indigenous people must play a more decisive role, yet here, as elsewhere, the crucial problem is their lack of training and experience. It therefore becomes imperative that governments provide the necessary institutions and facilities for training Africans and thus make possible the Africanization of such undertakings. This point was also discussed in the plenary session in connection with the problem of ethnic minorities as presented by Committee I. It was pointed out that, in taking "fair and appropriate measures" to increase the participation of the indigenous population in economic life, governments should recognize the fact that valuable contributions can be made to the economy by persons of other ethnic origin, who are willing to accept citizenship and demonstrate their loyalty to the country.

IV. *Prospects For Expanded Intra-African And World Trade*

This topic is closely related to Section II. National tax revenues, foreign aid, private capital—domestic and foreign—are all necessary ingredients of accelerated African development, but they must be supplemented by increased earnings from export trade with other countries in Africa, as well as in the wider international markets.

There is clearly ample room for increasing intra-African trade between Uganda, Kenya, Tanzania, Zambia, Burundi, Rwanda, the Congo, and others. Direct trans-African trade is more difficult; unfortunately, from Africa one has to go, it seems even to Heaven, through Europe instead of directly. Communications and transport links still remain largely as they were in colonial days, because the colonial metropolitan relationship was a basic factor in planning. But surely this should and can be changed.

For increasing and broadening intra-African trade, it was questioned whether African countries, indeed developing economies in general, should start on their difficult road to progress by coordinating their development plans or creating economic unions, common markets, etc. Such coordination and organization are undoubtedly necessary, but it might be more realistic for them first to take such joint practical steps as the development of road networks and other means of communications, and coordination of customs structures and procedures. (A great deal of illicit trade already takes place across frontiers, for instance, in West Africa.) The problem of different currencies should be considered—perhaps with less truculence than more comprehensive plans, and with more immediately beneficial results. Also, a West African Payments Union may offer more hope for practical realization than would ambitious plans which evoke deep emotional and political reactions and resistance.

Although the committee agreed upon the imperative need for concerted action among African countries, there was some difference of opinion as to what was feasible and what was merely pious aspiration. In any case, it became clear that the two approaches—immediate practical steps or more comprehensive aims—were necessary and not mutually exclusive.

To increase earnings from international trade, it was agreed that preferential treatment for African products must continue. Developing countries require more and more assistance, not only economic and technical, but in the form of more favorable price structures and trade practices, as well as readiness on the part of developing countries to import manufactured goods from the developing countries and to devise provisions for compensatory finance. These are the issues that occupied the UN Conference on Trade and Development for three months at Geneva in the summer of 1964.

The fear was expressed that, even at Geneva, a line may already have been drawn, despite high phrases, between the developed and the developing countries. The world seems to be dividing itself more sharply into rich and poor, and the division seems to run along broad north-south geographical lines, as well as on color lines —with the USA and the USSR possibly coming closer together. This line is, perhaps, one of the greatest potential sources of tension; in any case, it gives reason for the permanent establishment of the UN Conference on World Trade and Development to deal with it.

The discussion ended on a very sober and disquieting note. Sober because it was realized that intra-African trade is still very small, only 10 per cent of Africa's total trade; most African countries remain heavily dependent on the economies of former metropolitan powers. Disquieting for these reasons:

1. Advanced technology in North America, Western and Eastern Europe, and parts of Asia (China and Japan) is leading, or has led, to the production of synthetics which can easily replace the commodities from developing countries, thus enabling the developed countries to exploit their own resources more fully.

2. Africa's agricultural and mineral resources are therefore beginning to be confronted by a formidable challenge, and urgent joint action is required among Africa's actual and potential producers.

3. Commodities such as sugar, coffee, and cocoa are already being overproduced for the markets of developed countries and are consequently faced with the problem of further falling prices.

4. It is imperative that Africa begin to exploit her resources for domestic markets.

In brief, Africa must now learn to live more and more by depending on her own resources, to industrialize with a view to intra-African trade. Production and marketing surveys should be intensified. There is already a need for what might be called a diversification fund, which could be set up initially with the help of levies on commodities, and which would assist in the process of diversifying African products and promoting intra-African trade. The apron strings to former metropolitan countries can have only short-lived benefits. Africa should begin to be inward-looking in order to pull herself up by her own bootstraps. It will be some time, of course, before she can do so effectively, and in the process international aid and cooperation will continue to be of vital importance. Nations need to be independent and self-reliant in order to play their proper role in the interdependence which is the crucial fact in the economic world.

V. The Need for Technical Assistance and the Development of Skills

More than half of the world's technical assistance, in terms of people, now comes to Africa. This is understandable, since more newly independent African countries are experiencing an acute shortage of trained personnel. The assistants now being provided include advisory operational experts, education and training personnel, and technical specialists working on pre-investment surveys. Fellowship programs are also an important form of technical assistance. Literally thousands of operational experts are working in Africa today under both bilateral and multilateral schemes. This situation will change as more local people become adequately trained; but, until then, a vital function is being performed by such personnel.

Several important trends may be observed. One is the growing recognition that technical assistance and the supply of capital in the form of material and equipment must go together. Conversely, the supply of capital and equipment, to be effectively used, must often be accompanied by technical assistance. Under the US programs of technical assistance, one dollar is allowed for equipment to every three dollars of technical assistance. Another trend is toward longer-term programs of assistance, covering the building, operation, and maintenance of projects such as schools, up to the point where they can be taken over completely and effectively by local people.

A further tendency now is to supply experts—for example, teachers or professors—in larger numbers than before so that the team can be an entity and evolve an *esprit de corps*. This often means associating an institution, such as a university in a recipient country, with a similar institution in the donor country.

Finally, there is a trend toward recruiting specialists in certain fields from some developing countries to serve in other developing countries. Such experts, when they have had experience in certain problems, may be better equipped to handle special problems than experts from the more developed countries.

The committee strongly emphasized the value of *institution-building* in providing technical assistance. In certain cases, the provision of expatriate personnel or volunteer service corps for urgent specific needs in the less developed countries of Africa may be of great value, especially in the short run. But there is a growing realization that merely to send experts who remain for a few months or years and do not leave behind people or established institutions that can carry on by themselves falls short of meeting long-term needs. Some donors tend to relate their technical assistance to such institution-building. It is vitally important to increase these efforts in creating educational and research institutions, credit unions, and cooperatives, which become a permanent factor in accelerating development.

There is a special need for order, planning, and coordination in the provision of technical assistance, because of the multiplicity of the sources of assistance—multilateral, bilateral, nongovernmental, voluntary, etc. Furthermore, government requests for aid are often numerous and disorganized, resulting in interdepartmental confusion and overlapping requests from diverse sources to meet one and the same need.

Consideration was given to the need for effective local coordinating machinery on the part of recipient governments so that requests can be rationalized and integrated, duplication avoided, and projects effectively integrated with the development plan. It is often difficult to pinpoint the needs that require technical assistance. The problem is made easier where there already is a development plan, but in many countries it is necessary to make a country-wide study to identify areas where technical assistance is required.

Attention was called to the enormous contribution that science and technology can make toward progress in Africa, as well as in all developing areas. However, intensive study must be made and mechanisms established in order to adapt them to the needs and conditions of the countries concerned. The implications and problems involved in fully utilizing the benefits of science and technology were explored in the UN Conference on the Application of Science and Technology for the Benefit of the Less Developed Areas, Geneva 1963.

The level of technical assistance and transfer of know-how have changed considerably over the last few years. A careful study must be made as to the professional and technical qualifications of experts now required, and how to recruit those with experience, as well as the ability to adjust to changing conditions. At the present time, the availability and adaptability of these experts is a greater problem than the availability of money. Recruitment is more and more difficult, partly because the problems of the developing countries are becoming more sophisticated, and partly because technical assistance seldom offers permanent careers. All of these factors contribute to the need for better advance planning. It was suggested that more extensive career service bureaus, specifically for technical assistance, be established so that competent personnel could be found to serve for varying periods without sacrificing their own careers.

The question was raised as to whether it is possible to determine how long technical assistance in such fields as agriculture, teaching, etc., will continue to be required. It was agreed that a probable trend toward more assistance can be foreseen for some time ahead.

It is extremely important for developing countries to provide the necessary counterpart staff to work alongside the experts, since the purpose of technical assistance is to impart skills to the local people as quickly as possible in order to equip them eventually to run their own affairs. The countries giving and those receiving technical assistance should insist on the training of local people as a major part of any technical assistance agreements and programs. As much of this training as possible should be provided within the developing countries, under the same conditions in which the local people will carry on their work. However, for various reasons such as lack of facilities and adequate personnel, it will still be necessary for training to be provided to some extent in the developed countries.

Precautions must be taken to guard against certain dangers which are likely to occur in technical assistance. While experts should remain long enough to take full advantage of their experience and to build up local skills, projects should be self-liquidating and not overstay their usefulness. Assistance must not stifle local talent and ambition; it must not be paternalistic or lead to a dependent mentality on the part of the local government or people. A steady cultivation of local ability and initiative in economic, social, and cultural development must be maintained and promoted. Indigenous craftsmanship and industries, as well as local creative ideas and inspiration, must not be ignored, but appreciated and encouraged. They can be dynamic building tools.

On the question of special programs using relatively young and inexperienced people (Peace Corps, Volunteer Service Overseas), it was agreed that they are fulfilling a very important role and have been extremely useful. There is great value in the services of these youths, whose sympathy, eagerness, and enthusiasm are definite assets. Nevertheless, many more experienced and trained people are required, particularly to work as teachers. There is the danger that standards of education may drop as a result of using university undergraduates who are not trained or have had no experience as teachers.

Cooperation, vigorous research and planning are needed to keep abreast of the times, to train Africa's people, and to promote her progress through her own persistent efforts, while benefiting cooperatively from international economic and technical assistance. The keys to progress are self-help and cooperation toward mutual benefit; dynamic individuality of nations within the framework of international understanding; and interdependence, if not unity.

COMMITTEE IV—DEVELOPMENT OF HUMAN RESOURCES: EDUCATION, CULTURE, AND SOCIAL PROBLEMS

Committee IV met under the chairmanship of Monseigneur Bakole. The following account is based on the report prepared by W. Senteza Kajubi, who served as rapporteur. The discussion included the following main topics:

    I. Adapting education to the needs of African countries
    II. Education for civic and community responsibility
    III. Culture as a human resource
    IV. Health and health education
    V. Population dynamics.

I. Adapting Education to the Needs of African Countries

Education in Africa has passed through a period when it was largely oriented toward foreign cultures and colonial needs, or supposed needs. Even today, the content of education in many African countries has not been thought out afresh because the social and cultural objectives of African education have not been properly evaluated. Educational structures and systems are still based largely on those of the former metropolitan powers and on examinations controlled by them. Curricula, teaching materials, and research activities all need to be redirected toward objectives suitable for Africa.

African countries want to develop their human and natural resources in a great hurry, while at the same time preserving their cultural identity in the modern world. Revision of curricula and preparation of new teaching materials must take account of the need for more scientific and technical education, and of the equally urgent need for making the African child aware of his own environment and cultural heritage. Various immediate practical steps were considered to bring about these revisions.

Educational Research. Thoroughgoing revision of school curricula at all levels must await the results of greater research into the growth, development, and psychology of African children. The material now used in teaching child psychology, for example, was based upon the study of children in Europe and America. While a certain amount of this is doubtless of universal validity, there are obvious respects in which the social and physical environment of the African child can be expected to produce a somewhat different pattern of development. Little is known at present about the play habits of African children, the effects of different methods of weaning and the much more contant presence of the mother, of early exposure or nonexposure to constructive or mechanized toys.

Another field for psychological research is the effect of teaching young children in a language different from that used in their homes. Does this tend to deepen the division already existing between the world of the school and the world of the home? If so, what remedial steps might be taken to bring the two worlds into a comprehensible relation to each other? It must be remembered that one of the objectives of early missionary education was precisely to estrange the child from "pagan" relatives and surroundings, and from many customs, attitudes, and beliefs. This trend still lingers to some extent in existing curricula and teaching methods. To find the answers, more attention must be focused on educational research, experimentation, and innovation; the training of research workers and the production of research-minded students must be recognized as a necessary function of African universities. Educational research must cease to be regarded as an academic luxury which African countries cannot afford. What is more important, however, than fundamental and action research is the production of teachers who have a dynamic, problem-solving approach to teaching.

Cooperation in Research. A coordinated approach is most essential in studying the African child in his African environment. Research in this field should start by collecting in one place all the available information about the work which has been done in various African countries, the problems selected for study, and the methods employed in the investigations. The sharing of this information among research workers and teachers in African countries provides a promising opportunity for cooperation.

It was suggested, therefore, that research and demonstration centers should be established in those countries or regions where they do not already exist, corresponding with the Institutes of Education in English-speaking Africa. These centers should encourage innovation and experimentation in education and collect all available information on all projects, small and large, which may have been carried out in their respective countries. There should be liaison among such centers and a clearinghouse or other means to facilitate the exchange of information in order to prevent duplication of effort or unfilled gaps. It is to be hoped that such a clearinghouse would also draw on the experience of other continents.

Research, though basic to all real progress in this field, is very expensive in terms of finance and of trained personnel. This is a field in which international assistance is greatly welcomed, to provide funds, personnel, and the training of local people to undertake further research.

Preparation of Teaching Materials. The committee commended highly the study projects, such as the UNESCO Workshops on the New Mathematics, Elementary Science, and Programed Instruction, which have been held in Africa, bringing together local educators and outside experts to produce new teaching materials based on the African environment, dealing with African problems, and expressed in a comprehensible idiom. It was hoped that projects of this nature would be expanded to cover all school subjects as soon as possible. Schemes for promoting African authorship and publishing skills deserve encouragement and support.

The Problem of the School Leaver. The large number of primary-school leavers for whom neither wage-earning employment nor further education is available poses a great problem in all

African countries. These children for whom there is no place in the school system, too young and unprepared for paid employment (even if employment were available), but inspired with hopes of a standard of living which rural environment cannot satisfy, go into the world destined to be failures. Some questions discussed by the committee were: Is it possible to devise a curriculum that would prepare the primary-school leaver to enter effectively in society and, at the same time, give adequate preparation to those who will continue their education? Alternatively, is a two-stream system possible or desirable right from the beginning of elementary school, one preparing for agriculture at the completion of primary school, and the other an academic program for those continuing to secondary school? If so, how would selection of pupils be made?

The conclusion was that the aim of the elementary school should be to provide a broad basic education and basic skills, and not to prepare children for specific forms of employment. In other words, alleviation of the problem of the primary-school leaver seems to be in widening opportunities for post-primary training.

Secondary-level education must be expanded fast enough to cope with this problem. It is necessary to begin to think beyond traditional methods in terms of the latest innovations of educational technology and mass media. Correspondence courses, radio, television, and programed self-instructional materials could be considered as a possible means of extending secondary education to large numbers of children who at the moment cannot be accommodated in the schools.

The consensus was that even secondary schools should not concentrate too closely on preparing boys and girls for specialized employment. A broad general education should be the aim of the secondary school. Vocational training is also necessary, but if it is not based on this sound foundation it is bound to be sterile.

Priorities in Educational Planning. One problem facing all developing countries is that the demand for education is very great, and the means to provide it extremely limited. Illiteracy is crippling to a modern society; its elimination through universal elementary education and mass literacy campaigns would seem to be basic to economic and social development. But this would consume all the resources available for education at all levels. African education is facing a serious financial crisis. The targets set by the Conference of African States on the Development of Education in Africa (Addis Ababa, 1961) are too ambitious to be achieved within the periods specified. Since the educational problems of developing nations cannot be tackled on all fronts, it is necessary to establish priorities in the tasks that must be undertaken first in order to break the vicious circle of ignorance and poverty.

The committee felt that the greatest emphasis should be placed on:

(a) Expansion of secondary-level education, including vocational training. The shortage of high-level and middle-level trained manpower is one of the most serious bottlenecks in African social and economic development. Plans for economic and social development depend very much upon a larger supply of high school graduates, clerks, nurses, and many other middle-level skilled workers. More graduates are also needed to go on to universities and teachers colleges. Special effort should be devoted to the teaching of science subjects at the secondary-school level, so that the goals set by the UNESCO Conference on Higher Education at Tananarive, September 1962, may be achieved as soon as possible—namely, that the proportion of students enrolled in scientific and technical subjects, including medicine and agriculture, in institutions of higher learning should be at least 60 per cent, and those in the humanities 40 per cent.

(b) More and better facilities for teacher education. A major obstacle in the expansion of education in Africa is the critical shortage of teachers, particularly at the high-school level. Expansion and improvement of the facilities for the education and training of teachers was regarded as a very high priority if there is to be any significant increase in the quantity and quality of education in Africa.

(c) Improving the quality of elementary-school teaching. At the primary level, the greatest need is to improve the quality of education rather than to aim at universal and compulsory primary schooling. In many such schools, the buildings are poor and the teachers inadequately prepared, in many cases having no professional training. The result is that teaching methods are often formal, consisting of drill and rote-learning, and there is a high rate of wastage through children's repeating classes or failing to complete the primary course. Emphasis should be placed not on expansion, but on raising the standards of elementary-school teachers and improving the quality of teaching.

The Institutes of Education, or their counterparts, should concern themselves, among other things, with activities aimed at achieving these objectives—for example, through organization of frequent and intensive in-service courses to raise the academic and professional level of teachers or through research into teaching methods in order to reduce either student hours or the teacher/pupil ratio.

Need for International Cooperation. The staffing of African secondary schools and colleges will depend for a long time on the flow of expatriate teachers into Africa. Supplying teachers, professors, and teacher trainers, therefore, offers one of the widest fields for international cooperation. There are already a number of international projects which have significantly increased the flow of teachers. In the last analysis, however, the fundamental need is to provide more and better indigenous teachers. Crash programs of training aimed at attracting and retaining Africans in the teaching professions should receive great encouragement and support.

Many general approaches to education could be adapted to satisfy African needs. For example, teaching of a second language should benefit a great deal from international cooperation, because it is now common to all countries. The problems of teacher education, research, and the training of African research workers all offer limitless opportunities for international cooperation. Since the Institutes of Education act as the spearheads of educational innovation, they should receive sympathetic consideration from governments and from foreign and domestic donors.

While regional conferences and workshops in Africa can do much toward raising educational standards, there should be opportunities for many more African teachers than at present to take part in summer schools and conferences in developed countries where the latest educational techniques are discussed and demonstrated.

II. Education for Civic and Community Responsibility

Adult education must be integrated with the primary curriculum so that the school is brought to the community and the community nearer to the school. Adults should not merely be taught how to read. Through radio and television they can be given educational programs aimed at increasing their knowledge and their contribution to society.

The committee recognized the need to study more closely the contribution which the traditional forms of education can make to modern school education. In all parts of Africa there are traditional schools, such as the Poro and Bondo in West Africa, popularly referred to as secret societies. What is taught and learned in these schools may have much to contribute to civic and community responsibility in Africa.

Adult Education

1. The prerequisite for the effectiveness of any economic plan is an adequate level of literacy of the total population. Educational facilities for youth and adults have to be in line with the social and economic needs of the country, in both urban and rural areas.

2. The high rate of illiteracy in all African countries is a social burden, associated with ill-health, malnutrition, disease, and poverty. Yet adult education cannot concentrate only on reading, writing, and calculating—although these are essential for the transition

from a mainly emotional and traditional to a more modern way of life. Adult education must teach new techniques and concepts, such as the time factor, discipline, productivity, initiative, and a problem-solving attitude.

3. Adult education must also have the practical goal of improving employment. Rural underemployment is an acute problem in all African countries. For the immediate future, the majority of Africans will be employed in agriculture, the foundation of their economies. The expansion of agricultural output is urgently required. Adult education could decisively contribute to the modernization of agriculture and increase output by introducing new methods of soil conservation, land reclamation, irrigation and drainage, and reforestation, thus promoting self-help activities.

4. The rural environment will be improved through adult education and become more attractive to school-leavers, thus counteracting excessive rural-urban migration.

As the adult population receives an integrated education for a more modern way of life, the cultural gap and conflicts between the older and younger generations may be attenuated. Family and marital life will be healthier and happier if the wife has received an education—apart from the knowledge she gains of housekeeping and child rearing. This is of particular importance for the young African elites who receive a higher education, either in their own countries or abroad.

The Role of Women. Women have played a decisive role in the societies of all African countries. They took an active part in the fight for independence. The majority of all constitutions recently proclaimed by African nations guarantee the same legal rights to men and women.

Even though some African women hold high-ranking positions in governments and administrations and are members of parliament, the illiteracy rate is far higher among the female population. However, it is mainly the mothers at all social levels who mold the personalities of their children, and profoundly influence the prejudices and attitudes which are developed during their first six years.

Therefore, as the future educators of the next generation, it is extremely important for African girls to receive the education and training to enable them to prepare their children adequately for adult life in a modern community.

The Youth Movement. In certain countries youth movements have become a driving force in the process of nation-building. They provide a way of channeling the natural energy of youth into constructive and socially useful activities. While organized youth movements in the hands of unscrupulous politicians can be very dangerous, their potential as a means of positive education and social action in African countries was recognized. They could be of particular service to that large section of youth whose formal education at present ends with primary school. One or two years of training, comradeship, and social discipline with other youths might fit them to become useful and responsible members of society.

III. Culture as a Human Resource

In considering the importance of culture in education, it must be remembered that the transmission of African culture in the past had been largely oral. With the coming of modern school education, there was a danger that this chain of oral transmission, linking the child with the culture and tradition of his people, might be destroyed. As one member remarked: "When an old man dies in Africa, it is as if another library has burned down."

The preservation of African culture calls for the most urgent action. Therefore, it was suggested that the years 1965–1975 should be declared "The African History Decade." UNESCO at its 13th session invited member states to stimulate and encourage research projects in these ten years which would lead to the preparation and publication of an African history. The Bureau of the International Congress of Africanists has already declared its readiness to collaborate in this task. It was felt that this project should be widened to involve secondary-school children in Africa in the collection of primary information, which would be interpreted by experts. Information collected should cover all aspects of African culture, including historical traditions, stories, music, works of art, riddles, and dances.

IV. *Health and Health Education*

In discussing the place which health services should occupy in the list of priorities for development, it was first agreed that health should be regarded as including complete mental, physical, and spiritual well-being, not merely as the absence of disease. Just as education is basic to development, so also is health, since poor health prevents individuals from working as productively as they otherwise could.

The most important aspects of health in developing countries generally are: (1) the control and prevention of diseases, such as malaria, yaws, sleeping sickness, and tuberculosis, which affect large numbers of people or are readily contagious; (2) improvement in the nutrition of the population; and (3) education about the factors on which the maintenance of good health depends.

Dealing adequately with these problems requires wise decisions about priorities. More emphasis should be placed on public health programs which serve the needs of all the people more completely —such as rural health centers—than on elaborate hospitals.

Major emphasis should be placed on the training of health workers who can deal adequately with specific local problems. This requires a type of training different from that which prevails in developed countries. A good example of this new approach to training is the center at Gondar, Ethiopia.

At the same time serious efforts should be made to study the contributions which traditional African medicine might make to modern medicine—particularly in the use of herbs, etc., and in the psychological aspects of disease.

The problems of nutrition require an understanding of the customs and dietary restrictions and habits of the community, as well as a study of the ways in which more food and/or better qualities of foods can be produced, preserved, transported, and made available to all.

The special needs of the pre-school child were emphasized. From weaning up to the age of six, proper feeding is the foundation for good health, while improper feeding can lead to permanently underdeveloped or even maldeveloped bodies and minds.

It was agreed that education in health, nutrition, hygiene, etc., should be carried out at all levels, as well as through indigenous institutions and among special groups. The role of women in promoting sound health practices in the home and village was particularly emphasized.

In all aspects of health service there exist many opportunities for cooperation, not only among African countries but with the developed countries. The World Health Organization, UNICEF, FAO, and UNESCO have given and are giving much assistance to African countries. Several donor countries also place major emphasis on health needs in the technical aid which they offer, and full advantage should be taken of this source of assistance.

V. *Population Dynamics*

This was discussed from the point of view of planning for the best use of African resources for the benefit of the family. In some areas land is abundant, in others it is not. The starvation existing in other parts of the world is seldom seen here, but the pressures of rapid and suddenly rising rates of population growth are being felt in certain areas. The estimated rates, according to official UN figures just collected for the World Population Conference in Yugoslavia (September 1965), show a rise in annual population growth rates from 1.5 per cent in the 1940's to 2.5 per cent now. The essential problem is one of balancing the resources of a country—the ability of the people to use them effectively, and the numbers of people they must support.

As death rates fall and birth rates remain high, there are often imbalances of many kinds. The need increases for schools, teachers, hospitals, doctors, houses, and food. With lower infant mortality, economic pressures build up for many families.

There are wide variations in population dynamics within as well as among African countries. Tunisia, Egypt, and Morocco have had such rapid increases in population that they are launching programs to help families who wish to space their children. Modern medicine offers a choice of methods which can be used without offense to conscience or tradition. A full freedom of choice should be offered, as this is a decision for the individual family concerned. Families should not be denied access to knowledge on a subject so vital to their health and well-being. The large numbers of children in Kenya have led that nation to plan a study of this problem. The concern of the Catholic Church about the sudden increases in population in some parts of the world was noted, as well as the concern in the UN regarding the relation of such rapidly rising population growth rates to economic and social development.

It is true that other areas, such as Gabon and the Congo, are short of people for the labor market, and there is an increase in rural-urban migration, leading to other types of population imbalance. Therefore it was felt that Africans should study the population dynamics in their own countries—projecting population and economic growth rates, needs for schools, etc., in order to determine each country's probable ability to best provide for its families in the years to come. This was considered important not only for immediate action, but because of the decades required to correct imbalances which may develop in the population structure. This is an area in which technical assistance is available and can be helpful, because even the most developed countries are struggling with the same problem.

The problems created by rural-urban migration in terms of congestion in cities, inadequate housing, unemployment, and insufficient health services are all aspects of the dynamics of population. These are great factors in dissatisfaction, restlessness, and tension. They can be extremely explosive unless ingenuity, foresight, planning, and large resources are promptly devoted to them.

APPENDIX A

CHIEF S. O. ADEBO, Nigerian Ambassador Extraordinary and Plenipotentiary, Permanent Representative to the United Nations, and Commissioner-General for Economic Affairs, was formerly Chief Secretary to the Government of Western Nigeria and head of the Civil Service. Joint author of the 1952 report on the "Nigerianization" of the Civil Service, he carried out replacement of British senior officials by Nigerians in top posts of the Western Nigeria Civil Service during 1957–60. Chairman of the United Nations Working Group of Twenty-One, examining administrative and budgetary procedures, 1963–65. Graduate of King's College, Lagos; Bachelor of Arts and Bachelor of Laws, London University. Barrister-at-Law, Gray's Inn, London. Honorary doctorates of Laws, Western Michigan University, 1963; University of Nigeria (Nsukka), 1965; Honorary Doctorate of Civil Law, Union College, Schenectady, New York, 1965.

ADAM P. ADOSSAMA, Minister of National Education of the Republic of Togo; Chief of Radio in Lomé, 1955–58; member of the staff of the Minister of Education, 1958–59, and former director of the departmental staff of the Minister of Finance, Economic Affairs, and Planning.

LEONA BAUMGARTNER, M.D., Assistant Administrator for Technology Cooperation and Research, Agency for International Development of the United States Department of State; she has served as a public health administrator and educator, and as professor at Cornell University. She has been Adviser to the Governments of France (1945) and of India (1955–56). Formerly she was Commissioner of Health, New York City. Dr. Baumgartner received her M.D. and Ph. D. degrees from Yale University.

BERNARD T. G. CHIDZERO, of Rhodesia, is the Representative of the United Nations Technical Assistance Board and Director of UN Special Fund Programs in Kenya. Served for three years on the staff of the UN Economic Commission for Africa. Author of *Tanganyika and International Trusteeship*, 1960. Educated at the University of South Africa, Pius XII University College, Basutoland; M.A. in Political Science, Ottawa University; Ph. D., McGill University in Montreal, 1958. Two years' research at Nuffield College, England, on problems of Central African economic and political development.

SIR ANDREW COHEN, K.C.M.G., K.C.V.O., O.B.E., Permanent Secretary to the Ministry of Overseas Development since its establishment in 1964, was Director-General of the Department of Technical Cooperation, 1961–64. While serving as Permanent Representative of the United Kingdom on the Trusteeship Council of the United Nations 1957–62, he travelled and lectured in the United States. Governor of Uganda, 1952–57 and administrator in Malta during World War II. Educated at Malvern and Trinity College, Cambridge, he began his career in the Inland Revenue Department and joined the Colonial Office in 1933.

GERSHON B. O. COLLIER, Barrister-at-Law, is Ambassador of Sierra Leone to the United Nations and to the United States. During 1964 he was a member of his Government's delegations to the United Nations Trade Conference in Geneva, to the Commonwealth Prime Ministers' Conference in London, and to the Heads of African States Conference in Cairo. A founder-member of the People's National Party in 1958 and constitutional Legal Adviser at the London Conference for Sierra Leone's independence in 1960. He was educated at Durham University, Middle Temple, London.

CHIEF H. O. DAVIES, Barrister-at-Law, is a Member of Parliament, Nigeria, Minister of State, Cabinet rank, Minister of Industries, Federal Government of Nigeria. He was Chairman and Managing Director of the Nigerian National Press, 1960–62; Chairman of Federal Commission on Aids to African Businessmen, 1958; Chairman of the Company Law Revision Committee, 1962. President of the Rotary Club of Lagos, 1964–65. Author of *Nigeria: The Prospects for Democracy*. In 1959 he was a Fellow, Center for International Affairs, Harvard University.

A. S. DHAWAN is the High Commissioner of India in Kampala, Uganda. Previously he was First Secretary of the Indian Embassy in

Stockholm, 1960–62, and First Secretary of the Indian Embassy, Belgrade, 1957–59. Commissioner of India in Aden, 1953–57. Served in Ministry of Rehabilitation 1948–52, and as Under Secretary of the Ministry, 1952–53. He holds an M. A. degree, and joined the Civil Service in 1933.

RENÉ FOCH, French Croix de Guerre, has been Director, External Relations Department of the European Atomic Energy Community (EURATOM) since 1958. He was Liaison Officer, 1953–57, between the Council of Europe and the Organization for European Economic Cooperation, heading the Economic Section in the Secretariat of the Council of Europe in 1954. Staff writer, *Le Monde*, 1948–49; author of *La Haute Autorité de la Vallée du Tennessee*. A graduate of the Universities of Toulouse and Paris, he holds a Doctorate in Law.

JIŘÍ HÁJEK, has been Permanent Representative of Czechoslovakia to the United Nations since 1962, heading the Delegation at the 17th, 18th, 19th, and 20th sessions of the General Assembly, and serving as Representative in the Security Council in 1964. He was a delegate to 18 Nation Disarmament Conference in 1962; representative in the ECOSOC, 1963–65, Deputy Minister, Foreign Affairs 1958–62, Ambassador to the United Kingdom, 1955–58; head of the Delegation to the General Conference of UNESCO in 1954, Member of the National Assembly from 1945–53. University Lecturer in 1947, and in 1952 Professor of History and International Relations at Charles University in Prague from which he holds doctorates in Law and Science (History). A member of the resistance movement against German occupation, he was imprisoned in Germany until the Nazi regime ended. Author of *Munich* (translated into German and Russian), and other books.

PAUL G. HOFFMAN, who acted as General Chairman of the African Conference on Progress Through Cooperation, is Managing Director of the United Nations Special Fund. He served as President of The Ford Foundation and as Honorary Chairman of the Fund for the Republic. He was also the first Chairman of the Committee for Economic Development, and first Administrator of the Marshall Plan. Mr. Hoffman was formerly President of the Studebaker Corporation.

LOUIS IGNACIO-PINTO is Ambassador of the Republic of Dahomey to the United Nations, to the United States, and to Canada. Member of the Administrative Tribunal, United Nations. Head of the

Delegation of Dahomey to the World Conference on Trade and Development, Geneva, 1964. Head of the Delegation of Dahomey to the Conference of Members of the Organization of African Unity, Addis Ababa, 1963. Formerly served as Minister of Justice and of the Civil Service as well as Minister of Economics, Commerce and Industry of Dahomey. Served 1946–56 as Senator from Dahomey to the Senate of the French Republic in Paris. Has practiced law in Paris as well as in Dahomey. Received his education at the University of Bordeaux and the University of Paris.

W. SENTEZA KAJUBI is Director of the National Institute of Education, Makerere University College, Kampala, Uganda, where he was formerly Senior Lecturer in Geography Methods, Faculty of Education. He studied at Makerere and is a graduate of the University of Chicago.

JOHN KAREFA-SMART, M. D. of Sierra Leone has recently been appointed Assistant Director General of the World Health Organization, Geneva, having served as a Member of the Executive Board of WHO. Formerly Associate Director of International Health and Assistant Professor of Public Health Practice, School of Public Health and Administrative Medicine, Columbia University, New York, and Minister of External Affairs of Sierra Leone, 1961–64. He was educated at McGill University Medical School and Harvard University School of Public Health.

ALBERT KERVYN, a Belgian economist, became first head of the Belgian Economic Planning Office, after service with the Ministry of Finance. He also teaches at Louvain University. Mr. Kervyn served in various capacities with the United Nations in New York, Geneva, and Bangkok, and he has been a Research Associate at the Center for International Studies at Massachusetts Institute of Technology.

PUMLA E. KISOSONKOLE is a consultant to UNICEF, and was a Member of the Uganda Delegation to the 18th and 19th sessions of the United Nations General Assembly. Mrs. Kisosonkole is a Vice-President of the International Council of Women, and a Past President (1963–64) of the Uganda Council of Women. During 1955–58 she was a Member of Parliament.

SIR W. ARTHUR LEWIS of Jamaica is Professor of Economics and International Affairs, Woodrow Wilson School of Public and International Affairs, Princeton University and Vice President of the American Economic Association. He was formerly Vice-Chancellor, University of the West Indies, 1959–63; Director, Central Bank of Jamaica, 1962–63; Special Adviser to the Prime Minister of the West Indies, 1961–62; Economic Adviser to the Prime Minister of Ghana, 1957–58; Director, Colonial Development Corporation, United Kingdom, 1950–52; member of the Colonial Economic Advisory Council, U.K., 1945–49. His numerous publications on economic questions include *Principles of Economic Planning.*

TOM MBOYA became Kenya's Minister for Economic Planning and Development in 1964, previously serving as Minister for Justice and Constitutional Affairs, 1963; Secretary-General of Kenya African National Union in 1962; member of the Legislative Council in 1957; and Secretary of Kenya Federation of Labor, 1953. He was founder and Secretary of the Kenya Local Government Workers' Union, and with the Nairobi City Council as a Sanitary Inspector. Educated at Kabaa, Yala, and Mangu Secondary School he was awarded a one-year scholarship to Ruskin College, Oxford. He holds an honorary Degree of Doctor of Law from Howard University, Washington, D.C., 1959.

LEO MODEL, an international investment banker and economist, contributes much of his time to organizations dealing with international problems. Co-Chairman, Sponsors Committee, Washington World Conference on World Peace Through Law. He entered the investment banking business in the Stock Exchange in Germany in 1920. From the Amsterdam Stock Exchange, he came to the New York Stock Exchange in 1941 and started his own firm, Model, Roland & Co., Inc. He is a director of a number of companies in other countries as well as in the United States.

FRANÇOIS A. N'LIBA-N'GUIMBOUS of Cameroon has been Deputy Executive Secretary of the Economic Commission for Africa since November 1963. Educated in the Cameroon and at the University of Paris, Mr. N'Liba-N'Guimbous has served at various periods in the French Ministries of Finance and Economic Affairs. Appointed Commissioner at the Caisse Centrale de Co-opération Économique in 1956; served as Vice-President and later as District Manager of Crédit du Cameroon. A former Director General of the Cameroon Development Bank and Director of the Central Bank of Equatorial African States and Cameroon, Governor of the International Bank for Reconstruction and Development, and Chairman of the Board of the African and Malagasy Union of Development Banks.

A. MILTON OBOTE is Prime Minister of Uganda and President of the Uganda People's Congress.

SAMUEL N. ODAKA became Minister of State for Foreign Affairs of Uganda in 1964, having been Deputy Minister in 1963. He was elected Member of Parliament in 1962, and appointed Parliamentary Secretary for Finance. Elected to Legislative Council, 1961. Member of Jinga Municipal Council, 1959–62; Kampala Municipal Councillor, 1957–59. Member of Uganda Electricity Board of Directors, 1959–62. With Standard Vacuum Oil Company, 1955–62. B.A. from Makerere College.

TAIB SLIM is Permanent Representative of Tunisia to the United Nations and Ambassador to Canada. A member of the *bureau politique du Parti Socialiste Destourien*. He was formerly Ambassador to the United Kingdom. He has represented Tunisia at African Summit Conferences and at the Conferences of Nonaligned Nations in Belgrade, 1961 and Cairo, 1964.

ALHAJI YUSUFF MAITAMA SULE is now Minister of Mines and Power in the Federal Government of Nigeria, having been elected a Member for Kano City to the Nigerian Parliament in 1954. Formerly he held a teaching appointment with the Kano Native Administration, his principal subjects being History and English. He was also interested in adult education, organizing evening classes in Hausa and English. He attended a Higher Elementary Teachers' Training Course at Laria Middle School and received his college education at Kaduna College.

BARBARA WARD, economist, lecturer, author of numerous books, including *The Rich Nations and the Poor Nations, Five Ideas that Change the World, India and the West,* is a frequent contributor to *The New York Times Magazine, Foreign Affairs, Harper's Magazine,* and *The Economist.* Former foreign editor of *The Economist* and a governor of the British Broadcasting Corporation. Graduate of Somerville College, Oxford. In private life she is Lady Jackson, wife of the economist, Sir Robert Jackson.

WALTER H. WHEELER, JR., Chairman of the Board, Council on World Tensions, is an industrial executive with a special interest in the cause of peace and better understanding. He is a Director of the United Nations Association of the United States of America. In addition to his work as Chairman of the Board, Pitney-Bowes, Inc., New

York, he serves on the Citizens Committee for International Development and the Council on Foreign Relations. He is a Trustee Member of the Research and Policy Committee of the Committee for Economic Development; a Director of Foreign Policy Association, a Trustee of Worcester Academy, Member of Business Council, as well as a Director of several corporations.

WHITNEY M. YOUNG, JR., is Executive Director of the National Urban League, and President of the National Conference on Social Welfare. He is also a member of the National Advisory Council, Office of Economic Opportunity, and the National Commission on Technology, Automation and Economic Progress. He received an Outstanding Alumni Award, University of Minnesota and was a Rockefeller visiting scholar at Harvard University, 1960–61. Assisted in planning the 1963 Civil Rights March on Washington.

APPENDIX B

OFFICERS AND PARTICIPANTS OF THE AFRICAN CONFERENCE ON PROGRESS THROUGH COOPERATION

CONFERENCE CHAIRMAN
PAUL G. HOFFMAN
Managing Director, UN Special
Fund (USA)

CO-CHAIRMEN

Y. K. LULE
Principal, Makerere University College, Uganda

TAIEB SLIM
Ambassador of Tunisia to United Nations

ADVISORY COMMITTEE

*S. O. ADEBO, Ambassador of Nigeria to United Nations
*LORD CARADON, Ambassador of the United Kingdom to United Nations
*GERSHON COLLIER, Ambassador of Sierra Leone to United Nations
SIR ANDREW COHEN, Ministry of Overseas Development, United Kingdom
*ROBERT K. A. GARDINER, Executive Secretary, Economic Commission for Africa (Ghana)
PAUL-MARC HENRY, Assoc. Director, Bureau of Operations UN Special Fund (France)
*SIR ROBERT JACKSON, Consultant, UN Special Fund (Australia)
DR. JOHN KAREFA-SMART, Member of Parliament, Sierra Leone
APOLLO K. KIRONDE, Ambassador of Uganda to United Nations
SIR ARTHUR LEWIS, Woodrow Wilson School of Public and International Affairs, Princeton University (Jamaica)
WALDEMAR A. NIELSEN, President, African-American Institute (USA)
*JOSEPH E. SLATER, Assoc. Director, International Affairs Program, The Ford Foundation (USA)

PARTICIPANTS

ADAM PIERRE ADOSSAMA, Minister of National Education, Togo
A. L. ADU, Regional Rep. UN Tech. Assistance Board & Director Special Fund Program (Ghana)

* Members of Advisory Committee not present at Kampala.

286

D. G. ANGLIN, Professor, Carleton University, Canada
ANDRE GUSTAVE ANGUILE, Minister of State, National Planning, Gabon
MOHAMED AWAD, Chairman, UN Committee on Racial Discrimination (UAR)
MONSEIGNEUR BAKOLE, Vice-Rector, Lovanium University, Democratic Rep. of the Congo
DR. LEONA BAUMGARTNER, Asst. Administrator for Technical Cooperation & Research, AID (USA)
WM. H. BEATTY, JR., Vice-President, International Dept., Chase Manhattan Bank
CHARLES BENTON, Director, Council on World Tensions (USA)
J. BULIRO, Assistant Secretary-General, Organization for African Unity
BERNARD CHIDZERO, Rep. UN Tech. Assistance Board, Nairobi (S. Rhodesia)
JOSEPH CIMPAYE, Director of Public Relations, Sabena Airlines, Burundi
WILLIAM CLARK, Director, Overseas Development Institute, Ltd. (U.K.)
EVERETT R. CLINCHY, President, Council on World Tensions (USA)
JAMES S. COLEMAN, Director, African Studies Center, University of California
H. O. DAVIES, Federal Minister of State, Nigeria
A. S. DHAWAN, Indian High Commissioner, Kampala
ROSCOE DRUMMOND, Washington Columnist, *New York Herald Tribune*
BEN ENWONWU, Cultural Advisor to Nigerian Government
RENÉ FOCH, Director, International Relations, EURATOM (France)
MELVIN GORDON, Director, Council on World Tensions (USA)
JIRÍ HÁJEK, Ambassador of Czechoslovakia to UN (Not present at conference but prepared paper)
PAUL-MARC HENRY, Assoc. Director, Bureau of Operations, UN Special Fund (France)
MRS. ANNA ROSENBERG HOFFMAN, Public and industrial relations consultant (USA)
LOUIS IGNACIO-PINTO, Ambassador of Dahomey to UN and USA
J. KAKONGE, Director, Uganda Planning Commission
W. SENTEZA KAJUBI, Director, Institute of Education, Makerere University College, Uganda
ALBERT KERVYN, Head of the Belgian Planning Office
ERISA KIRONDE, Chairman, Uganda Electricity Board
MRS. PUMLA KISOSONKOLE, Member, Uganda Delegation to United Nations
RALPH KNIGHT, Vice-President, Kaiser Aluminum & Chemical Corp. (USA)
GEORGE LOFT, Vice-President, African-American Institute (USA)
JAYANT MADHVANI, Industrialist, Uganda
LIDJ KASSA WOLDE MARIAM, President, Haile Selassie University, Ethiopia
KELETIGUI MARIKO, Director of Rural Development, Niger
TOM MBOYA, Minister of Economic Planning, Kenya
MAHENDRA N. MEHTA, Industrialist, Uganda

LEO MODEL, Investment Banker, New York (Not present at conference but prepared paper)
A. NEKYON, Minister of Economic Planning, Uganda
A. VALENTIN N'GAKOUTOU, Director of Planning and Development, Chad
FRANÇOIS N'LIBA N'GUIMBOUS, Deputy Executive Secretary—Economic Commission for Africa (Cameroon)
A. MILTON OBOTE, Prime Minister of Uganda
SAMUEL N. ODAKA, Minister of State for External Affairs, Uganda
AYRE ODED, First Secretary, Embassy of Israel, Uganda
DANIEL PEPY, Director, Training Centre for Economic & Technical Cooperation, France
L. RELJIC, Chargé d'Affaires, Yugoslav Embassy, Kampala
MRS. AGDA ROSSEL, Ambassador of Sweden to Yugoslavia
J. D. RUBADIRI, Former Ambassador of Malawi to USA and UN
MISS M. E. SENKATUKA, Senior Community Development Officer, Ministry of Planning, Uganda
ABDEL-RAZZAK SIDKY, Asst. Director-General, Near East Affairs, FAO (UAR)
CARLETON SPRAGUE SMITH, Professor, New York University
SHEPARD STONE, Director, International Affairs Program, The Ford Foundation (USA)
MAITAMA SULE, Minister of Mines and Power, Nigeria
FRANCIS X. SUTTON, Ford Foundation Representative for East Africa (USA)
A. Z. NSILO SWAI, Minister of State, Directorate of Development & Planing, Tanzania
WILLARD L. THORP, Chairman, Development Assistance Committee, OECD (USA)
MAMOUDOU TOURE, in charge of the European Office of UNICEF, Paris (Mauritania)
BARBARA WARD, Author and Economist (U.K.)
SAMUEL WESTERFIELD, JR., Deputy Asst. Secretary for Economics, Bureau of African Affairs, U.S. Dept. of State
WALTER H. WHEELER, JR., Chairman of the Board, Council on World Tensions (USA)
MRS. GABRIELE WUELKER, Former Minister of State, Federal Republic of Germany
WHITNEY YOUNG, JR., Executive Director, National Urban League (USA)

NOTE: Although the Council made every effort to arrange that participants would be present from all independent African countries as well as several additional countries of other continents, a number of those invited were unable to attend.

Date Due